MW00718984

Relocating to Atlanta and Surrounding Areas

Relocating to
ATLANTA
and Surrounding Areas

Everything You Need to Know Before You Move

and After You Get There!

H. M. CAULEY

PRIMA PUBLISHING
3000 Lava Ridge Court • Roseville, California 95661
(800) 632-8676 • www.primalifestyles.com

© 2000 by Prima Publishing

All rights reserved. No part of this book may be reproduced or transmitted in any form or by any means, electronic or mechanical, including photo-copying, recording, or by any information storage or retrieval system, with-out written permission from Prima Publishing, except for the inclusion of brief quotations in a review.

Section 2 © 2000 by Monstermoving.com

The RELOCATING series is a trademark of Prima Communications Inc. Prima Publishing and colophon are trademarks of Prima Communications Inc., registered with the United States Patent and Trademark Office.

Every effort has been made to make this book complete and accurate as of the date of publication. In a time of rapid change, however, it is difficult to ensure that all information is entirely up-to-date. Although the publisher and author cannot be liable for any inaccuracies or omissions in this book, they are always grateful for corrections and suggestions for improvement.

All products mentioned are trademarks of their respective companies.

Library of Congress Cataloging-in-Publication Data
Cauley, H. M.
    Relocating to Atlanta and surrounding areas : everything you need to know before you move and after you get there! / H. M. Cauley.
        p. cm.
    Includes index.
    ISBN 0-7615-2564-5
    1. Atlanta Region (Ga.)—Guidebooks. 2. Moving, Household—Georgia—Atlanta Region—Handbooks, manuals, etc. I. Title.
F294.A83 C38 2000
975.8′231044—dc21
                                                                    00-044090
        00 01 02 03 04 05 HH 10 9 8 7 6 5 4 3 2 1
            Printed in the United States of America

HOW TO ORDER:

Single copies may be ordered from Prima Publishing, 3000 Lava Ridge Court, Roseville, CA 95661; telephone (800) 632-8676, ext. 4444. Quantity discounts are also available. On your letterhead, include information con-cerning the intended use of the books and the number of books you wish to purchase.

Visit us online at www.primalifestyles.com

CONTENTS

"We have raised a brave and beautiful city. . . ."
—HENRY GRADY, JOURNALIST, "THE NEW SOUTH," DECEMBER 22, 1886

At the edge of Woodruff Park in the heart of downtown Atlanta towers the triumphant sculpture of a robed lady, her arms outstretched above her head. Her hands gently clasp a phoenix, the mythical bird of immortality, said to rise from its own ashes to live for hundreds of years. This granite and bronze *Atlanta from the Ashes*, created in the late 1960s, was overhauled and given a prominent new home in the renovated park prior to the 1996 Olympic Games. The move was as symbolic as the statue itself: Once again, Atlanta was pulling itself up from obscurity to become the center of attention.

"Atlanta from the Ashes" is also a suitable title for the history of a town that started as a pioneer wilderness and made it to the turn of the millennium as one of the leading cities of the South and the world. It was—and is—a city that continued to face adversity and survive, stronger and more determined than ever.

The groundwork for Atlanta was a small settlement not far from present-day Woodruff Park. In the early 1880s it was called Terminus, an apt moniker for a town whose claim to fame—and reason for existence—was the convergence of several rail lines. It had little else to offer, far removed from the coast's blossoming cities, Savannah and Charleston, and surrounded by heavily wooded mountains and ridges. But determined pioneers transformed the oversized rest stop into a bustling town that attracted all sorts of entrepreneurs who saw a future in the continual influx of businessmen and visitors. In 1843, the settlers gave the city a more distinguished name, Marthasville, in honor of a former governor's daughter, then changed it two years later to Atlanta, denoting the Georgia end of the Atlantic railroad. By the time it was incorporated in 1847, Atlanta was not only a railroad hub but the state capital as well.

The same railroads that brought people and goods to Atlanta proved to be the town's undoing during the Civil War. In 1864, Atlanta was a crucial communications, supply, and transportation center for the Confederacy. Exhausted troops and frightened residents endured months of sweltering heat and constant bombardment from Union forces, but in September of that year the city fell to General William Tecumseh Sherman. The Union leader left the remaining warehouses, magazines, stores, and homes a pile of smoldering ashes before heading to Savannah, the destination of his famous "March to the Sea." Today, some good-humored natives joke about Sherman's misplaced zeal for urban renewal, but a great many still despise his name.

Three years after burning to the ground, Atlanta was scrambling back to its feet. The capital was relocated to Milledgeville in the center of the state, but the change didn't deter people from pouring into town. From a prewar population of about 10,000, the city more than doubled by 1870. Increases continued through the turn of the century as the city came into the nation's eye, hosting spectacular events such as the 1895 Cotton States and International Exposition, an event that featured a visit by the Liberty Bell and drew almost a million spectators.

From the turn of the century on, Atlanta has continued to attract people who eventually adopt the city as their own. They were lured by renowned schools such as Emory University and the Georgia Institute of Technology, as well as some of the country's leading black colleges: Spelman, Morehouse, and Clark Atlanta University. Others found it a friendly place for supporters of the Civil Rights movement, Martin Luther King Jr. prominent among them, along with Andrew Young, who served as mayor of the city and ambassador to the United Nations. (When much of the rest of the South was wrestling violently with segregation, Atlanta had relatively few confrontations, earning it the nickname "The City Too Busy to Hate.")

To this day, Atlanta boasts a reputation as a transport crossroads. Along with the still-busy railroads, the nation's busiest airport and an excellent interstate system make getting people and goods in and out of the city a cinch. (As business travelers joke, "You can't get to heaven or hell without passing through Atlanta.") The appeal of such convenience isn't lost on businesses headquartered here, including Delta Airlines, Coca-Cola, and CNN News.

The city's allure is just as powerful for folks looking for a good place to live. Affordable housing and a significantly lower cost of living than the rest of the East Coast play a big part in wooing buyers from more expensive areas of the country. Residential architecture comes in every style imaginable, from turn-of-the-century Victorian cottages in shady city neighborhoods to sprawling million-dollar mansions that back up to new suburban golf courses. Homeowners can live as far as forty-five miles from the official city limits, on a Cherokee County horse farm or in a historic town in Newton County, and still be considered part of the Atlanta metropolitan area. A recent return to in-town living has fueled a renovation of the city's midtown and downtown neighborhoods, where just about any building or warehouse left standing idle is being renovated to meet the demand for lofts.

No matter where they live, Atlantans enjoy all the advantages of a cosmopolitan city. The Atlanta Ballet and world-class Atlanta Symphony sparkle in a sea of cultural attractions, from the High Museum of Art and the stages of the Alliance and Fox theaters to small neighborhood playhouses, art galleries, dance troupes, and music venues. Sports fans are enthralled with the Philips Arena, built in 1999 and home of the city's first National Hockey League franchise; Turner Field, the former Olympic stadium that houses the Braves baseball team; and the Georgia Dome, the indoor home of the Falcons football team. Thrill seekers flock to Six Flags Over Georgia's seven twisting roller coasters or ride the skylift to the top of Stone Mountain, the world's largest granite outcropping, towering 825 feet. History buffs can walk Civil War trenches in the Kennesaw battlefields, tour Jimmy Carter's presidential library, and visit various venues of the 1996 Olympic Games. And you foodies haven't been forgotten: Atlanta's diverse community supports elegant restaurants as well as down-home barbecue joints, ethnic eateries, coffeehouses, and outdoor cafés.

One of Atlanta's most endearing qualities is its weather. The spring and fall seasons are lengthy and awash with the color of azaleas, camellias, and magnolias. Trees that sprout bright, fragrant buds in

April turn ruby red in October, and many flaunt their greenery year-round. The mild months make the intense heat and humidity of July and August more bearable. (Of course, having buses, trains, and most public buildings coolly air-conditioned helps, too.) The winter temperatures are mild, typically hovering in the 40s. Occasionally, the city is sideswiped by a vicious ice storm or dusted with a sprinkling of snow, but the good news is that Atlantans view these onslaughts as a great excuse to crawl back under the covers. Just the hint of ice or snow sends people out in droves for bread and milk, and the real thing keeps everyone indoors until the offending front departs. Count on living quite comfortably without snow boots and long underwear.

Of course, not everything about living in a metropolitan area with 3.7 million people is ideal. Traffic is horrific during rush hour and only marginally bearable the rest of the time—a fact of life that's beginning to influence people's decisions about where to live. (Radio traffic reporters claim that Friday morning's rush hour starts on Thursday night, and Friday night's crush continues into Sunday. After a few hours on Atlanta's roadways, you may start to believe them!) It is true that Atlanta was ranked sixth among the nation's most congested metro areas in a Texas Transportation Institute report released in the fall of 1999. And the same report recorded that most Atlanta drivers spend an average of sixty-eight hours per year stuck in the gridlock. The addition of High Occupancy Vehicle (HOV) lanes in the late 1990s has encouraged car pooling, but not to the degree that negotiating the interstates has gotten significantly smoother.

Unchecked growth is a concern in each of the city's twenty metropolitan counties. Neighbors are more organized and active than ever in their attempts to thwart the demands of commercial and residential developers. For years, Atlanta has held onto its reputation as one of the most heavily wooded cities in the country, and efforts to keep that title have sparked many a battle between pro-growth factions and those who would take a slower approach. But there's no disputing that most residents have benefited from the city's invigorating growth and the homes, jobs, and recreational opportunities it's created.

No introduction to Atlanta would be complete without going back to where much of it all started. In many ways, the Civil War was a community-defining event that is far from passing into obscurity. Battles took place on the very streets and parks where people live and play today, and many native Atlantans keep the memories of those horrific days alive in family folklore. Many newcomers are surprised, some appalled, to hear their indigenous neighbors talking about the "War of Northern Aggression," or to see the Confederate battle banner prominently incorporated into the state flag. No matter what side of the conflict a newcomer claims, it doesn't hurt to approach the whole issue with respect and a sense of humor.

Keep in mind the words of Atlanta journalist Henry Grady, who in 1886 offered General Sherman his take on the town that indeed rose from the ashes. As an Atlanta newcomer, you're not an outsider; you are now part of a "brave and beautiful city."

Atlanta Statistics

Average Temperature by Season
Spring: 62 degrees F
Summer: 78 degrees F
Fall: 63 degrees F
Winter: 44 degrees F

Average Rainfall by Season
Spring: 14 inches
Summer: 12 inches
Fall: 10 inches
Winter: 14 inches
Last significant snowfall on record:
            7.9 inches in 1983

City and Area Population
City of Atlanta: 403,819 (1998)
20-county metropolitan area: 3.746 million (1998)

Population by Ethnicity (1998 estimates from the Census Bureau)

68%   *white*

25%   *black*

1%   *American Indian*

3%   *Asian*

3%   *Hispanic*

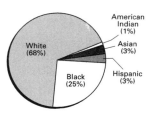

Population by Gender (1990 census info for city of Atlanta)

48%   *male*

52%   *female*

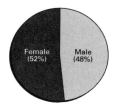

Population by Age (1990 census info for city of Atlanta)

Median age: 31.5

Average Income

1990: $35,607

1998: $47,393

Average Rent

$410 per month

Average Price of Houses (1998, according to AJC annual real estate wrap up)

Existing homes: *$144,158*

New homes: *$179,353*

All homes: *$155,570*

Cost of Living (100 is considered average)

Atlanta: 103.3
New York: 232.1
San Diego: 125.6
D.C.:   123.7

Resources

Metro Atlanta Chamber of Commerce

235 International Boulevard
Atlanta, GA 30303
(404) 586-8403

www.metroatlantachamber.com

U.S. Census Bureau

www.census.gov

Atlanta Convention and Visitors Bureau

233 Peachtree Street
Atlanta, GA 30303
(404) 521-6600

www.acvb.com

Atlanta Journal–Constitution

72 Marietta Street
Atlanta, GA 30303
(404) 526-5151

www.ajc.com

Web Sites

www.onlinecityguide
www.lycos.com

Books

Atlanta and Environs: A Chronicle of Its People and Events, Vols. I &
II, Franklin Garrett; Vol. III, Harold Martin

Metropolitan Frontiers: A Short History of Atlanta, Darlene R. Roth
and Andy Ambrose

ATLANTA AREA

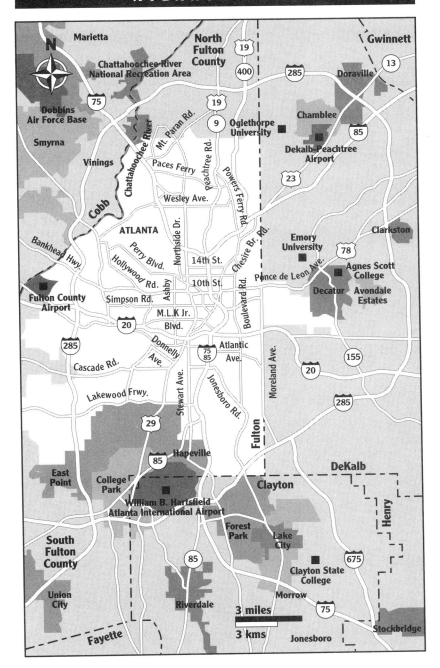

N

Marietta

North Fulton County

Gwinnett

19

400

285

13

Doraville

Chattahoochee River National Recreation Area

75

19

Dobbins Air Force Base

Chamblee

Smyrna

9

Oglethorpe University

85

Chattahoochee River

Mt. Paran Rd.

Peachtree Rd.

Dekalb-Peachtree Airport

Vinings

Paces Ferry

Powers Ferry Rd.

23

Cobb

Wesley Ave.

Clarkston

ATLANTA

Northside Dr.

Emory University

78

Bankhead Hwy.

Perry Blvd.

14th St.

Chesire Br. Rd.

Agnes Scott College

Hollywood Rd.

10th St.

Ponce de Leon Ave.

Decatur

Avondale Estates

Ashby

Fulton County Airport

Simpson Rd.

Boulevard Rd.

20

M.L.K Jr. Blvd.

285

Donnelly Ave.

Atlantic Ave.

75 85

Moreland Ave.

155

20

Cascade Rd.

285

Stewart Ave.

Lakewood Frwy.

Jonesboro Rd.

Fulton

29

85

Hapeville

DeKalb

East Point

College Park

Clayton

Henry

William B. Hartsfield Atlanta International Airport

South Fulton County

Forest Park

Lake City

85

Clayton State College

675

Union City

Riverdale

Morrow

75

3 miles

3 kms

Jonesboro

Stockbridge

Fayette

Places to Live

CHAPTER 1

Neighborhood Descriptions

Atlanta is a big place, and it's getting bigger by the year. Since 1990, the twenty-county metro area has welcomed more than 786,000 newcomers; only Los Angeles drew more. And the influx doesn't seem to be slowing as Atlanta closes in on the 4 million mark.

One of the features that makes Atlanta so attractive is its diverse housing market. Want to live in town, where restaurants and stores are within walking distance? Many city neighborhoods are dotted with lofts in converted warehouses, high-rise condominiums, townhouses, and affordable single-family homes, as well as multimillion-dollar mansions. Perhaps a new home in a nearby suburb where the focus is on family and schools suits your needs. And if you're yearning for wide open spaces and a barn for your horse, there are those options as well. There are even places where you can have a few acres in a suburban county but be close to a small town with a quaint square lined with shops and restaurants. In fact, deciding where to live in Atlanta will be easy once you determine two things: where you'll be working and what kind of lifestyle you want.

In the early days, Atlanta's housing growth surrounded its downtown. The hub was Five Points, where the main business district sprang up at the crossroads of Decatur, Peachtree, and Marietta

Streets. Since the swankiest address to have was (and in many cases still is) Peachtree Street, residents built their way northward along that road into Buckhead, a crossroads with a tavern adorned with an enormous buck's head over the door. Soon, neighborhoods were being carved out of farms and pastures, and the city limits expanded to include them.

By the turn of the century, elaborate gingerbread houses were springing up east and south of the city in Grant Park, West End, and Inman Park. Electric trolleys connected these neighborhoods with downtown and made living in the first suburbs enormously popular. By the mid-1950s, the city had expanded into DeKalb County on the east and to the Chattahoochee River on the west, as well as north to Buckhead and south to the border of East Point, Hapeville, and College Park, three municipalities with their own histories, governments, and services.

The expansion of the interstate system around Atlanta created a building boom in the 1960s. The I-285 Perimeter, the sixty-three-mile route that detours traffic around the heart of downtown, spurred the arrival of "edge cities"—communities such as Sandy Springs and Perimeter Center in Fulton County and Cumberland and Vinings in Cobb County that boast their own business centers, commercial districts, and neighborhoods. The widening of I-75 and I-85 to the north and south made commuting downtown from counties beyond the Perimeter a possibility. The opening of Georgia Highway 400 north from downtown to Forsyth County created another building bonanza in the early 1990s. And despite Atlanta's reputation for abominable traffic, growth experts predict that expansion will continue to cluster along these routes into the far northern and southern edges of the metro area. In fact, the far-flung sprawl is already credited with a recent housing trend: families with city residences for the work week and mountain or lakeside houses for escape on weekends.

A study of the twenty-county area shows a remarkably lopsided explosion of growth across the city's northern arc. Southern counties such as Clayton, Fayette, and Henry have been slower to develop than Cobb, Gwinnett, and northern Fulton, despite the fact that they offer more affordable housing alternatives and less congestion. A number of reasons have contributed to the imbalance. In southern Fulton, Hartsfield Atlanta International Airport took out entire neighbor-

hoods and attracted major manufacturing centers as it grew. Some
northern counties offer more resources in terms of schools, libraries,
cultural centers, and shopping districts, but they also assess higher
sales and real estate taxes to support them. The ability of some easily
accessed counties, such as Gwinnett along I-85, to attract corporate
headquarters helps pull in people who want to live near the office. But
as the entire metro area has mushroomed, the southern counties are
quickly catching up on all levels—from population and housing units
to traffic.

The easiest way to get a grip on all this growth is to think of the
metro area as three circular sections. The inner loop includes all of the
city limits. And even though most locals refer to everything inside the
Perimeter as "intown," the unincorporated parcels of Fulton and
DeKalb counties inside I-285 are included in the descriptions of those
counties.

The second circle consists of the "close-in" counties that ring the
Perimeter and a few on the southside that do not, but have tradition-
ally been considered suburban. Lastly, the "exurbs" are those counties
outside the second ring.

The areas covered in this chapter are:

City of Atlanta
- Downtown
- Midtown
- Buckhead
- East
- West
- South

Suburbs
- Clayton
- Cobb
- DeKalb
- Douglas
- Fayette
- Gwinnett

- Henry
- North Fulton County
- South Fulton County

Exurbs
- Bartow
- Cherokee
- Coweta
- Forsyth
- Paulding
- Rockdale

Grab a map and fill up the gas tank for a tour of what might be your new neighborhood.

City of Atlanta

As recently as the mid-1990s, residents inside the city limits could be pigeonholed into a few categories: the very rich, who owned lavish, gated Buckhead estates; the very young, both single and married, who weren't worried about schools or sprawling lawns; and the very pioneering, who willingly moved into ramshackle neighborhoods where houses were cheap but close to downtown.

Two things had a tremendous effect in turning the inner city into a hotbed of housing activity. The first was the summer of 1996, when Atlanta hosted the Olympic Games. Suddenly, this leading Southern city was in the international spotlight, and it took great pains to look its best. Many areas were overhauled, particularly the downtown district where today Centennial Olympic Park is a major tourist attraction, with its summertime fountains and winter ice rink. Out-of-towners who knew little about the city saw something they liked and moved in. Suburbanites spent two weeks in the city and discovered it was safe, clean, and easily navigated. Companies took advantage of the city's transportation facilities, inviting business climate, and available housing and decided Atlanta was the place to be. Newcomers, particularly from cities where urban living is a viable alternative, helped fuel a demand for condominiums, lofts, town-houses, and houses inside the city limits.

The second force driving the intown market is, in a way, the result of so many folks arriving into town. As noted, all those rumors you may have heard about Atlanta's traffic are unfortunately true. Anecdotes about two-hour commutes are typical water cooler conversation. Empty-nesters (couples whose children are grown) are trading in their suburban tract homes for the convenience of walking to work, restaurants, and entertainment venues. Young professional singles and couples are enthralled with the unusual loft spaces carved out of former warehouses, factories, and office buildings. Neighborhoods are enjoying a resurgence of families moving in who support the local schools and commercial districts. Civic leaders have emphasized a return to pedestrian-friendly areas and vetoed projects that are car-dependent.

As a result, housing prices in the city limits have climbed. Areas that once drew only drug dealers are brimming with urban pioneers who have driven property values up. Though house hunters will find similar price ranges around the metro area, properties in the city generally come with a smaller house and yard than their suburban counterparts.

Sorting out the particulars about Atlanta's neighborhoods requires a close look at several districts. We'll start in the heart of Downtown, where it all started.

Neighborhood Statistical Profile

Population: 425,200

Median income: $36,051

Percentages by Ethnicity

22%	*Anglo*
2%	*Hispanic*
68%	*Black*
<1%	*American Indian*
1%	*Asian*

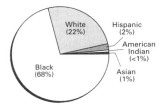

Population by Gender

48%   *male*

52%   *female*

Population by Age

24%   *under 21*

28%   *21–34*

24%   *35–49*

13%   *50–64*

11%   *65 and over*

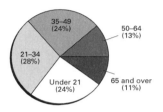

Crime Statistics (from the Metro Atlanta Crime Commission, 1998)

Murder   149

Rape   385

Robbery   4,658

Aggravated
   assault 7,432

Burglary 9,093

Larceny   28,513

Car theft 7,899

DOWNTOWN

Five Points, the intersection of Decatur, Peachtree, and Marietta Streets and the site of the famed phoenix statue in Woodruff Park, was once the sole domain of banks and businesses. In recent years, it's become the focus of major renovations that have turned former department stores and office buildings into homes. And it's become a fun place, close to the CNN Center with its food court and movie theaters; Philips Arena, home of the Hawks and Thrashers; the Georgia Dome; Turner Field, home of the Braves; and the Georgia State University campus. The demand for homes has stretched beyond the heart of downtown into adjacent areas such as Fairlie-Poplar,

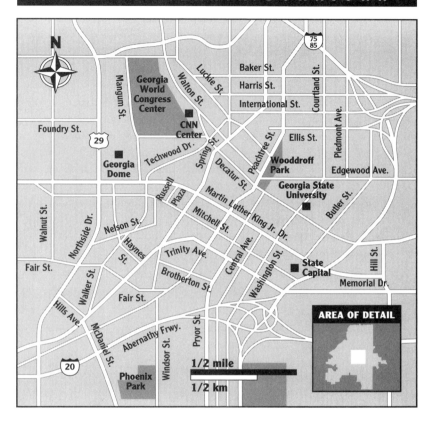

CITY OF ATLANTA/DOWNTOWN

Castleberry Hill, and Vine City. The western district, crisscrossed with train tracks, has the largest assortment of warehouses and factories that have become lofts. Centennial Place, an upscale apartment complex near the park, is one of the few rental properties; most are condominiums.

Downtown draws a range of residents, from the president of Georgia State (who bought a condominium in a restored clothing store) to artists and photographers who enjoy living in their work space. For others, the appeal is to walk to work, or to have a "reverse commute"—one that takes them to the suburbs against the rush hour traffic.

The thirty-three-story Equitable Building and the fifty-two-story Georgia Pacific headquarters overshadow some of the city's first high-rises, such as the Candler and the Rhodes Haverty Buildings. Macy's operates a large store on Peachtree Street just north of Five Points, opposite one of the city's top hotels, the Ritz-Carlton Atlanta. Other hotels cater to the city's burgeoning convention business, making downtown a bustling place during the day. However, typical community services have been slow to arrive. It often requires a drive to find a grocery or drug store, and many of the area restaurants cater more to the lunch crowds than to locals looking for dinner. There are signs of improvement, with the opening of a Kroger grocery store near City Hall and several new hotels and restaurants coming into the area. An active neighborhood association has worked closely with the city's development efforts in the area and has combated problems such as homeless men and women sleeping in the parks.

Average price of house: $77,950 to $140,130
Estimated commute times:

to Buckhead	*15 minutes*
to Marietta	*25 minutes*
to Decatur	*15 minutes*
to the airport	*15 minutes*

Important Places Nearby

Grocery Stores

Kroger
235 Central Avenue
(404) 586-7390

Sweet Auburn Curb Market
209 Edgewood Avenue
(404) 659-1665

Pharmacies

Kroger
235 Central Avenue
(404) 586-7390

Banks

Bank of America
35 Broad Street
(404) 893-8282
www.bankofamerica.com

Wachovia
2 Peachtree Street
(404) 865-4000

www.wachovia.com

Hardware Stores

Ace Hardware
626 Glen Iris Drive
(404) 872-6651

Fast Food

McDonald's
55 Decatur Street
(404) 521-3553

Wendy's
1 CNN Center
(404) 659-1698

Wall Street Deli
100 Peachtree Street
(404) 681-5542

Hospitals/Emergency Rooms

Grady Memorial Hospital
80 Butler Street
Atlanta, GA 30335
(404) 616-4307

www.gradyhealthsystem.org

MIDTOWN

North and west of Downtown along Peachtree Street stretches one of the city's hottest residential real estate markets. Generally referred to as Midtown, the area had the most new single-family home and condominium sales in 1998 of any part of the city. The 311 properties that changed hands had an average price of $201,326.

Midtown offers something for every housing preference, from luxurious penthouses fifty stories above the skyline at The Grand on 10th Street to modest Craftsman bungalows and cozy Tudors in Virginia Highland and Morningside. Some of the city's first subdivisions along Peachtree are now the mature, lushly wooded neighborhoods of Ansley Park, Sherwood Forest, and Brookwood Hills. The variety is reflected in the price range, from the low $100,000s to more than $1 million.

Midtown has some of the city's most colorful corners. Restaurants, shops, and condominiums are sprouting up on Peachtree, and the scene along Ponce de Leon Avenue, Highland Avenue, and 10th and 14th Streets has always been one of activity, with plenty of places to eat, grab a beer, or catch a show. The Fox Theatre, the High Museum of

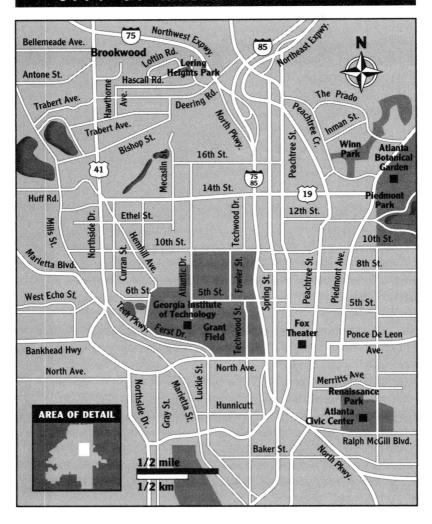

CITY OF ATLANTA/MIDTOWN

Art and the Woodruff Arts Center are some of the city's chief cultural attractions. In addition, popular neighborhood commercial districts at the intersections of Virginia and Highland Avenues (Virginia-

CITY OF ATLANTA/MIDTOWN

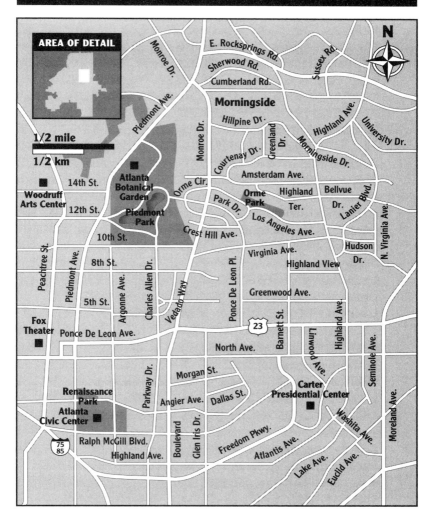

Highland) and Moreland and Euclid Avenues (Little Five Points) draw visitors from around the metro area to the antique, consignment, health food and specialty stores. Piedmont Park, a 185-acre green space that includes the Atlanta Botanical Garden, is a huge attraction for joggers, in-line skaters and cyclists, as well as crowds who pack the lawns for free outdoor concerts during the summer.

Along with families who have turned Morningside Elementary into one of the city's leading schools, Midtown has a large gay and lesbian community. Energetic neighborhood associations and business alliances keep sharp watch on commercial and residential development.

Average price of house: *$105,250 to $268,950*
Estimated commute times:

to Downtown	*10 minutes*
to Marietta	*20 minutes*
to Decatur	*10 minutes*
to the airport	*20 minutes*

Important Places Nearby

Grocery Stores

Kroger
725 Ponce de Leon Avenue
(404) 875-2701

Publix
1544 Piedmont Road
(404) 898-1850

Pharmacies

APP Pharmacy
1710 Peachtree Street
(404) 875-9717

Drug Emporium
2953 Druid Hills Road
(404) 636-6108

www.drugemporium.com

Eckerd Drugs
1512 Piedmont Avenue
(404) 876-2263

www.eckerd.com

Banks

Bank of America
600 Peachtree Street
(404) 607-4850

www.bankofamerica.com

First Union
999 Peachtree Street
(404) 865-3010

www.firstunion.com

Hardware Stores

Intown Hardware & Garden
854 Highland Avenue
(404) 874-5619

Fast Food

Harry's in a Hurry
1501 Ponce de Leon Avenue
(404) 439-1100

Kentucky Fried Chicken
425 Ponce de Leon Avenue
(404) 874-1400

The Varsity
61 North Avenue
(404) 881-1706

Hospitals/Emergency Room

Crawford Long Hospital
550 Peachtree Street
Atlanta, GA 30365
(404) 686-4411

Georgia Baptist Health Care System
303 Parkway Drive
Atlanta, GA 30312
(404) 265-4000
www.gbhcs.org

BUCKHEAD

In the early 1900s, Atlanta's wealthy citizens left the summer heat of the city for the cooler climes to the north. There, on acres of woods crisscrossed by streams, they built getaway cottages in the area called Buckhead.

Eventually, Atlanta's growth caught up to those warm-weather retreats. As trolley lines made commuting downtown feasible, it wasn't long before the well-heeled were selling off their Midtown mansions and hiring noted architects to design and build fabulous abodes in Buckhead. Many of those estates still stand along Tuxedo, Blackland, and Habersham Roads. In the 1960s, the Governor's Mansion was built on West Paces Ferry Road, around the corner from where golf-great Bobby Jones had an estate. The city's showplace home, the Swan House on Andrews Drive, is part of the Atlanta History Center. Several sections of the surrounding neighborhood are listed on the National Register of Historic Places. Though many of the sprawling estates have been subdivided for developments and infill houses, many of the old homes can be found nearby, still overlooking several manicured acres.

CITY OF ATLANTA/BUCKHEAD

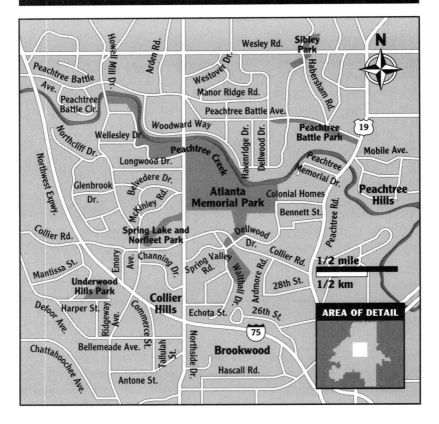

While Buckhead boasts streets of million-dollar homes where tour buses frequently stop for photos, the community isn't exclusively the bastion of the super-rich. On the community's southern and western border, Garden Hills, Loring Heights, and Collier Hills have one-story cottages and some larger traditional homes that draw families with children as well as professional singles. The houses and prices get bigger as you head north into Haynes Manor along Peachtree Battle Road and into the northwest along the Chattahoochee River.

CITY OF ATLANTA/BUCKHEAD

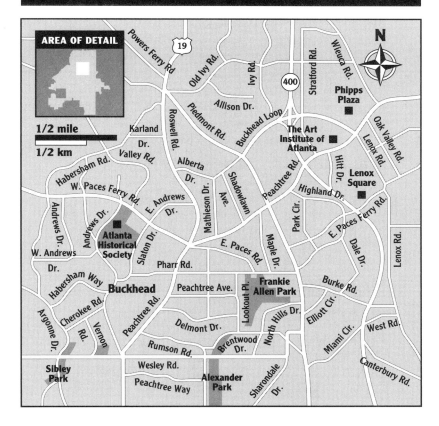

Buckhead's portion of Peachtree (which becomes Peachtree Road as it enters the neighborhood) is often referred to as "the Beverly Hills of the South" for its shopping and restaurant districts. Lenox Square, the largest shopping center in the Southeast, and Phipps Plaza, its upscale counterpart, sit catty-corner from each other under the gaze of the elegant Ritz-Carlton Buckhead. Other fancy boutiques, art galleries, and glitzy hotels dot the area, beside high-rise office towers, condominiums, and townhouses. Commercial encroachment is a hot button issue for dedicated Buckhead residents, who are among some of the most vocal, active, and well-heeled in the city. It's not unusual for them to turn out by the busload to object to almost any proposal that suggests taking out trees or creating more traffic for neighborhoods.

Along with several outstanding public schools, Buckhead is home to the city's most elite independent schools: the Westminster Schools, Pace Academy, the Galloway School, and the Lovett School. The area is also known for its large and wealthy churches, including the biggest Presbyterian congregation in the country, the 12,000-member Peachtree Presbyterian on Roswell Road.

Average price of house: $286,800 to $341,000
Estimated commute times:

to Downtown	*15 minutes*
to Marietta	*20 minutes*
to Decatur	*15 minutes*
to the airport	*25 minutes*

Important Places Nearby

Grocery Stores

Harris Teeter
3954 Peachtree Road
(404) 814-5990

www.harristeeter.com

Publix
2628 Peachtree Road
(404) 848-0330

Pharmacies

Drug Emporium
2625 Piedmont Road
(404) 233-1201

www.drugemporium.com

Eckerd Drugs
4540 Roswell Road
(404) 257-1873

www.eckerd.com

Banks

Bank of America
600 Peachtree Street
(404) 607-4850

www.bankofamerica.com

First Union
999 Peachtree Street
(404) 865-3010

www.firstunion.com

Hardware Stores

General Hardware
4218 Peachtree Road
(404) 237-5209

Home Depot
815 Sidney Marcus Boulevard
(404) 231-1411
www.homedepot.com

Fast Food

Chick-fil-A
3500 Peachtree Street
(404) 848-9550

Einstein Bros. Bagels
1870 Piedmont Road
(404) 853-1678

Steak N Shake
3380 Northside Parkway
(404) 262-7051

Hospitals/Emergency Rooms

Piedmont Hospital
1968 Peachtree Road
Atlanta, GA 30309
(404) 605-5000

EAST

In the late 1800s, trolley lines running east from downtown opened up residential areas that have become some of the city's most historic neighborhoods. MARTA trains have long since replaced the trolleys, but continue to make commuting easy to such areas such as Inman Park, Druid Hills, Candler Park, Lake Clair, Kirkwood, East Atlanta, and East Lake.

Renowned for their Victorian and early twentieth-century architecture, many homes in Grant Park, Inman Park, and Druid Hills have been turned into showplaces. (In fact, the entire Druid Hills neighborhood was on display when it served as the backdrop for the movie *Driving Miss Daisy.*) Along with the more modest areas of Candler Park, Lake Clair, Kirkwood, and Ormewood Park, these communities benefit from two busy and colorful business districts: Little Five Points, where Euclid, McLendon, and Moreland Avenues intersect, and East Atlanta Village, centered at Flat Shoals and Glenwood Avenues. Both draw crowds to ethnic restaurants, consignment shops, health food stores, coffeehouses, and the sidewalks, where musicians frequently hold forth for the public's entertainment.

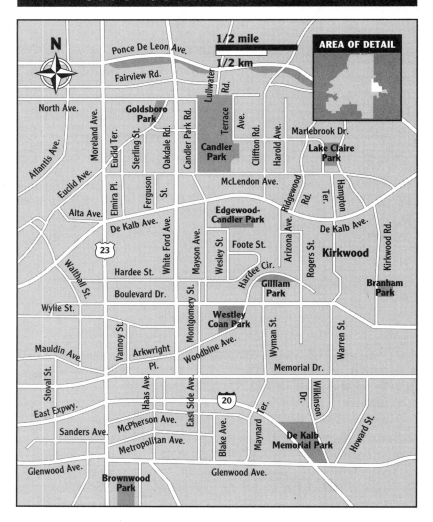

CITY OF ATLANTA/EAST

In the late 1990s, the housing stock in many of these neighborhoods soared as a proposed highway project was killed and replaced instead with bike and jogging paths that meander through the area. Young families, gay couples, and singles are restoring the Craftsman

CITY OF ATLANTA/EAST

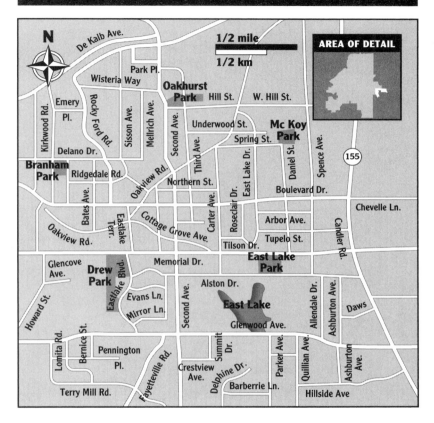

bungalows and small Tudor houses. In East Lake, a housing project was torn down to make way for mixed-income apartments and town-houses near the East Lake Golf Course, a restored oasis of green with a historic clubhouse. The club's owners have partnered with the area's public schools to tutor kids and teach the fundamentals of the game.

Average price of house: $87,697 to $171,058
Estimated commute times:

to Downtown	*10 minutes*
to Marietta	*25 minutes*
to Decatur	*10 minutes*
to the airport	*20 minutes*

CITY OF ATLANTA / EAST

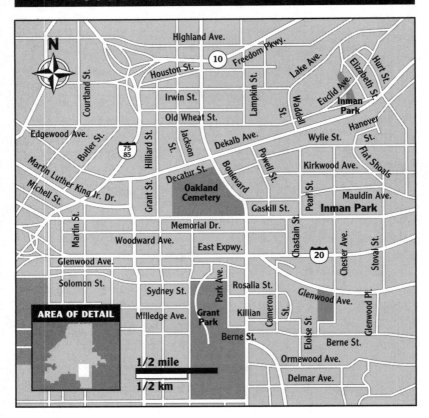

Important Places Nearby

Grocery Stores

Kroger
1700 Moreland Avenue
(404) 872-0782

Sevananda Natural Foods Market
457 Moreland Avenue
(404) 681-2831

Pharmacies

Eckerd Drugs
1410 Moreland Avenue
(404) 622-5348

Banks

Bank of America
411 Flat Shoals Avenue
(404) 330-0750

www.bankofamerica.com

Hardware Stores

Ace Hardware
1231 Glenwood Avenue
(404) 627-5757

Fast Food

Fellini's Pizza
1634 McLendon Avenue
(404) 687-9190

Church's
1405 Moreland Avenue
(404) 622-7207

Zesto's
377 Moreland Avenue
(404) 523-1973

Hospitals/Emergency Rooms

Georgia Baptist Medical Center
303 Parkway Drive
Atlanta, GA 30312
(404) 265-4000

www.gbhcs.org

WEST

Victorian-era trolley lines west of the city made West End one of the most popular neighborhoods in Atlanta. Some of the city's leading citizens, including writer Joel Chandler Harris, built lavish mansions that are part of the neighborhood's historic district today. The community also supports the West End Mall and a business district along Abernathy Boulevard.

Close by, other early 1900s neighborhoods have earned city-designated historic status: Adair Park is a neighborhood of modest cottages south of West End; Whittier Mill is a collection of tiny homes originally built for millworkers along the Chattahoochee River. Washington Park, home of Atlanta's first black high school, the Auburn Avenue area where Martin Luther King Jr. lived and preached,

CITY OF ATLANTA/WEST

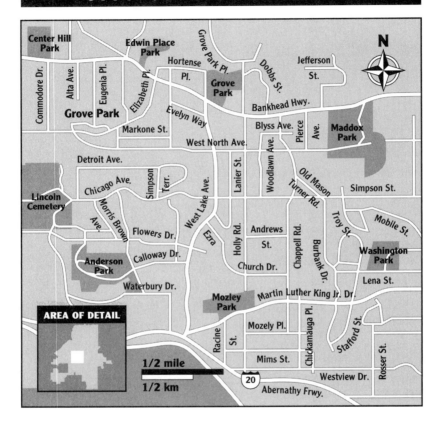

and Cabbagetown, another millworkers' village adjacent to the factory that now sports apartments, have been given landmark status. Beyond West End, neighborhoods such as Mozley Park, Grove Park, and Collier Heights have long been stable black communities of well-built brick ranch houses.

The northwestern corner of the city, though crowded with rail lines, has promoted its proximity to downtown and Georgia Tech, and an assortment of new and older housing, to draw home owners to Underwood Hills, Berkeley Park, and Bolton. Many of these com-

CITY OF ATLANTA/WEST

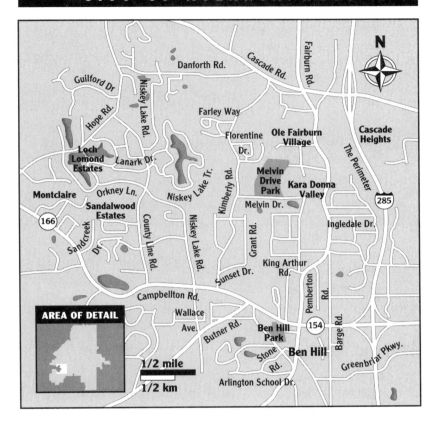

munities have large numbers of student residents as well as strong neighborhood associations that tackle issues of crime, congestion, and zoning.

Atlanta's southwestern border, along Cascade and Campbellton Roads, is home to some of the African American community's wealthiest professionals, civic leaders, and entrepreneurs. Contemporary mansions in new housing developments are now part of middle- and upper-income black areas such as Adams Park, Niskey Lake, and Loch Lomond Estates. The enormous popularity of the area has brought shopping centers and restaurants to a once under-served community.

Average price of house: *$49,704 to $172,434*
Estimated commute times:
     to Downtown   *15 minutes*
     o Marietta   *20 minutes*
     to Decatur   *20 minutes*
     to the airport   *15 minutes*

Important Places Nearby

Grocery Stores

Kroger
1715 Howell Mill Road
(404) 355-7886

Publix
3655 Cascade Road
(404) 505-2870

Pharmacies

Bolton Professional Pharmacy
2608 Bolton Road
(404) 351-3811

CVS
2076 Campbellton Road
(404) 758-4526

www.cvs.com

Banks

First Union
3680 Cascade Road
(404) 865-4900

www.firstunion.com

SouthTrust Bank
874 Abernathy Boulevard
(404) 752-8400

www.southtrust.com

Hardware Stores

Cascade Heights Hardware
3910 Campbellton Road
(404) 346-1552

Fast Food

Burger King
2760 Greenbriar Parkway
(404) 344-5926

Church's
529 Cascade Road
(404) 758-6374

Hospitals/Emergency Rooms

Georgia Baptist Health Care System
303 Parkway Drive
Atlanta, GA 30312
(404) 265-4000
www.gbhcs.org

Grady Memorial Hospital
80 Butler Street
Atlanta, GA 30335
(404) 616-4307

SOUTH

For years, neighborhoods such as Mechanicsville and Summerhill just south of Downtown have been battered by Atlanta's development. These predominantly black communities were divided in the 1960s when Interstate 20 cut through the residential district. Before the 1996 Olympics, the construction of Turner Field on the site of the old Fulton County Stadium tore up much of the area. But resilient residents have formed land trusts and development groups to encourage a rebirth of the area's vacant lots and abandoned houses. Success stories include single-family houses in Victorian styles and contemporary townhouses with garages that now stand within view of the stadium and the state capitol. Though the area is slowly drawing young singles and couples, it suffers from a lack of neighborhood amenities as well as from traffic and congestion—a real plague during the baseball season.

Farther south, the area is dotted with middle-class black neighborhoods such as Lakewood, Thomasville, and Sylvan Hills. But along with assets such as Lakewood Park with its entertainment amphitheater and the Browns Mill Golf Course, the area includes a federal prison on McDonough Road, the Carver Homes housing project, and Metropolitan Avenue—one of the city's most notorious strips for drug deals and prostitution.

CITY OF ATLANTA/SOUTH

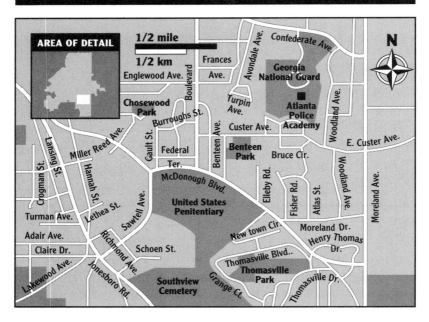

Average price of house: $53,500
Estimated commute times:
    to Downtown   10 minutes
    to Marietta   20 minutes
    to Decatur   15 minutes
    to the airport   15 minutes

Important Places Nearby

Grocery Stores

Sweet Auburn Curb Market
209 Edgewood Avenue
(404) 659-1665

Pharmacies

Kroger
235 Central Avenue
(404) 586-7390

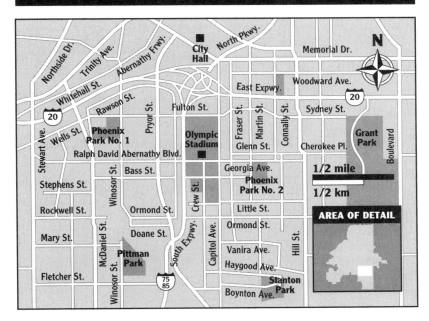

CITY OF ATLANTA/SOUTH

Sweet Auburn Curb Market
209 Edgewood Avenue
(404) 659-1665

Banks

First Union
2791 East Point Street
(404) 865-2625

www.firstunion.com

Hardware Stores

East Point True Value Hardware
2891 Church Street
(404) 761-2640

Fast Food

Church's
2558 Martin Luther King Drive
(404) 691-8065

CITY OF ATLANTA/SOUTH

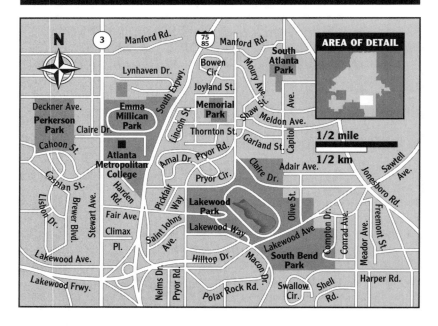

McDonald's
150 Cleveland Avenue
(404) 766-7779

Hospitals/Emergency Rooms

Grady Memorial Hospital
80 Butler Street
Atlanta, GA 30335
(404) 616-4307

Southwest Hospital
501 Fairburn Road
Atlanta, GA 30331
(404) 699-1111

Suburbs

Just outside the I-285 Perimeter is the ring of close-in communities that make up the bulk of Atlanta's suburbs. Though largely developed with new home communities, these areas also include several old towns with thriving shopping districts that offer an alternative to sprawling subdivisions. Here's an overview of what each county has to offer.

CLAYTON

Chamber of Commerce

8712 Tara Boulevard
Jonesboro, GA 30236
(404) 608-2770

www.claytoncham.org

Alas for fans of *Gone With the Wind,* Tara was just a figment of Margaret Mitchell's imagination. But if you want to see grand homes of the sort that inspired the writer, visit Clayton County. Mixed in with the antebellum showplaces are moderately priced older homes and new subdivisions not far from downtown Atlanta.

Clayton County capitalizes on its *GWTW* connection, with streets named Tara, tours of the area's historic mansions, and frequent Civil War reenactments. Jonesboro, the county seat and site of a key Civil War battle, has its visitors' center in the restored train depot, surrounded by the courthouse, shops, and antique stores.

Life in the municipalities of Riverdale, Lake City, and Lovejoy is laid back, as you'd expect from such small communities. Forest Park, the town closest to Hartsfield Atlanta International Airport, has faced the most setbacks as it has struggled to survive alongside the world's busiest flight center. Over the years, the city has lost houses and citizens to new runways and noise pollution. Morrow is home to Clayton State College, whose performance venue, Spivey Hall, attracts musicians from around the world. It also boasts an impressive pipe organ.

East of Jonesboro, new upscale housing developments around Lake Spivey's waterfront and golf course have prospered. The area includes Southlake Mall, the Beach water park, and one of the few funeral museums in the south.

ATLANTA SUBURBS

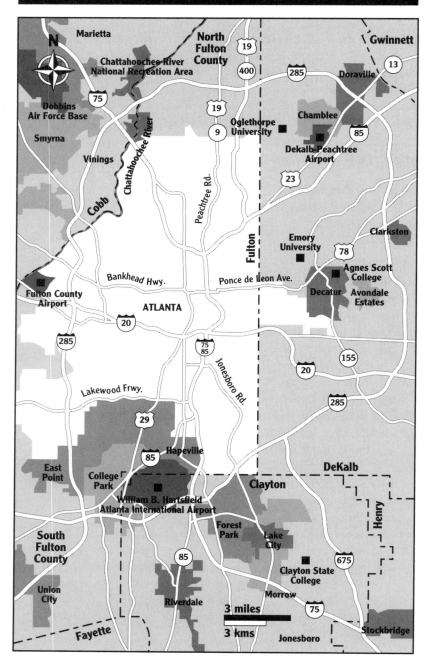

Neighborhood Statistical Profile

Population: 208,999

Population by Ethnicity

72%	*white*
24%	*black*
<1%	*American Indian*
3%	*Asian*
1%	*other*

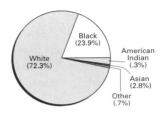

Population by Gender

49%	*male*
51%	*female*

Population by Age

33%	*under 21*
27%	*21–34*
23%	*35–49*
11%	*50–64*
6%	*65 and over*

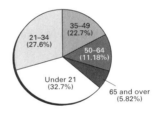

Crime Statistics (from the Georgia Bureau of Investigation, 1998)

Murder	*11*
Rape	*36*
Robbery	*381*
Aggravated assault	*396*
Burglary	*2,418*
Larceny	*8,186*
Car theft	*1,806*

Other Statistics

Median income:	$36,379
Percentage living at poverty level:	13.3%
Average price of house:	$95,558
Estimated commute times:	

to Downtown	*15 minutes*
to Marietta	*25 minutes*
to Decatur	*20 minutes*
to the airport	*10 minutes*

Important Places Nearby

Grocery Stores

Publix
7899 Tara Boulevard
Jonesboro
(770) 603-5900

Georgia State Farmers Market
16 Forest Parkway
Forest Park
(404) 675-1782

Pharmacies

Arrowhead Pharmacy
1880 Upper Riverdale Road
Jonesboro
(770) 991-2020

Christian's Pharmacy
1032 Main Street
Forest Park
(404) 366-4320

Banks

**First Citizens Bank
of Clayton County**
223 North Main Street
Jonesboro
(770) 477-2424

SouthTrust Bank
1893 Mt. Zion Road
Morrow
(770) 968-6400

www.southtrust.com

Hardware Stores

Ace Hardware
7459 Georgia Highway 85
Riverdale
(770) 996-2442

Campbell True Value
810 Morrow Road
Forest Park
(404) 361-6080

Fast Food

Chick-fil-A Dwarf House
4959 Jonesboro Road
Forest Park
(404) 361-3443

Mrs. Winner's
6273 Jonesboro Road
Morrow
(770) 961-2381

Hospitals/Emergency Rooms

Promina Southern Regional Health System
11 Upper Riverdale Road
Riverdale, GA 30274
(770) 991-8000

COBB

Chamber of Commerce
240 Interstate Parkway North
P.O. Box Cobb
Marietta, GA 30006
(770) 980-2000

www.cobbchamber.org

For years, the east side of Cobb County north from the Chattahoochee River has been noted for its new upscale neighborhoods, good schools, access to I-75 and Buckhead, and taxes lower than Fulton's. But as available land in the area dwindles and traffic heading to town becomes increasingly snarled, developers and buyers have shifted their attention to the rest of the county.

Growth in the more rural west and north has been explosive, with new houses cropping up on former farms and woodlands. Road improvements have made the areas more accessible, but the accompanying traffic has increased proportionately. Still, the areas continue to draw upscale families to new communities. The spread of commercial districts to serve the growing population has prompted the formation of some strong citizens groups.

Several sleepy small towns on the county's southwest have come alive as Atlanta's growth moves west along I-20. Mableton, Austell, and Powder Springs have benefited from the high-speed Thornton Highway off I-20 and the East-West Connector that links drivers to I-285.

The proximity to I-75 has fueled growth in Kennesaw and Acworth to the north. Both quaint antebellum towns have historic districts surrounded by new developments. Acworth's crown jewel is a lengthy stretch of Lake Allatoona waterfront that brings many seasonal visitors to town. Kennesaw, the town that made headlines when it legislated that every homeowner be armed, takes in much of the area's commercial explosion in the Town Center mall area along Barrett Parkway as well as the preserved Civil War battlefields around Kennesaw Mountain.

Along Cobb's southeastern edge is the Galleria district, where I-75 crosses I-285. This regional hub is booming with office parks, shopping malls, and restaurants, as well as condominiums, apartments, and cluster homes popular with singles and empty-nesters. The city of Smyrna, long an area of middle-income neighborhoods, has garnered national attention for revitalization efforts that have created a new town square for city hall, a library, and a community center. Smyrna also benefits from the overflow of affluent singles and families pouring into Vinings, a charming unincorporated district along the Chattahoochee River. This tiny district has become the darling of people who want to be close to Buckhead just across the water, but who don't want to pay Fulton taxes. As the demand for Vining's pricey new homes and condominiums spills into Smyrna, real estate experts have taken to calling the area "Smyrna-Vinings." Vinings' commercial district has several upscale restaurants, shops, and coffeehouses.

Marietta, the county seat, has a scenic old town square where bands play in the summer and wedding and prom parties stop to pose for photos. The heart of town is built up with county and city buildings, shops, restaurants, churches, and old neighborhoods. The city has also benefited from the metro area's loft craze, as several old warehouses along the train tracks have been converted to condominium and apartment spaces.

Getting to I-75 from Cobb's western neighborhoods during peak drive times is difficult because of the congestion around Marietta. And once you've arrived at the highway, things are often worse; the I-75 stretch to Atlanta is one of the metro area's most heavily traveled roads, despite its eight southbound and high-occupancy-vehicle lanes. Two particularly nasty sections are the junctions of I-575 coming out of Cherokee County and I-285 at the Galleria.

Neighborhood Statistical Profile

Population: 566,203

Population by Ethnicity

87%	*white*
10%	*black*
<1%	*American Indian*
2%	*Asian*
1%	*other*

Population by Gender

49%	*male*
51%	*female*

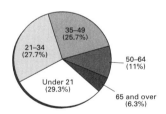

Population by Age

29%	*under 21*
28%	*21–34*
26%	*35–49*
11%	*50–64*
6%	*65 and over*

Crime Statistics (from the Georgia Bureau of Investigation, 1998)

Murder	*16*
Rape	*127*
Robbery	*639*
Aggravated assault	*790*
Burglary	*3,617*
Larceny	*13,246*
Car theft	*2,314*

Other Statistics

Median income:	$50,018
Percentage living at poverty level:	7.4%
Average price of house:	$157,127
Estimated commute times:	
to Downtown	25 minutes
to Decatur	30 minutes
to the airport	45 minutes

Important Places Nearby

Grocery Stores

Harry's Farmers Market
70 Powers Ferry Road
Marietta
(770) 578-4400

Harris Teeter
2960 Shallowford Road
Marietta
(770) 977-7724

www.harristeeter.com

Pharmacies

CVS
1169 Powder Springs Street
Marietta
(770) 919-1281

www.cvs.com

Eckerd Drugs
5105 Austell Road
Austell
(770) 941-2645

Banks

Fidelity National
1223 Johnson Ferry Road
Marietta
(770) 973-5494

www.fidelitynational.com

Independent Bank and Trust
4484 Marietta Street
Powder Springs
(770) 943-5000

www.independentbank.com

Hardware Stores

Ace Hardware
775 Whitlock Avenue
Marietta
(770) 422-1646

Home Depot
449 Roberts Circle
Kennesaw
(770) 424-1309

www.homedepot.com

Fast Food

The Square Bagel
45 S. Marietta Parkway
Marietta
(770) 426-4475

Tommy's Sandwich Shop
148 Roswell Road
Marietta
(770) 422-3185

Krystal
30 Whitlock Avenue
Marietta
(770) 422-2200

Hospitals/Emergency Room

Cobb Hospital
3950 Austell Road
Austell, GA 30106
(770) 732-4000

Kennestone Hospital
677 Church Street
Marietta, GA 30060
(770) 793-5000

DEKALB

Chamber of Commerce
750 Commerce Drive, Suite 201
Decatur, GA 30030
(404) 378-8000

There's something about living in DeKalb that makes folks fiercely loyal. Whether they're in a condominium near Emory University, a bungalow in a Decatur historic district, or a new home in the expanding southwest section, residents of this county (founded in the early 1820s) wouldn't trade their proximity to Atlanta and the Perimeter or their quaint communities for anything else in the area.

Decatur, the county seat, houses a historical society in the old courthouse. The streets around the square are booming with shops, coffeehouses, and some of the area's best restaurants. With its good school system and variety of housing options, Decatur has benefited from the surge of single and family buyers returning to close-in communities.

Other municipalities include Chamblee and Doraville, two of the most culturally diverse communities around Atlanta. The influence of Asian and Hispanic residents is evident in the variety of ethnic groceries and restaurants that line Buford Highway. Avondale Estates, east of Decatur, has a charming section of Old English–style stores and affordable houses. Stone Mountain, home to the park and granite outcropping of the same name, has a pretty business district with a restored train depot and a variety of restaurants and antique shops.

Unincorporated Dunwoody, one of the northside's most prestigious addresses, includes Perimeter Mall, the Dunwoody Country Club, and an array of upscale subdivisions and shopping centers built with tightly controlled architectural standards that limit everything from building colors to the height of the McDonald's arches. The Murphy-Candler area has numerous established developments around one of the county's largest parks. Along I-20, southwest DeKalb, Lithonia, and Panola have an assortment of affordable new houses that are popular with middle-class black families. The area also includes South DeKalb Mall.

DeKalb boasts some of the south's finest centers of higher learning, including Emory University, Oglethorpe University, and Agnes Scott College, along with a regional airport called DeKalb-Peachtree. Its traffic hot spots are I-20 heading into Atlanta and the Stone Mountain Freeway, two heavily traveled routes that back up regularly during rush hours.

(Note: DeKalb's western neighborhoods that are inside the Atlanta limits are included in the city section.)

Neighborhood Statistical Profile

Population: 593,850

Population by Ethnicity

54%	white
42%	black
<1%	American Indian
3%	Asian
1%	other

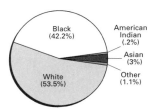

Population by Gender

48%   male
52%   female

Population by Age

28%   under 21
28%   21–34
23%   35–49
12%   50–64
9%   65 and over

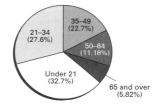

Crime Statistics (from the Georgia Bureau of Investigation, 1998)

Murder   56
Rape   153
Robbery   2,034
Aggravated
*   assault 983*
Burglary   8,527
Larceny   25,155
Car theft   7,241

Other Statistics

Median income:	*$38,189*
Percentage living at poverty level:	*15.7%*
Average price of house:	*$147,800*
Estimated commute times:	
* to Downtown*	*15 minutes*
* to Marietta*	*25 minutes*
* to the airport*	*25 minutes*

Important Places Nearby

Grocery Stores

DeKalb Farmers Market
3000 East Ponce de Leon Avenue
Decatur
(404) 377-6400

Kroger
2835 Wesley Chapel Road
Decatur
(770) 987-0633

Pharmacies

Avondale Drug
1 North Clarendon Avenue
Avondale Estates
(404) 294-5070

CVS
2738 North Decatur Road
Decatur
(404) 508-2225

www.cvs.com

Banks

Colonial Bank
3361 Clairmont Road
Atlanta
(404) 321-0004

Regions Bank
1457 Mt. Vernon Road
Dunwoody
(770) 395-9611

www.regionsbank.com

Hardware Stores

Cofer Bros. Hardware
2300 Main Street
Tucker
(770) 938-3200

Ace Workbench Hardware
5466 Peachtree Industrial
Boulevard
Chamblee
(770) 458-8058

Fast Food

Arby's
2788 Candler Road
Decatur
(404) 243-0220

Burger King
5654 Buford Highway
Doraville
(770) 451-0908

Hardee's
5516 Peachtree Industrial
Boulevard
Chamblee
(770) 458-2433

Hospitals/Emergency Rooms

Decatur Hospital
450 North Candler Street
Decatur, GA 30030
(404) 501-6700

DeKalb Medical Center
2701 North Decatur Road
Decatur
(404) 501-5200
www.drhs.org

St. Joseph's Hospital
5665 Peachtree Dunwoody Road
Atlanta, GA 30342
(404) 851-7001
www.stjosephsatlanta.org

DOUGLAS

Chamber of Commerce
2145 Slater Mill Road
Douglasville, GA 30135
(770) 942-5022

Douglas County straddles I-20 on the metro area's western edge. For years, the area has been a largely rural community around the county seat of Douglasville. In recent years, Douglas has been discovered by buyers looking for affordable housing, low taxes, and less congestion. It's been particularly popular with those heading to work in the Marietta and the Fulton Industrial district. The drive to Atlanta isn't bad, either; the eastbound stretch of I-20 into downtown is the only interstate section in the metro area that didn't have enough traffic to warrant construction of high-occupancy-vehicle lanes.

Douglas developers have catered to the demands of first-time buyers looking for three-bedroom starter homes, as well as more upscale, older customers who enjoy the amenities at golf course communities. The county's first major shopping mall, Arbor Place, opened in late 1999, and is the sixth biggest in the state.

Neighborhood Statistical Profile

Population: 89,843

Population by Ethnicity

91%   *white*

8%   *black*

<1%   *American Indian*

1%   *Asian*

<1%   *other*

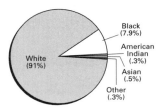

Population by Gender

50%   *male*

50%   *female*

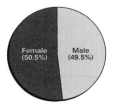

Population by Age

33%   *under 21*

25%   *21–34*

24%   *35–49*

11%   *50–64*

7%   *65 and over*

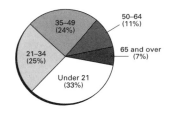

Crime Statistics (from the Georgia Bureau of Investigation, 1998)

Murder   4

Rape   10

Robbery   50

Aggravated assault 191

Burglary   651

Larceny   2,774

Car theft   409

Other Statistics

Median income:	*$44,894*
Percentage living at poverty level:	*8.8%*
Average price of house:	*$129,019*
Estimated commute times:	

to Downtown	*20 minutes*
to Marietta	*20 minutes*
to Decatur	*35 minutes*
to the airport	*20 minutes*

Important Places Nearby

Grocery Stores

Kroger
3875 Chapel Hill Road
Douglasville
(770) 947-7144

Cub Foods
5901 Stewart Parkway
Douglasville
(770) 920-4800

Pharmacies

Eckerd Drugs
9559 Georgia Highway 5
Douglasville
(770) 949-0904
www.eckerd.com

Banks

Douglas County Bank
6157 Fairburn Road
Douglasville
(770) 949-2500

SunTrust Bank
819 Thornton Road
Lithia Springs
(770) 739-3850
www.suntrust.com

Hardware Stores

Home Depot
7399 Douglas Boulevard
Douglasville
(770) 577-8311
www.homedepot.com

Fast Food

McDonald's
2777 Chapel Hill Road
Douglasville
(770) 947-2882

KFC
5620 Fairburn Road
(770) 489-0182

Hospitals/Emergency Rooms

Douglas Hospital
8954 Hospital Drive
Douglasville, GA 30134
(770) 949-1500

FAYETTE

Chamber of Commerce
200 Courthouse Square
Fayetteville, GA 30214
(770) 461-9983
www.henrycounty.com

If you fly for a living, Fayette County may be just the spot for you. This southwest area is the "in" place for employees of the airline industry who work for and around Hartsfield Atlanta International Airport. It's less attractive to those who must head into Atlanta; the drive up I-85 is relatively snarl-free but long.

Many of those well-paid airline employees enjoy escaping to Fayette's rolling countryside, golf courses, upscale neighborhoods, and picturesque small towns, such as Fayetteville, the county seat, anchored by one of the state's oldest Victorian-era courthouses on a shady square. The county's biggest town, Peachtree City, is a planned resort and residence community whose pricey subdivisions sit alongside lakes and golf links. The architecturally controlled town, where even the height of the stop signs is regulated, is linked by a series of golf-cart paths that take residents from the greens to the grocery store. The alternative wheels are so popular that most homes feature golf-cart garages.

The county is one of the few where zoning demands one-acre lots in many neighborhoods. With its large properties, low crime rate, and good school system, Fayette continues to attract affluent buyers.

Neighborhood Statistical Profile

Population: 88,609

Population by Ethnicity

92%	*white*
5%	*black*
<1%	*American Indian*
2%	*Asian*
1%	*other*

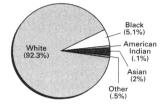

Population by Gender

49%	*male*
51%	*female*

Population by Age

33%	*under 21*
19%	*21–34*
29%	*35–49*
12%	*50–64*
7%	*65 and over*

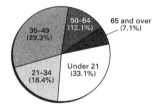

Crime Statistics (from the Georgia Bureau of Investigation, 1998)

Murder	0
Rape	4
Robbery	19
Aggravated assault	37
Burglary	263
Larceny	1,196
Car theft	115

Other Statistics

Median income:	*$66,080*
Percentage living at poverty level:	*3.5%*
Average price of house:	*$181,195*

Estimated commute times:

to Downtown	*40 minutes*
to Marietta	*50 minutes*
to Decatur	*45 minutes*
to the airport	*15 minutes*

Important Places Nearby

Grocery Stores

Kroger
564 Crosstown Road
Peachtree City
(770) 487-3602

Publix
108 Pavilion Parkway
Fayetteville
(770) 460-4100

Pharmacies

CVS
181 Banks Station
Fayetteville
(770) 461-3431

www.cvs.com

Banks

Bank of America
219 Banks Station
Fayetteville
(770) 460-3510

www.bankofamerica.com

SunTrust Bank
103 City Circle
Peachtree City
(770) 487-7675

www.suntrust.com

Hardware Stores

Home Depot
103 Pavilion Parkway
Fayetteville
(770) 461-9819

www.homedepot.com

Fast Food

Arby's
170 North Glynn Street
Fayetteville
(770) 460-8695

KFC
494 Crosstown Drive
Peachtree City
(770) 631-3786

Taco Bell
1140 Crosstown Court
Peachtree City
(770) 631-9193

Hospitals/Emergency Rooms

Fayette Community Hospital
1255 Georgia Highway 54 West
Fayetteville, GA 30214
(770) 719-7000

GWINNETT

Chamber of Commerce
5110 Sugarloaf Parkway
Lawrenceville, GA 30034
(770) 513-3000

www.gwinnettchamber.org

The sign on the giant water tower overlooking I-85 says it all: Gwinnett is Great. In this sprawling county, everything is big, especially its geographic stretch from Lilburn, Norcross, and Peachtree Corners in the south to Buford and Suwanee in the north. Its western boundary is the Chattahoochee River, where upscale housing developments back up to the banks. The southern end is crowded with technology parks and middle-income neighborhoods to house the people who work there. The southeastern portion around Snellville is also packed with new homes favored by middle-income families. Farther north, the swank golf course communities at Sugarloaf, Hamilton Mill, and the Apalachee River Club were once thought too far from anywhere to be popular, but they've attracted upper-income families who like the extensive recreational facilities in their new neighborhoods. Beyond these still is the enormous Mall of Georgia, which opened in late 1999.

Though the county is often ridiculed as an example of growth gone awry, it does have several picturesque small towns. Old Norcross has an area of Victorian homes around a restored downtown with a train depot, antique shops, and restaurants. Historic Suwanee is a strip of antebellum homes and shops beside the railroad tracks. Buford, once a town whose sole support was its saddle factory, brags its own school system and a large artists' colony whose members have renovated old stores into lofts and studios. Lawrenceville, the county seat, has a restored courthouse, museums, and shops around the square.

As the sixth-fastest-growing metro county, Gwinnett has more than its share of traffic headaches. The good news is that there are alternative routes along Peachtree Industrial Boulevard and Buford Highway to avoid I-85. But traffic jams regularly at I-285, the Stone Mountain Freeway, and Georgia Highway 316 out of Lawrenceville. During the summer, the volume of cars heading to Lake Lanier and the Georgia mountains adds to the congestion. Still, with building land available, the county continues to attract residential development.

Neighborhood Statistical Profile

Population: 522,095

Population by Ethnicity

91%	*white*
5%	*black*
<1%	*American Indian*
3%	*Asian*
1%	*other*

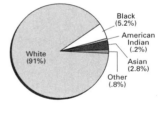

Population by Gender

50%	*male*
50%	*female*

Population by Age

31%	*under 21*
29%	*21–34*
26%	*35–49*
9%	*50–64*
5%	*65 and over*

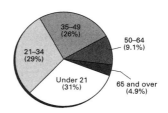

Crime Statistics (from the Georgia Bureau of Investigation, 1998)

Murder	*17*
Rape	*115*
Robbery	*500*
Aggravated assault	*562*
Burglary	*2,999*
Larceny	*13,103*
Car theft	*2,006*

Other Statistics

Median income:	*$54,083*
Percentage living at poverty level:	*5.2%*
Average price of house:	*$150,756*
Estimated commute times:	
to Downtown	*25 minutes*
to Marietta	*35 minutes*
to Decatur	*30 minutes*
to the airport	*45 minutes*

Important Places Nearby

Grocery Stores

Ingles
675 Buford Drive
Lawrenceville
(770) 995-1033

Cub Foods
5495 Jimmy Carter Boulevard
Norcross
(770) 662-5990

Pharmacies

Drug Emporium
4015 Holcomb Bridge Road
Norcross
(770) 263-9552

www.drugemporium.com

CVS
112 Proctor Square
Duluth
(770) 622-6573

www.cvs.com

Banks

Wachovia
1625 Indian Trail
Lilburn
(770) 279-4600

www.wachovia.com

SouthTrust Bank
36 South Harris Street
Buford
(770) 932-7120

www.southtrust.com

Hardware Stores

Gwinnett Ace Hardware
4624 Jimmy Carter Boulevard
Norcross
(770) 934-0200

Howard Brothers
3616 Buford Highway
Duluth
(770) 476-3006

Fast Food

Chick-fil-A
2835 Lawrenceville-Suwanee Road
Suwanee
(770) 932-5797

Fuddruckers
3384 Holcomb Bridge Road
Norcross
(770) 448-4912

McDonald's
730 North Clayton Street
Lawrenceville
(770) 963-8377

Hospitals/Emergency Rooms

Gwinnett Medical Center
1000 Medical Center Boulevard
Lawrenceville, GA 30045
(770) 995-4321

Joan Glancy Memorial Hospital
3215 McClure Bridge Road
Duluth, GA 30096
(678) 584-6800

HENRY

Chamber of Commerce

1310 Georgia Highway 20
McDonough, GA 30253
(770) 957-5786

www.henrycounty.com

Between 1990 and 1998, Henry County led Atlanta's suburban growth blitz, increasing its population 75 percent. It also ranked fourth on the nation's list of fastest-growing counties. The expansion of the business and industrial base along the I-75 and I-675 corridors has turned employees into buyers for the plethora of new neighborhoods in a range of prices. Golf course communities at Eagles Landing and the Georgia National Golf Club have been magnets for upscale developments. Panola Mountain State Park and the Atlanta Motor Speedway are other area draws.

Even with the housing boom, Henry has retained much of its bucolic countryside. The county seat at McDonough is a wonderful old town of historic homes, a courthouse square, and antique shops, surrounded by outskirts of new subdivisions. The town's biggest coup was nabbing an 800,000-square-foot distribution center for Amazon.com, the Internet company, whose local presence will be felt for years in the county's housing and employment circles.

Though the area is about thirty miles south of downtown Atlanta, it's usually a hassle-free drive north on I-75. The commute into Gwinnett or DeKalb isn't too bad, either, along I-675 and Georgia Highway 155.

Neighborhood Statistical Profile

Population: 104,667

Population by Ethnicity

89%   white
10%   black
<1%   American Indian
1%   Asian
<1%   other

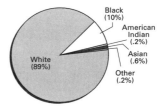

Population by Gender

49%   male
51%   female

Population by Age

32%   under 21
24%   21–34
23%   35–49
13%   50–64
8%   65 and over

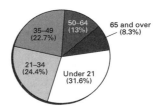

Crime Statistics (from the Georgia Bureau of Investigation, 1998)

Murder   3
Rape   27
Robbery   42
Aggravated
   assault   154
Burglary   818
Larceny   2,245
Car theft   294

Other Statistics

Median income: $50,410
Percentage living at poverty level: 6.3%
Average price of house: $124,949

Estimated commute times:

to Downtown	*25 minutes*
to Marietta	*45 minutes*
to Decatur	*30 minutes*
to the airport	*20 minutes*

Important Places Nearby

Grocery Stores

Kroger
1750 Hudson Bridge Road
Stockbridge
(770) 507-7732

Publix
11155 Tara Boulevard
Hampton
(770) 473-4779

Pharmacies

CVS
1240 Eagle's Landing Parkway
Stockbridge
(770) 506-9072
www.cvs.com

Moye's Pharmacy
230 Covington Street
McDonough
(770) 957-1851

Banks

Eagle National Bank
850 Eagle's Landing Parkway
Stockbridge
(770) 507-5855

First Union
17 South East Main Street
Hampton
(770) 946-4246
www.firstunion.com

Hardware Stores

Lowe's Home Improvement Warehouse
3505 Mt. Zion Road
Stockbridge
(770) 506-9665
www.lowes.com

Stockbridge True Value Hardware
5529 North Henry Boulevard
Stockbridge
(770) 474-8751

Fast Food

Big Chick
690 McDonough Road
McDonough
(770) 957-1329

Chick-fil-A
11161 Tara Boulevard
Hampton
(770) 472-6101

Hardee's
182 Keys Ferry Street
McDonough
(770) 954-1581

Hospitals/Emergency Rooms

Henry Medical Center
1133 Eagle's Landing Parkway
Stockbridge, GA 30281
(770) 389-2200

NORTH FULTON COUNTY

Greater North Fulton Chamber of Commerce
1025 Old Roswell Road, Suite 101
Roswell, GA 30076
(770) 993-8806

www.gnfchamber.org

Fulton County north of the Atlanta city line includes several pockets of unincorporated land as well as the municipalities of Roswell, Alpharetta, and Mountain Park. For years, this affluent county has enjoyed a building boom that has brought newcomers in record numbers. Much of the growth followed the opening of Georgia Highway 400, the north-south expressway that links to I-85 in Buckhead. At its northern tip is Windward, a planned community of variously priced neighborhoods with extensive recreational facilities, from lakes to golf courses. Old farming communities Shakerag and Birmingham are marked only by crossroads, but still noted for their beautiful horse farms. Mountain Park and Crabapple have attracted major retailers and restaurants along Holcomb Bridge Road, a major access road to Georgia Highway 400. The area is favored by relocating buyers drawn to the new subdivisions, good schools, and access to downtown and the Perimeter.

Closer to Atlanta, unincorporated Sandy Springs straddles the Perimeter. The area has many active neighborhood associations that have struggled to form an official city for years, without receiving the backing needed from the state to become an independent town. However, its proximity to business campuses along the Perimeter, Buckhead, and downtown has boosted property values of 1950s brick ranch houses as well as new infill homes.

Roswell in the northwest portion of the county has a scenic square surrounded by restaurants, antique shops, and several streets of antebellum homes. The quaint shopping area extends north to the Canton Street historic district. With the recent annexation of several subdivisions, Roswell's eastern boundary now extends across Georgia Highway 400. The town has a state-of-the-art cultural center that hosts a variety of professional works.

Alpharetta also has a charming downtown with the city hall, shops, restaurants, and older homes. The town includes North Point Mall off Georgia Highway 400. Nearby, some of the metro area's famous faces reside in the gated golf course communities of St. Ives and Country Club of the South.

Neighborhood Statistical Profile

Population: 213,717

Population by Ethnicity

48%	*white*
50%	*black*
<1%	*American Indian*
1%	*Asian*
1%	*other*

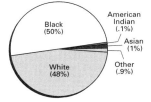

Population by Gender

48%   male
52%   female

Population by Age

29%   under 21
27%   21–34
23%   35–49
11%   50–64
10%   65 and over

Crime Statistics (from the Georgia Bureau of Investigation, 1998)

Murder   178
Rape   533
Robbery   5,625
Aggravated
*   assault 8,840*
Burglary   12,818
Larceny   45,611
Car theft   11,720

Other Statistics

Median income:	*$35,932*
Percentage living at poverty level:	*20.9%*
Average price of house:	*$251,486*
Estimated commute times:	

to Downtown	*30 minutes*
to Marietta	*30 minutes*
to Decatur	*40 minutes*
to the airport	*45 minutes*

Important Places Nearby

Grocery Stores

Harry's Farmers Market
1180 Upper Hembree Road
Alpharetta
(770) 664-9394

Publix
885 Woodstock Road
Roswell
(770) 552-4580

Kroger
4920 Roswell Road
Sandy Springs
(404) 843-3080

Pharmacies

Drug Emporium
11060 Alpharetta Highway
Roswell
(770) 587-5129

www.drugemporium.com

Kroger
6650 Roswell Road
Sandy Springs
(404) 256-2779

Northside Alpharetta Pharmacy
3400-A Old Milton Parkway
Alpharetta
(770) 667-4023

Banks

Fidelity National Bank
10920 Crabapple Road
Crabapple
(770) 993-3438

www.fidelitynational.com

Milton National Bank
11650 Alpharetta Highway
Roswell
(770) 664-1990

SunTrust Bank
6615 Roswell Road
Sandy Springs
(770) 980-2255

www.suntrust.com

Hardware Stores

Home Depot
5950 State Bridge Road
Alpharetta
(770) 476-4460

www.homedepot.com

Roswell Hardware
685 South Atlanta Street
Roswell
(770) 993-6686

Sandy Springs True Value Hardware
6125 Roswell Road
Sandy Springs
(404) 255-2151

Fast Food

Taco Bell
106 South Main Street
Alpharetta
(770) 664-5107

Wendy's
6240 Roswell Road
Sandy Springs
(404) 252-4092

Hospitals/Emergency Rooms

North Fulton Regional Hospital
3000 Hospital Boulevard
Roswell, GA 30076
(770) 751-2500

Northside Hospital
1000 Johnson Ferry Road
Atlanta, GA 30342
(404) 851-8000

www.northside.com

SOUTH FULTON COUNTY

South Fulton Chamber of Commerce
6400 Shannon Parkway
Union City, GA 30291
(770) 964-1984

www.southfultonchamber.com

Though the southern side of Fulton County has fewer upscale neighborhoods and affluent residents than its northern counterpart, it is rapidly gaining popularity for its easy access to downtown, proximity to the airport, and traffic-free streets. It has long been noted for the business presence along Fulton Industrial Boulevard on the west, Georgia Highway 138 in the south, and I-85 from top to bottom. South Fulton is also home to the Fort McPherson army base and the southeast region's National Archives and Federal Records Center.

Several old South Fulton municipalities bump up to Atlanta's southern border. East Point, served by southbound MARTA trains, has enjoyed a revival as single professionals and gay couples moved in to restore the affordably priced older homes. Hapeville is home to a Ford Motor Company marketing, manufacturing and customer service center not far from the spruced up its downtown with antique stores and businesses. College Park boasts the state's second-largest meeting space, the Georgia International Convention Center.

On the county's southern tip, Union City mixes the new and old with a charming early 1900s section along the train tracks and a bustling commercial district off of I-85 that includes Shannon Southpark Mall. Palmetto is crossed by train tracks that meander past Victorian homes and cottages and through a countryside dotted with farms and pastures.

South Fulton is expected to grow through the early 2000s, as developers who have discovered the wide-open spaces plan new housing developments, golf courses, and business parks in the area.

Neighborhood Statistical Profile

Population: 118,176

Population by Ethnicity

48%	white
50%	black
<1%	American Indian
1%	Asian
1%	other

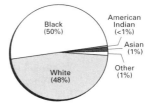

Population by Gender

48%	male
52%	female

Population by Age

29%   under 21
27%   21–34
23%   35–49
11%   50–64
10%   65 and over

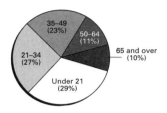

Crime Statistics (from the Georgia Bureau of Investigation, 1998)

Murder   178
Rape   533
Robbery   5,625
Aggravated
    assault   8,840
Burglary   12,818
Larceny   45,611
Car theft   11,720

Other Statistics

Median income:	$35,932
Percentage living at poverty level:	20.9%
Average price of house:	$78,352

Estimated commute times:

to Downtown	20 minutes
to Marietta	45 minutes
to Decatur	45 minutes
to the airport	10 minutes

Important Places Nearby

Grocery Stores

Kroger
4550 Jonesboro Road
Union City
(770) 969-0269

Ingles
7490 Old National Highway
Fairburn
(770) 996-4151

Pharmacies

Chapman Drug Co.
615 Central Avenue
Hapeville
(404) 761-1136

CVS
4853 Old National Highway
College Park
(770) 909-5670

www.cvs.com

Banks

Bank of America
2818 East Point Street
East Point
(404) 765-1966

www.bankofamerica.com

Fairburn Banking Co.
65 Washington Street
Fairburn
(770) 964-0631

www.fairbanco.com

Hardware Stores

Dorn Ace Hardware
3737 Main Street
College Park
(404) 767-8666

Tri-City Hardware Co.
597 North Central Avenue
Hapeville
(404) 767-1554

Fast Food

Blimpie
1509 Virginia Avenue
College Park
(404) 762-6226

Chick-fil-A
461 North Central Avenue
Hapeville
(404) 762-1746

Hospitals/Emergency Rooms

South Fulton Medical Center
1170 Cleveland Avenue
East Point, GA 30344
(404) 305-3500

Exurbs

Beyond the city's suburban ring, residential growth has spilled into neighboring counties that make up the area's "exurbs." Affordable housing, available land, access to major interstates and highways, and lower tax rates make these areas enormously popular. Many of the folks in these communities work in the business and commercial centers on the edge of the Perimeter, so the long distance from downtown is not an issue. However, they may not have entirely escaped the problems of overcrowded schools and traffic that the rest of the metro area battles.

BARTOW

Chamber of Commerce

120 Main Street
Cartersville, GA 30120
(770) 382-1466

www.cartersvillechamber.com

In the past ten years, the growth stretching from Atlanta north along I-75 has been so strong it spilled over into Bartow County. The area is home to several major carpet manufacturers, including Shaw Industries, the area's largest employer. There's also a major Anheuser Busch brewery and several industries that support the county's carpet production.

Cartersville, the county seat, features a restored downtown district around the courthouse, where the restored Grand Theater is home to the Cartersville Opera, a local opera company that celebrated its tenth anniversary in 1998. The area is rich in history, from the Cherokee Indians' burial mounds along the Etowah River to Roselawn, the Victorian mansion that houses the local historical society. Sporting and recreational opportunities abound along Lake Allatoona and in the shade of Red Top Mountain. From 1990 to 1998, Bartow's population swelled by 28 percent.

Neighborhood Statistical Profile

Population: 71,929

Crime Statistics (from the Georgia Bureau of Investigation, 1998)

Murder   *3*
Rape   *10*
Robbery   *37*
Aggravated
   assault *116*
Burglary   *610*
Larceny   *884*
Car theft *222*

Other Statistics

Median income: *$35,274*
Percentage living at poverty level: *11.8%*
Average price of house: *$140,000*
Estimated commute times:
    to Downtown   *60 minutes*
    to Marietta   *30 minutes*
    to Decatur   *60 minutes*
    to the airport *70 minutes*

CHEROKEE

Chamber of Commerce

3605 Brown Memorial Highway
Canton, GA 30114
(770) 345-0400

www.cherokee-chamber.com

As a neighbor to burgeoning Cobb County, Cherokee is an attractive option for home buyers, particularly families looking for larger lots, more affordable homes, and lower taxes. Residential development has been intense along the I-575 corridor that links to I-75 and downtown Atlanta. Grappling with growth is such a hot-button issue that recent elections have swept out most development supporters in favor of slow-growth advocates. The county has also battled the state school board over accreditation.

Despite its distance from Atlanta and the notoriously wicked rush hour traffic around the I-575/I-75 interchange, Cherokee continues to draw buyers. Property values have risen steadily over the past several years. Along with mega golf communities such as Towne Lake and Bradshaw Farm, the county is dotted with tiny crossroads villages and horse farms.

Neighborhood Statistical Profile

Population: 134,498

Crime Statistics (from the Georgia Bureau of Investigation, 1998)

Murder   4
Rape   8
Robbery   21
Aggravated
    assault 121
Burglary   356
Larceny   1,369
Car theft   136

Other Statistics

Median income: $53,091
Percentage living at poverty level: 6.2%
Average price of house: $149,130
Estimated commute times:

to Downtown	55 minutes
to Marietta	25 minutes
to Decatur	55 minutes
to the airport	65 minutes

COWETA

Chamber of Commerce

23 Bullsboro Drive
Newnan, GA 30263
(770) 253-2270

www.ncchamber.org

One of the most beautiful Victorian towns in the metro area is Newnan in Coweta County. Dubbed the "City of Homes," Newnan is a showplace of historic houses around a courthouse square. Another cozy village is Senoia on the county's southeastern edge. Both attract old-home lovers as well as fans of the laid-back lifestyle small towns afford.

Sharpsburg, just over the Coweta line from the amenities of Peachtree City, has been the darling of developers, who have turned the rural countryside into a booming real estate market. Several projects under way in the area will have more than two hundred houses. New schools have opened to serve the growing community of families. The influx has put Coweta fourth on the metro area's list of fastest-growing counties.

Commuters from Coweta County to downtown Atlanta have a long ride, but one that's relatively hassle-free along I-85 north.

Neighborhood Statistical Profile

Population: 85,028

Crime Statistics (from the Georgia Bureau of Investigation, 1998)

Murder   4
Rape   14
Robbery   37
Aggravated
  assault 172
Burglary   622
Larceny   1,680
Car theft 243

Other Statistics

Median income:	*$42,790*
Percentage living at poverty level:	*10.7%*
Average price of house:	*$122,998*
Estimated commute times:	

to Downtown	*45 minutes*
to Marietta	*60 minutes*
to Decatur	*60 minutes*
to the airport	*25 minutes*

FORSYTH

Chamber of Commerce

110 Old Buford Road, Suite 120
Cumming, GA 30040
(770) 887-6461

www.forsythchamber.org

From 1990 to 1998, Forsyth's population grew by a whopping 92 percent, ranking it first among Atlanta's fastest-growing counties. The two chief reasons for the explosion is the easy access to Georgia Highway 400 and work centers at Windward, the Perimeter, and Downtown, and the enormous number of new houses at various prices. First-time buyers will find modestly priced homes; families looking for something spacious will gravitate to the many neighborhoods with pools and tennis courts. Posh developments with homes on multi-acre lots along Lake Lanier or with fabulous amenities such as equestrian centers are available as well. Experts predict that the demand for Forsyth's lower land costs and taxes will continue to creep into the far northern reaches of the county. Cumming, the county seat, has a small shopping district, but the bulk of the retail businesses are located in new malls along the county's southern edge.

Neighborhood Statistical Profile

Population: 86,130

Crime Statistics (from the Georgia Bureau of Investigation, 1998)

Murder   2
Rape   9
Robbery   21
Aggravated
  assault 312
Burglary   510
Larceny   1,952
Car theft   216

Other Statistics

Median income: *$56,347*
Percentage living at poverty level: *5.9%*
Average price of house: *$197,013*
Estimated commute times:
    to Downtown   *45 minutes*
    to Marietta   *40 minutes*
    to Decatur   *45 minutes*
    to the airport   *55 minutes*

PAULDING

Chamber of Commerce

455 Jimmy Campbell Parkway
Douglasville, GA 30132
(770) 445-6016

www.pauldingcountygeorgia.com

Like Cobb County's northern neighbors, Paulding County to the west lures buyers over the boundary to new homes with lower prices and lower taxes. The bulk of Paulding's growth has been crowded along the Cobb border in Hiram and Dallas, where there's quick access to Georgia Highway 120 to Marietta and Thornton Road to I-20 in the south. Unfortunately, Paulding commuters find themselves joining the congestion to Cobb that heads down the same routes on the way to work.

Neighborhood Statistical Profile

Population: 73,534

Crime Statistics (from the Georgia Bureau of Investigation, 1998)

Murder   *0*
Rape   *5*
Robbery   *13*
Aggravated
  assault   *155*
Burglary   *466*
Larceny   *1,040*
Car theft   *126*

Other Statistics

Median income:	*$44,201*
Percentage living at poverty level:	*8.0%*
Average price of house:	*$106,039*
Estimated commute times:	

to Downtown	*45 minutes*
to Marietta	*25 minutes*
to Decatur	*55 minutes*
to the airport	*50 minutes*

ROCKDALE

Chamber of Commerce

1186 Scott Street
Conyers, GA 30012
(770) 483-7049

www.conyers-rockdale.com

Rockdale received a good deal of bad press in recent years after high school shootings and a television documentary about teens gone awry. But like most suburban and exurban counties, Rockdale is coping with the unprecedented growth of population and housing in a once-rural environment. Bisected by I-20 on the east side of Atlanta, the county is conveniently situated for businesses and developments. It's enormously popular with families and folks who don't have to drive as far as Atlanta to work.

Building has boomed around Conyers, the historic county seat with stores, antique shops, and restaurants. Rockdale is also home to the Georgia International Horse Park, where the 1996 Olympic equestrian events were staged.

Neighborhood Statistical Profile

Population: 68,305

Crime Statistics (from the Georgia Bureau of Investigation, 1998)

Murder	1
Rape	10
Robbery	43
Aggravated assault	312
Burglary	382
Larceny	2,154
Car theft	217

Other Statistics

Median income:	$46,925
Percentage living at poverty level:	8.1%
Average price of house:	$130,864
Estimated commute times:	

to Downtown	40 minutes
to Marietta	60 minutes
to Decatur	30 minutes
to the airport	35 minutes

CHAPTER 2

Advice on Finding an Apartment

As the metro area's population closes in on the 4 million mark, the geographic boundaries that constitute "Atlanta" stretch farther and farther out from the heart of the city.

For a newcomer, trying to find a place to live amid the sprawl can be a daunting job. One way to make the transition easier is to take up temporary residence in one of the area's 1,600 apartment complexes while you explore the nooks and crannies of the city and surrounding counties.

Relocation experts estimate that eighty to ninety thousand new-comers arrive in Atlanta each year, and the vast majority of them spend some time in a rental unit. They may be looking for the ideal neighborhood, having a house built, or just trying to find their way around town before making a decision about where to settle down for good.

But Atlanta's apartments also draw residents who prefer renting to buying a home. They enjoy the freedom that an apartment lifestyle brings, with no grass to cut and no house to maintain. And their numbers are significant: The majority of Atlanta's apartment complexes report occupancy rates around 90 percent. Some of the most attractive locations have only ten to fifteen units available at any given time, which prompts experts to observe that the demand exceeds the supply. New communities are particularly popular, filling up to 95 percent within the first few months of opening the doors.

In many of the city's new and upscale complexes, renters no longer have to sacrifice the perks frequently identified with home ownership, from an attached garage to a laundry room off the kitchen. Apartments now boast vaulted ceilings, detailed crown moldings, gourmet kitchens, and garages. Upgrades include granite countertops, hardwood floors, spa tubs, and marble fireplaces. Many have tossed out the traditional, garden-variety flat floor plan in favor of carriage homes, lofts, and townhouses. Apartment builders are paying an enormous amount of attention to amenities, too. Now, swimming pools and tennis courts are just one part of a package that includes business centers with computers and faxes, gymnasiums and fitness centers, conference rooms, mini-theaters with big screens and reclining seats, gardens, and walking trails.

Renters will find an array of options available throughout the city and in the close-in suburban counties, and even some in the exurban areas. But the greatest number of rental units—a whopping 96 percent of them—lie within a relatively small geographic area:

- Midtown and Buckhead inside the city limits
- Sandy Springs and Dunwoody in north Fulton County
- Cobb County along the I-75 corridor
- Clayton County around the airport
- The northeast, south, and southeast sections of DeKalb County
- Douglas County along I-20
- Gwinnett County along the I-85 corridor

As you might guess, rental ranges tend to be lower the farther away you get from the city center, but units are also a bit harder to find. Apartment industry experts suggest, as a general rule of thumb, that city apartments rent for about $1 per square foot. That is, a two-bedroom unit of 1,000 square feet would run approximately $1,000 per month. A small one-bedroom unit in the Buckhead area costs a minimum of $700 per month. As you move farther out of town, you'll find one-bedroom units in the $600 range, but there's not much available for less than that. Of course, those figures are all estimates; the only way to get a firm cost is to contact the individual property or an apartment finder who has current rate sheets.

The city's northside lures apartment dwellers with some of the best accessibility to major highways, city amenities, and major work centers. But if there's a downside to renting in this district, it's that the area's enormous popularity makes apartment buildings a prime target for converters who want to change the properties to condominiums. Atlanta's condominium market in this vicinity has been particularly strong in the past few years, and, with no end in sight, there's always the possibility that you'll find a notice in your mailbox announcing that your apartment is up for sale. That could be good news for renters looking to buy anyway, who usually have the first option to purchase. But if you're only interested in renting, it means you'd better start apartment shopping before your lease runs out. Although no one has a crystal ball, it's a good idea to ask leasing agents about the possibilities of a condominium conversion before you move in.

City Fact

In the past ten years, 650,000 people moved into the Atlanta area. In that same decade, 350,000 new jobs were added.

Fortunately, Atlanta has some terrific resources for making your apartment hunt easier. Around town, you'll find several free publications as well as real estate sections in local newspapers that will help you get started. After a few days of reading, you'll probably notice a few names that keep cropping up. Post Properties, one of the city's leading builders, has about forty apartment buildings and complexes across the northside, with amenities from urban vegetable gardens and lavish landscaping to privacy gates and garages. Julian LeCraw & Co. is another noted builder, with more than two dozen complexes from Douglasville to Stone Mountain. Gables Residential, Amli, and Sentinel are other major apartment companies. Most of these companies have Web sites offering virtual tours of their properties.

Along with publications and Internet sites, newcomers may want to check out the companies in town that specialize in finding apartments for free. (In the vast majority of cases, the cost of the service is paid for by the apartment company.) Working with an apartment finder can save time and money. Roger Gilliam of A&A Apartment Locators points out that his fifteen-year-old company has in its office information on about 1,500 communities that are looking for tenants, and many offer special deals to renters through A&A. "We know where the best specials and better properties are because we go out and see them," said Gilliam. "We know what's out there. The apartment companies pay us because we bring them great clients and tenants, and save them money."

Professional apartment finders can answer queries by e-mail or fax, and will escort newcomers on tours—a terrific time-saver in itself if you've only got a long weekend to find a place to live and you're not familiar with Atlanta's geography. They also have at their fingertips the latest occupancy rates, so, if you're in a hurry, you won't waste time checking out a complex that has a six-month waiting list.

If you do decide to rent, whether short term or longer, it's always smart to have renters' insurance. The policies, available through major insurers, are fairly inexpensive, but they protect tenants against theft and damage to personal possessions. Keeping an accurate inventory of your apartment's contents, including a visual record on videotape, is a smart idea.

Pros and Cons

Renting has its advantages. Take the time to learn your way around town, check out various neighborhoods, and find financing for the house you love. It also comes with a carefree existence: No lawns to mow or windows to wash!

On the flip side, renting can be expensive. And many complexes put restrictions on things from pets to number of cars. Short-term leases, particularly in Atlanta's most popular northern arc, may be difficult to find.

Pros

- Short leases: a sixth-month lease can give you time to learn about your new city while you figure out exactly which community you want to make your permanent home.

- House hunting: It's often easier to find a house while living in an intown apartment than on a three-day shopping trip! And you'll have time to line up a mortgage, hunt for the best sale deals, and check out the rush-hour drive time to work.

- Amenities: Most apartments have amenities to make your free time fun: swimming pools, tennis courts, barbecue grills, fitness centers, and social activities to help you make friends.

- Doing business: Having a business center at your complex eliminates the need for a computer or fax while you're job hunting.

- Traffic: An apartment close your job is convenient, and may be cheaper than owning a house in the same neighborhood.

MOVING TIP

Confirm that your subscriptions, credit/charge card statements, and outstanding bills, are forwarded to your new address. You'll miss your favorite magazines and might inadvertently harm your credit rating if you overlook this detail.

Cons

- Availability: Some of the city's most popular complexes and buildings, particularly on the northside of town, may have waiting lists.

- Prices: The rental prices of some close-in apartments may be as much as a house payment.

- Bare essentials: If you're relocating from a house to an apartment, you may have to pay storage fees for the furniture you can't cram into a scaled-down space.
- Going condo: Atlanta's thriving condominium market makes many upscale rental properties ripe for conversion, which may leave you searching for yet another apartment.
- Pets: Most apartments place some restrictions on pets. Find out if the complex you're considering accommodates your furry roommates.

Things to Ask or Consider While Looking

Making the decision about where to rent and for how long is based on a myriad of considerations, from how much space you'll need for your furniture to the distance you want to be from work. And when you call or visit various complexes, don't forget to mention any special requirements you may have, such as pets, extra-large household items, or the need for a handicap-accessible unit.

- Kids: What school district serves the apartment complex you like? Does it fit the needs of your children? Does the school bus come into the complex, or must you provide transportation?
- Separate bedrooms: Do you need more than two bedrooms for your family?
- Public transportation: Is commuting to work on the train or bus important?
- Special considerations: Do you require features such as wheelchair accessibility, or high ceilings to accommodate large pieces of furniture?
- Details: Do you prefer a furnished or unfurnished unit? Is a washer and dryer in your apartment an essential? What about a fireplace, sunroom, office area, garage?
- Safety: Is a gated complex, or one with individual security systems, important?
- Rules: What rules and regulations govern the property?

Resources for Renters

Atlanta Apartment Book
3098 Piedmont Road, Suite 150
Atlanta, GA 30305
(404) 816-4242

www.atlaptbook.com

www.apartmentsnationwide.com

Atlanta Apartment Guide
3139 Campus Drive
Norcross, GA 30071
(770) 417-1717

www.aptguides.com

Apartment Blue Book
2305 Newpoint Parkway
Lawrenceville, GA 30043
(770) 822-4340; 800-222-3651

www.apartmentbluebook.com

**Atlanta Journal-
Constitution**—Sunday
Homefinder section
72 Marietta Street
Atlanta, GA 30303
(404) 526-5151

www.ajc.com

Creative Loafing
750 Willoughby Way
Atlanta, GA 30312
(404) 688-5623

www.creativeloafing.com

For Rent Magazine
3290 Cumberland Club Drive
Atlanta, GA 30339
(770) 434-6347

www.aptsforrent.com

Know Atlanta Magazine
1303 Hightower Trail, Suite 101
Atlanta, GA 30350
(770) 650-1102

www.knowatlanta.com

Neighbor Newspapers
580 Fairground Street
Marietta, GA 30060
(770) 795-3000

MOVING TIP

The Atlanta Board of Realtors Web site, *www.realtorsatlanta.com*, can help you locate an agent who specializes in the area of town you want to explore.

APARTMENT LOCATOR SERVICES

A&A Apartment Locators
*1862-B Independence Square
Dunwoody, GA 30338
(404) 261-8540; (800) 999-1202*

www.atlantaapartments
4rent.com

About Atlanta Apartments
*3838 Green Industrial Way
Atlanta, GA 30341
(770) 688-0804*

www.aboutatlanta
apartments.com

Allpoint Rents
*2030 Beaver Ruin Road
Norcross, GA 30071
(770) 441-7707*

Atlanta Apartment Connection
*P.O. Box 80189
Atlanta, GA 30366
(770) 668-0811; 800-336-7066*

www.atlantaaptconnection.com

Apartment Advantage
*810 Mabry Road
Atlanta, GA 30328
(770) 396-1165; 800-215-5979*

members.aol.com/aptadv

Apartment Finders
*2250 North Druid Hills Road
Atlanta, GA 30329
(404) 633-3331; 800-278-7327*

www.therentsource.com

Apartment Locators of Atlanta
*6065 Roswell Road, Suite 600
Atlanta, GA 30328
(404) 256-5133*

www.aloatlanta.com

Apartment Hunters Inc.
*1640 Powers Ferry Road
Marietta, GA 30067
(770) 980-2582*

CITY
FACT

Looking for a great return on your investment? Last year, buyers in the Northside Drive area of Buckhead saw the value of real estate in their area increase 75 percent over 1998.

Apartment Network
3423 Piedmont Road
Atlanta, GA 30305
(404) 257-8809

www.aptment.com

Apartment Seekers
1690-A Cobb Parkway
Marietta, GA 30060
(770) 952-5202

Apartment Selectors
350 Northridge Road
Atlanta, GA 30350
(770) 552-9255; (800) 543-0536

www.aptselector.com

Apartment Services
3355 Lenox Road
Atlanta, GA 30326
(404) 633-1006; (888) 655-1006

www.aptservicesatl.com

Apartments Available
616 Barrington Hills Drive
Atlanta, GA 30350
(770) 512-0942; (888) 411-0942

www.apartmentsatlanta.com

Apartments Today
11285 Elkins Road
Roswell, GA 30076
(770) 664-4957

Corporate Lodgings
2135 DeFoor Hills Road
Atlanta, GA 30318
(404) 351-7033; (800) 261-3565

www.rent.net

Leasing Atlanta
2652 North Peachtree Road
Atlanta, GA 30305
(770) 455-3897

Nationwide Corporate Rentals
281 South Atlanta Street
Roswell, GA 30075
(770) 641-8393

www.rentalrelocation.com

Promove
3620 Piedmont Road
Atlanta, GA 30305
(404) 842-0042; (800) 950-6683

www.promove.net

Rental Relocation, Inc.
8891 Roswell Road
Atlanta, GA 30350
(770) 641-8393; (800) 641-RENT

www.rentalrelocation.com

TB Corporate Lodging
P.O. Box 627
Lawrenceville, GA 30046
(678) 442-9700; (800) 428-9997

Temporary Quarters
3620 Piedmont Road
Atlanta, GA 30305
(404) 848-0088; (800) 789-4901

www.temporaryquarters.com

Temporary VIP Suites
8725 Roswell Road
Atlanta, GA 30350
(800) 842-7970

www.vipsuites.com

Internet Resources

www.rent.net

www.apartmentguide.com

Living on Your Own Versus with a Roommate

Being on your own in a new town can be hard—and expensive. Having a roommate is a good way to make friends and at the same time share the costs of living in Atlanta.

Some of the major apartment-finding services will also work with you to find a compatible roommate, but don't count on it. "Very few of the apartment search companies stick with the roommate business," says Keri Glover, president of Roommate Finders. "It's not a big income producer, and it's very labor intensive." This is a personal service and one the search companies usually charge back to you if they offer it—the apartment rental companies that cover most of the searchers' bills aren't that benevolent. Finder's fees usually come to about $100 for each of the parties in the search.

The good news is that a professional search company will do

MOVING TIP

Good credit, steady employment in the same line of work for at least two years, and some money in the bank can help you pre-qualify for a loan over the phone in minutes. Pre-qualifying is a tremendous tool for finding the housing price range that's right for your budget.

the legwork, including in-depth interviews, lifestyle preferences, credit and employment checks, and personal references. The company's offices can be used as a safe and neutral meeting place for prospective roomies. The companies also provide roommate contracts that spell out the details of the arrangement.

The largest free listings of folks looking for compatible roommates are in the local newspapers, as well as in various free publications distributed in area bookstores and libraries. The leader among these is *Creative Loafing,* an entertainment and arts paper distributed weekly to stands inside the entrances of many restaurants and stores.

Another good source for finding roommates—as well as making friends—is any of Atlanta's many churches. The myriad of congregations in the city offer recreational, educational, and social programs for single adults. Many of the larger churches in Buckhead and Midtown have weekly singles dinners and workshops on topics from interpersonal relationships to finding a job.

Before you start the process, here are a few considerations leasing experts suggest you keep in mind:

- Spell out the specific rules. Before you sign a lease with a roommate, or agree to take one in, make sure you're both in agreement about specific issues. Consider setting up guidelines about everything from visitors to utility bills and cleaning.

- Decide in advance if you are comfortable rooming with a pet owner. Also, how do you feel about rooming with someone who has children, or whose children visit on a regular basis?

- Most people interested in sharing prefer to be in a roommate situation for longer than three months. If you're on a shorter time frame, finding a roommate might be difficult.

- Think beyond rooming with someone your own age. Many times, elderly home owners are happy to take in renters. They've even been known to reduce the rent in exchange for help with household chores.

- If you're on a limited budget, it is more cost-effective to share living expenses. Many folks looking for roommates are waiting for a house to be built or a family to arrive from out of town, and need to save wherever possible.

ROOMMATE FINDER SERVICES

Roommate Finders

2250 North Druid Hills Road
Atlanta, GA 30329
(404) 633-8118

www.therentsource.com

This Atlanta-based company has been finding compatible roommates for sixteen years. Fees average about $100 for the property owner and prospective roommate.

www.roommatesbbs.com

This New York-based company provides a free roommate-matching service on the Internet. There's no cost to list what you're looking for or to browse the write-ups of people looking to share the rent.

Extended-Stay Housing and Short-Lease Apartments

You don't have to live out of a suitcase while you get your bearings around Atlanta. Scattered around the Perimeter are an assortment of extended-stay facilities where all you need to live comfortably is your toothbrush.

CITY FACT

Downtown, the city's oldest commercial district, is also one of its hottest new neighborhoods. Experts predict that by 2003, 5,000 new residents will make their home there.

Many of these recently built properties feature furnished studios or suites, some as large as three bedrooms. While many welcome guests who plan to stay just a few days, most require a fourteen- to thirty-day stay to get the reduced extended-stay rates.

Though most of the facilities listed here offer common amenities (such as on-site laundry rooms and fully equipped kitchens), it's always a good idea to find out exactly what each unit includes before making a final decision.

Corporate Apartment Community

2805 Northeast Expressway Access Road
(404) 329-9800

www.rentnet.com

Rates range from $1,200 to $1,300 per month for one-bedroom apartments inside the Perimeter. Each of the eighty-two units comes with a queen or king bed, fully equipped kitchen, linens, and television; there is a swimming pool, tennis court, and laundry facility on the property. A minimum two-week stay is required.

Crestwood Suites

2353 Barrett Creek Parkway
Marietta, GA 30066
(770) 528-9880

www.crestwoodsuites.com

Furnished suites with fully equipped kitchens, data ports, cable TV, and weekly housekeeping services are priced from $189 to $259 weekly at this facility, located near Town Center Mall in Cobb County.

Extended StayAmerica

3115 Clairmont Road
Atlanta, GA 30329
(404) 679-4333; 800-EXT-STAY

www.exstay.com

All of the studio rooms at this DeKalb property are furnished with queen-sized beds, kitchenettes, an eating area, and a work space. Laundry facilities are on-site. Weekly rates average $279.

Guest House Inn

4649 Memorial Drive
Decatur, GA 30032
(404) 836-8100

2250 Pelican Drive
Norcross
(770) 417-1088

This extended-stay hotel features furnished efficiencies. Kitchens are fully equipped with refrigerator, two-burner stove, microwave, and coffeemaker. Rooms include cable TV and a queen-sized bed, two twins, or two doubles. A twenty-four-hour laundry is on-site. Rates run from $187 to $237 per week, and require a $100 security deposit.

MOVING TIP

If you store boxed items in your new garage, be careful. Very few garages are fully insulated, and temperature-sensitive items (e.g., photographs, paintings, video-cassettes, and food) may be permanently damaged.

Homestead Village

1050 Hammond Drive
Atlanta, GA 30328
(770) 522-0025

1339 Executive Park Drive
Atlanta, GA 30329
(404) 325-1223

3103 Sports Avenue
Smyrna, GA 30080
(770) 432-4000

www.stayhsd.com

Homestead's studios are designed with full, queen, or king beds, as well as fully equipped kitchens, data ports and voice mail, ironing boards and irons, and a television. Weekly rates start at $422 and go as high as $511.

Homewood Suites Hotel

3566 Piedmont Road
Atlanta, GA 30305
(404) 365-0001; (800) 225-5466

3200 Cobb Parkway
Atlanta, GA 30339
(770) 988-9449

www.homewoodsuites.com

The two-room suites at Homewood have king-sized beds, sleep sofas, ironing boards and irons, hair dryers, refrigerators, and cable TV. The properties include workout rooms, spas, and complimentary breakfast. Daily rates for extended stays start at $125.

Intown Suites

1944 Piedmont Circle
Atlanta, GA 30324
(404) 875-0047

2570 Cobb Parkway
Kennesaw, GA 30152
(770) 590-0825

Suites complete with a full-sized bed, microwave, refrigerator, and stove are rented from $160 per week. A $100 room deposit and $10 phone deposit are required. Laundry facilities are on the grounds.

Sierra Suites Hotel

3967 Peachtree Road
Atlanta, GA 30319
(404) 237-9100; 800-474-3772

6330 Peachtree Dunwoody Road
Atlanta, GA 30328
(770) 379-0111

2010 Powers Ferry Road
Atlanta, GA 30339
(770) 933-8019

www.sierrasuites.com

The double, queen, or king suites at Sierra have fully equipped kitchens, sleep sofas, cable TV, irons and ironing boards, dining tables, and voice mail. For stays of thirty days or more, nightly rates start at $49.

Staybridge Suites

3980 North Point Parkway
Alpharetta, GA 30005
(770) 569-7200

www.basshotels.com

A fitness center, library with Internet connections, twenty-four-hour business center, convenience store, and complimentary breakfast are part of this extended-stay facility. The studios and one- or two-bedroom units include televisions with VCRs and desk areas with a data port. For stays longer than five nights, rates range from $89 to $129 per day.

MOVING TIP

Some safety features to look for in a good storage facility include: electronic security gates, good lighting, motion detectors, fire precautions, and twenty-four-hour security.

Stratford Inn

585 Parkway Drive
Atlanta, GA 30354
(404) 607-1010

This residential hotel has two hundred rooms with full-sized beds, refrigerator, microwave, cable TV, desk area, and voice mail. Extended-stay weekly rates, available for stays of more than seven days, go from $165 to $180; a $100 security deposit and $5 application fee are required.

StudioPLUS

3115 Clairmont Road
Atlanta, GA 30329
(404) 679-4333

7065 Jimmy Carter Boulevard
Norcross, GA 30092
(770) 582-9984

2474 Cumberland Parkway
Atlanta, GA 30339
(770) 436-1511

www.extstay.com

Weekly rates range from $319 for a studio with a queen bed to $409 for a suite with two beds and a sleep sofa. Each unit comes with a fully equipped kitchen, television with cable hookup, and free local calls. The property has laundry facilities, an outdoor pool, and a small workout room.

Suburban Lodge

1375 Northside Drive
Atlanta, GA 30318
(404) 350-8102; 800-951-7829

1638 Church Street
Decatur, GA 30033
(404) 267-3701

www.suburbanlodge.com

Weekly rates, from $149 to $203, require a one-week deposit. Each room has one or two beds and an equipped kitchenette, but no television. Laundry facilities are on-site.

Summerfield Suites Hotel

505 Pharr Road
Atlanta, GA 30305
(404) 262-7880

www.summerfieldsuites.com

Daily rates for extended-stay guests range from $89 to $119; extended-stay rates require a thirty-day stay. Each suite has a full kitchen, queen-sized beds, television and VCR, separate living area. There's also an outdoor pool and spa, barbecue area, and laundry facilities.

Sun Suites

3000 Highlands Parkway
Smyrna, GA 30082
(770) 433-1200

www.sunsuites.com

Weekly rates are $262.50 and include local calls. Each suite has a kitchenette with a small refrigerator, microwave, and all utensils; queen-sized beds; a separate living area with cable TV. Weekly housekeeping services are provided.

CHAPTER 3

Advice on Finding a House

Many Atlanta newcomers whose jobs bring them to town have only days to find a place to live. Making that big a decision with little time can be tough, but armed with a list of your likes and dislikes, you won't waste precious time visiting properties that don't really suit your lifestyle.

Before you even start to think about the kind of house you want and where it should be, consider whether or not buying a house or condominium is the right choice. The Atlanta housing market has been booming since the early 1990s, with more houses being built and property values gradually increasing. Even condominiums, almost unsalable in the 1980s, are in unprecedented demand, as are houses in intown neighborhoods once considered too blighted to be habitable. Local real estate experts expect that the market will slow down during the 2000s, as land in certain areas dwindles and inventory of new homes sells out. On the other hand, Atlanta's strong economic climate is expected to draw more companies and their employees, many of whom will want houses.

But, of course, no one has a crystal ball.

As with any large investment, a house may not be the best place for your money depending on your circumstances. Employees who know they are likely to be transferred within a few months might be financially better off renting than spending money on closing costs and mortgage points that they may not be able to recoup. Others may prefer the flexibility and freedom an apartment, townhouse, or leased home affords. And for those who can't decide on which part of the metro area they prefer, renting for a few months allows the time to explore the area in depth and at leisure.

On the positive side:
- Atlanta's housing prices have increased steadily for the last several years.
- Owning can often be more financially rewarding than renting.
- Home owners have the freedom to build, or decorate and improve on, the property to their own personal preferences.

And for the negative side:
- A house is a major investment. Will you live in it long enough to recoup the expense of moving in?
- Are you uncertain about which area of town is right for you?
- Do you prefer the freedom of renting to the chores of owning?

More Things to Consider before House Hunting

Once you've settled on buying, it's time to go back to your preferences list and take a look at the features that are most important to make your house an ideal home.

As in most major metropolitan areas, getting around town with the greatest of ease is at the top of the house-hunting agenda. Today, there is almost no part of the Atlanta vicinity that is unaffected by traffic. Commuting to work, getting to the grocery store, and dropping the kids off at school with the least amount of aggravation are issues of pressing concern to many residents. As convenient as it is, MARTA does not serve the bulk of the metro area, and you need a car to get in and out of most counties. Additionally, in many locations you can't even go to the video store or mall without getting in the car. If being able to walk to amenities or take the train to work outweigh your craving for a property on a suburban cul-de-sac, living intown, within range of a MARTA station, or in a close-in suburb may be best.

For many families with young children, the quality of the school system is an important factor in deciding where to live. Atlanta is fortunate in having several outstanding public and independent schools. Later on in this book, we will take a closer look at the various county systems. But it is also a good idea to contact the schools in areas where you might consider buying and talk with administrators to discuss specific questions and to get an idea of what the district can offer your child.

MOVING TIP

Mortgages with less than a 20-percent down payment require mortgage insurance, which can add extra dollars to your monthly payment.

Along the same lines, you may want to investigate and compare what each county offers in the way of amenities. Some have extensive parks and recreational facilities, from lakes and soccer fields to gymnasiums and indoor pools. Some have extensive library systems with many neighborhood branches; others may have just one or two libraries in the entire county. Many counties have organized sports leagues for the kids. Check off which counties and towns have the features you expect before you move in and find they are lacking.

About the only thing Atlanta doesn't offer buyers is houses that are very old. When we talk about historic homes, we're referring to ones fortunate enough to have survived the Civil War. The bulk of Atlanta's housing stock was burnt to a cinder during General Sherman's 1864 march through town. Many small towns in the suburban and outlying counties have pockets of antebellum homes that were spared the torch, yet in recent years even those numbers have dwindled in the path of progress.

No matter what your taste in home styles and floor plans may be, there's an excellent chance that the metro area's extensive housing assortment will have it. And, if you don't happen on an existing home that suits your needs, a wealth of new developments are available where you can build your dream house. You may want to jot down particulars about houses you've seen or read about that you can refer to later. For instance, do you prefer a two-story home to a ranch? Is a master bedroom on the main level a must? How important is a large garage, a teen suite, or a finished basement? Do you need a home office? Knowing the answers will make finding a home a less daunting task.

Atlanta's housing smorgasbord does make matching your wants to your wallet a good deal easier. Homes to fit every price range exist across the area. It's interesting to note, though, that the same dollars buy different things in different counties. For instance, $150,000 can buy a spacious house in several suburban communities, but the same money only covers a condominium or a two-bedroom bungalow inside the city limits!

Key Questions to Get You Started

- How much am I able (or willing) to spend on a house each month?
- How close to work, shopping, entertainment, or schools do I want to live?
- What is the maximum amount of time I want to spend driving to work?
- Do I want to live close to public transportation?
- How important are these factors in deciding where to live?

  Quality of schools

  Quality of recreational facilities and other amenities

  Proximity to a mall

  Proximity to a shopping center for groceries, dry cleaners, pharmacy, and so on

  Availability of cultural offerings

  A single-family house

  A condominium, loft, or townhouse

  A rental unit on the property

  A yard

A new house

An existing house

A fixer-upper

House style: bilevel, contemporary, European, ranch, split-level, two-story traditional, Tudor

Approximate size of house in square feet

Number of bedrooms

One- or two-car garage

A basement

A home office

Contemporary features: high ceilings, open floor plan, two-story foyer

Classic features: hardwood floors, front porch, formal living and dining rooms

CITY FACT

Each metropolitan county collects a local sales tax, in addition to state sales tax. The various rates range from 5 to 7 percent, and is levied on most purchases.

Pros and Cons of Looking on Your Own or with an Agent

On the Internet, it's possible to get a sneak preview of Atlanta's housing market. There are several sites that showcase available homes, communities, and prices. With all the information available, you may think finding a house without a real estate agent would be a cinch. But unless you're willing to devote a significant amount of time to learning the metro area's quirks, it is probably in your best interest to take advantage of the expertise and insight an agent can provide.

No matter where their company may be located, many agents specialize in marketing the real estate in specific areas and neighborhoods. If you have a general idea of where you'd like to be, hooking up with an agent who can show you specific properties is easy to do. The leading real estate firms have Web sites where you can find their agent for the area you want.

In addition to their knowledge of the city, agents are also trained in handling real estate transactions in the state. They'll be your best source of information on what you'll need to buy a home in Georgia. They'll also offer a connection to mortgage companies and lenders so you can do some comparative shopping for loans. Best of all, if you're trying to close a deal while living in another state, having a real estate agent working for you saves a lot of time and energy. Many brokerages also offer the services of buyers' agents, who work exclusively for the buyer.

MOVING TIP

Find a pediatrician or ask a nurse for assistance by calling (404) 250-KIDS, the phone referral service of Children's Healthcare of Atlanta.

If you're the adventurous type and not in a hurry to make a decision, it's fun to go exploring on your own. Take a few months to visit the area's wealth of neighborhoods, talk to residents, and see first-hand which parts of town you prefer. It may take longer to settle down, but you'll have the satisfaction of knowing you checked out all the choices first.

Resources for Finding a House

Atlanta Journal-Constitution's Sunday HomeFinder

72 Marietta Street NW
Atlanta, GA 30303
(404) 526-5802

www.ajc.com

weekly profiles of neighborhoods, new developments, condominiums and apartments

Communities Magazine guide to new homes, condominiums, and townhouses
2100 Powers Ferry Road, Suite 400
Atlanta, GA 30339
(770) 541-7575

www.atlantacommunities.com

free bimonthly publication of new metro area developments by price range; includes special features on golf course communities and leading builders

Target Atlanta
6205 Barfield Road NE
Atlanta, GA 30328
(404) 255-5603
(800) 875-0778

www.targetatlanta.com

seasonal guide to relocation resources in the city and suburbs

Know Atlanta
1303 Hightower Trail
Dunwoody, GA 30350
(770) 650-1102

www.knowatlanta.com

information on new communities around the metro area

The Real Estate Book
2305 Newpoint Parkway
Lawrenceville, GA 30043
(770) 242-0540

www.realestatebook.com

one of the most compact collections of house photos in various geographic areas of town

Real Estate Agencies

Buy Owner
4177 Northeast Expressway
Doraville, GA 30340
(770) 491-7000
(800) 468-1999

www.buyowner.com

Century 21
2749 Lavista Road
Decatur, GA 30033
(404) 636-0313
(800) 647-9963

www.c21atlanta.com

MOVING TIP

Never place flammable and perishable

items in storage!

Century 21 Southern Crescent
635 Glynn Street
Fayetteville, GA 30214
(770) 461-5111

www.c21atlanta.com

Coldwell Banker Buckhead Brokers
5395 Roswell Road
Atlanta, GA 30342
(404) 252-7030

www.coldwellbankeratlanta.com

Coldwell Banker The Condo Store
900 Peachtree Street
Atlanta, GA 30309
(404) 292-6636

www.condostore.com

ERA Atlanta
2030 Beaver Ruin Road
Norcross, GA 30071
(770) 446-3832

www.eraatlanta.com

Harry Norman Realtors
5229 Roswell Road
Atlanta, GA 30342
(404) 255-7505

www.harrynormanrealtors.com

Jenny Pruitt & Associates
990 Hammond Drive
Sandy Springs, GA 30328
(770) 394-5400

www.jennypruitt.com

Metro Brokers/Better Homes & Gardens
415 East Paces Ferry Road NE
Atlanta, GA 30305
(404) 843-2500

www.metrobrokers.com

Prudential Atlanta Realty
863 Holcomb Bridge Road
Roswell, GA 30076
(770) 992-4100
(800) 241-2441

www.prudentialgeorgia.com

Northside Realty
6065 Roswell Road NE
Atlanta, GA 30328
(404) 252-3393

www.northsiderealty.com

Re/Max
5163 Roswell Road
Atlanta, GA 30342
(404) 847-0808

www.remax-greateratlanta.com

Additional Internet Sites

www.Atlantas-realestate.com

www.homesandlifestyles.com

www.homegain.com

www.citysearch.com

www.zipreality.com

Packing Up and Moving Out

By Monstermoving.com

CHAPTER 4

Getting Organized and Planning Your Move

Written for both the beginner and the veteran, this chapter contains information and resources that will help you get ready for your move. If money is foremost on your mind, you'll find a section on budgeting for the move and tips on how to save money throughout the move—as well as a move budget-planning guide. If time is also precious, you'll find time-saving tips and even suggestions for how to get out of town in a hurry. You'll find help with preliminary decisions, the planning process, and packing, as well as tips and advice on uprooting and resettling your family (and your animal companions). A budget worksheet, a set of helpful checklists, and a moving task time line complete the chapter.

Paying for Your Move

Moving can certainly tap your bank account. How much depends on a number of factors: whether your employer is helping with the cost, how much stuff you have, and how far you are moving.

To get an idea of how much your move will cost, start calling service providers for estimates and begin listing these expenses on the move budget-planning guide provided at the end of this chapter.

If you don't have the money saved, start saving as soon as you can. You should also check out other potential sources of money:

- Income from the sale of your spare car, furniture, or other belongings (hold a garage or yard sale).
- The cleaning and damage deposit on your current rental and any utility deposits. You probably won't be reimbursed until *after* your move, though, so you'll need to pay moving expenses up front in some other way.
- Your employer, who may owe you a payout for vacation time not taken.

Taxes and Your Move

Did you know that your move may affect your taxes? As you prepare to move, here are some things to consider:

- Next year's taxes. Some of your moving expenses may be tax-deductible. Save your receipts and contact your accountant and the IRS for more information. Visit *www.irs.gov* or call the IRS at (800) 829-3676 for information and to obtain the publication and forms you need.
- State income tax. If your new state collects income tax, you'll want to figure that into your salary and overall cost of living calculations. Of course, if your old state collects income tax and your new one doesn't, that's a factor, too, but a happier one—but remember to find out how much if any of the current year's income will be taxable in the old state.
- Other income sources. You'll want to consider any other sources of income and whether your new state will tax you on this income. For example, if you are paying federal income tax on an IRA that you rolled over into a Roth IRA, if you move into a state that collects income tax, you may also have to pay state income tax on your rollover IRA.
- After you move or when filing time draws near, consider collecting your receipts and visiting an accountant.

The Budget Move (Money-Saving Tips)

Here you'll find some suggestions for saving money on your move.

Saving on Moving Supplies

- Obtain boxes in the cheapest way possible.

  Ask a friend or colleague who has recently moved to give or sell you their boxes.

  Check the classified ads; people sometimes sell all their moving boxes for a flat rate.

  Ask your local grocery or department store for their empty boxes.

- Borrow a tape dispenser instead of buying one.

- Instead of buying bubble wrap, crumple newspaper, plain unused newsprint, or tissue paper to pad breakables.

- Shop around for the cheapest deal on packing tape and other supplies.

- Instead of renting padding blankets from the truck rental company, use your own blankets, linens, and area rugs for padding. (But bear in mind that you may have to launder them when you arrive, which is an expense in itself.)

MOVING TIP

If you are renting a truck, you'll need to know what size to rent. Here is a general guideline. Because equipment varies, though, ask for advice from the company renting the truck to you.

10-foot truck:

   one to two furnished rooms

14- to 15-foot truck:

   two to three furnished rooms

18- to 20-foot truck:

   four to five furnished rooms

22- to 24-foot truck:

   six to eight furnished rooms

Saving on Labor

- If you use professional movers, consider a "you pack, we drive" arrangement, in which you pack boxes, and the moving company loads, moves, and unloads your belongings.
- Call around and compare estimates.
- If you move yourself, round up volunteers to help you load and clean on moving day. It's still customary to reward them with moving-day food and beverages (and maybe a small cash gift). You may also have to volunteer to help them move some day. But you may still save some money compared to hiring professionals.
- Save on child and pet care. Ask family or friends to watch your young children and pets on moving day.

Saving on Trip Expenses

Overnight the Night Before You Depart

- Where will you stay the night before you depart? A hotel or motel might be most comfortable and convenient, but you could save a little money if you stay the night with a friend or relative.
- If you have the gear, maybe you'd enjoy unrolling your sleeping bag and "roughing it" on your own floor the night before you leave town. If you do this, try to get hold of a camping sleeping pad or air mattress, which will help you get a good night's sleep and start your move rested and refreshed.

Overnight on the Road

- Look into hotel and motel discounts along your route. Your automobile club membership may qualify you for a better rate. Check out other possibilities, too—associations such as AARP often line up discounts for their members, as do some credit cards.
- When you call about rates, ask if the hotel or motel includes a light breakfast with your stay.
- If your move travel involves an overnight stay and you're game for camping, check into campgrounds and RV parks along your route. Be sure to ask whether a moving truck is allowed. Some

parks have size restrictions; some RV parks may not welcome moving trucks; and some limit the number of vehicles allowed in a campsite.

Food While Traveling

Food is one of those comfort factors that can help make the upsetting aspects of moving and traveling more acceptable. Eating also gives you a reason to stop and rest, which may be exactly what you or your family needs if you're rushing to get there. Here are a few pointers to consider:

- Try to balance your need to save money with your (and your family's) health and comfort needs.

- Try to have at least one solid, nutritious sit-down meal each day.

- Breakfast can be a budget- and schedule-friendly meal purchased at a grocery or convenience store and eaten on the road: fruit, muffins, and juice, for example.

- Lunch prices at sit-down restaurants are typically cheaper than dinner prices. Consider having a hot lunch and then picnicking in your hotel or motel on supplies from a grocery store.

Scheduling Your Move

Try to allow yourself at least three months to plan and prepare. This long lead time is especially important if you plan to sell or buy a home or if you are moving during peak moving season (May through September). If you plan to move during peak season, it's vital to reserve two to three months in advance with a professional moving company or truck rental company. The earlier you reserve, the more likely you are to get the dates you want. This is especially important if you're timing your move with a job start date or a house closing date, or are moving yourself and want to load and move on a weekend when your volunteers are off work.

WHEN IS THE RIGHT TIME TO MOVE?

If your circumstances allow you to decide your move date, you'll want to make it as easy as possible on everyone who is moving:

- Children adjust better if they move between school terms (entering an established class in the middle of a school year can be very difficult).
- Elders have special needs you'll want to consider.
- Pets fare best when temperatures aren't too extreme, hot *or* cold.

THE "GET-OUT-OF-TOWN-IN-A-HURRY" PLAN

First the bad news: Very little about the move process can be shortened. Now the good news: The choices you make might make it possible to move in less time. The three primary resources in a successful move are time, money, and planning. If you're short on time, be prepared to spend more money or become more organized.

MOVING TIP

Before buying anything for your new apartment or home, stop and consider what you'll need immediately and what you might be able to do without for a while. You'll spend a lot less if you can afford to wait and look for it on sale or secondhand.

Immediately check into the availability of a rental truck or professional moving service. Next, give your landlord notice or arrange for an agent to sell your home. (If you own your home, you may find it harder to leave town in a hurry.) If your employer is paying for your move, ask if it offers corporate-sponsored financing options that will let you buy a new home before you sell your old one.

Then consider the following potentially timesaving choices:

- Move less stuff. Of all the moving tasks, packing and unpacking consume the most time. The less you have to deal with, the quicker your move will go. Consider drastically lightening the load by selling or giving away most of your belongings and starting over in your new location. Although buying replacement stuff may drain your pocketbook, you can save some money by picking up some items secondhand at thrift stores and garage sales. (And after all, everything you have *now* is used, isn't it?)

· Make a quick-move plan. Quickly scan through chapters 4 and 5, highlighting helpful information. Use the checklists and the task time line at the end of this chapter to help you.

· Get someone else to do the cleaning. Before you vacate, you'll need to clean. You can be out the door sooner if you hire a professional cleaning company to come and clean everything, top to bottom, including the carpets. Again, the time you save will cost you money—but it may well be worth trading money for time.

Planning and Organizing

Start a move notebook. This could be as simple as a spiral-bound notepad or as elaborate as a categorized, tabbed binder. Keep track of this notebook. You'll find it invaluable later when the chaos hits. In your notebook, write notes and tape receipts. Of course, keep *this* book with your notebook! You may find the checklists and moving task time lines at the end of this chapter helpful. You may also find it helpful to assign a "do-by" date to each task on the checklist. To help you gauge what you face in the coming weeks, perhaps you will find it useful at this point to scan through the task time lines before reading further.

The section of the Moving Task Time Line that will help you the most at this point is "Decision Making: Weeks 12 to 9," which you'll find at the end of this chapter.

Preliminary Decisions

Before you even begin to plan your move, there are a number of decisions you'll need to make regarding your current residence, how you will move (do it yourself or hire a professional), and your new area.

LEAVING YOUR CURRENT HOME
(RENTED PROPERTY)

Leaving a rental unit involves notifying your landlord and fulfilling your contractual obligations. This won't be a problem unless you have a lease agreement that lasts beyond your desired move date.

Your rights and options are dictated by state and local landlord/tenant laws and by your lease agreement. Exit fees can be expensive, depending on the terms of your lease. Here are some tips that may help you get out of a lease gracefully and save a few bucks at the same time.

- Know your rights. Laws governing landlord/tenant agreements and rights vary by state and municipality. Consult state and local law and call and obtain a pamphlet on renter's rights for your state and municipality.

- Review your lease agreement. There's no point in worrying until you know whether you have anything to worry about—and no use finding out too late that there were things you could have done.

- Look for a way out. Ask your landlord to consider letting you find a replacement tenant to fulfill your lease term (in some areas, this is a right dictated by law). If your move is due to a corporate relocation, your landlord or the property management company *may* be more willing to be flexible with exit fees—especially if you provide a letter from your employer. (And you may be able to get your employer to pick up the cost if you can't get the fees waived.)

- Adjust the timing. If you need to stay a month or two longer than your current lease allows and you don't want to sign for another six months or longer, ask your landlord for a month-to-month agreement lasting until your move date.

LEAVING YOUR CURRENT HOME
(OWNED PROPERTY)

If you own your home, you'll either sell it or rent it out. If you sell, you'll either hire a real estate agent or sell it yourself. If you rent it out, you'll either serve as your own landlord or hire a property management agency to manage the property for you. Here are a few quick pros and cons to help you with the decisions you face.

Hiring a Selling Agent: Pros

- Your home gets exposure to a wide market audience, especially if the agent you choose participates in a multiple listing service.

- Homes listed with a real estate agent typically sell more quickly.

- Your agent will market your home (prepare and place ads and so on), and will also schedule and manage open houses and showings.

- Your agent will advise you and represent your interest in the business deal of selling including offers, negotiation, and closing, guiding you through the stacks of paperwork.

MOVING TIP

Start packing as soon as you get boxes. Some things you can pack long before the move. For example, off-season holiday decorations and off-season clothes can be boxed right away. The more you do early on, the less there is to do closer to move day, when things are hectic anyway.

Hiring a Selling Agent: Cons

- Hiring an agent requires signing a contract. If, for whatever reason, you want out, you may find it difficult to break the contract (it's wise to read carefully and sign only a short-term contract. Typical real estate agent contracts are ninety to 120 days in length).

- You pay your agent a fee for the service, typically a percentage of the selling price.

Selling Your Home Yourself: Pros

- You don't pay an agent's fee.

- You retain more control over showings, open houses, walk-throughs, and so on.

Selling Your Home Yourself: Cons

- Selling a home takes time. You must arrange your own showings and schedule and conduct your own open houses. Combined with everything else that happens during move preparation (working, interviewing for jobs, finding a new home, planning your move, packing, and so on), you will probably be swamped already. Add home showings (which are based around the buyer's schedule, not yours), and you may find yourself looking for an agent to help you after all.

- You pay for marketing costs, which can add up. Consider the cost of flyers, newspaper ads, or listing your home on a "homes for sale by owner" Web site.

- Since you don't have a real estate agent to represent you in the sale, you may need to hire an attorney at that point, which could take up some of the savings.

MOVING TIP

Take a tape measure and your notebook with you. Measure rooms; sketch your new home and write room measurements on your sketch. Before you move, you'll know whether your current furniture will fit and will have a good idea of how it should be arranged.

RENTING OUT YOUR PROPERTY

If you prefer to rent out your home, you can turn it over to a property management agency or be your own landlord. The services an agency will perform depend on the agency and your agreement with them. The following table details some of the rental issues you'll need to consider. As you review these, ask yourself how far away you're moving and whether or not you can handle these issues from your new home. Remember that every piece of work you must hire out cuts into the money in your pocket at the end of the month.

Rental Issue	You As Landlord	Hired Property Manager
Vacancy	You interview candidates, show the property, and choose tenants	The agency finds and selects tenants
Cleaning	You clean or arrange for cleaning services between tenants	The agency arranges for cleaning services between tenants
Late Rent	You collect rent and pursue late rent	The agency collects rent and pursues late rent
Rental Income	The rent you collect is all yours	The agency charges a fee, usually a percentage of the monthly rent
Repairs	You handle repairs and emergencies or find and hire a contractor to do the work	The agency handles repairs and emergencies

Strategic Financial Issues
Related to Renting Out Your Old Home

If your property is located in a desirable neighborhood that is appreciating in value 3 percent or more annually, keeping it may in the long run defray or overcome the cost of management fees. If you rent out your property, it ceases being your primary residence. Find out from your accountant if this will affect your federal or state income taxes or local property taxes (some counties/municipalities give owner-occupied credits that reduce the tax burden). If there is an impact, you'll want to figure the difference into your decision of whether or not to sell and into the total you charge for rent.

Deciding How to Move: Hiring Professionals or Moving Yourself

At first, you may be inclined to handle your own move to save money. But there are other factors to consider, and, depending on your situation, you may actually *save* money if you use professional services. Consider the range of service options some professional companies offer. The right combination could save you some of the headache but still compete with the cost of a do-it-yourself move. For example, some professional moving companies offer a "you pack, we drive" arrangement, in which you pack boxes, and the moving company loads, moves, and unloads your belongings. Call around and inquire about rates. Also consider the following list of pros and cons to help you decide what's best for you.

The section of the Moving Task Time Line that will help you the most at this point is "Decision Making: Weeks 12 to 9," which you'll find at the end of this chapter.

The Pros of Using Pros

- *Time.* You may not have the hours it will take to pack, move, and unpack, but professional movers do—that's their day job.
- *Materials.* The moving company provides boxes and packing materials.*
- *Packing.* The movers pack all boxes (unless your contract states that you will pack).*
- *Loading and Unloading.* The movers load your belongings onto the moving van and unload your belongings at your destination.*
- *Unpacking.* The movers remove packed items from boxes and place items on flat surfaces.*
- *Debris.* The movers dispose of packing debris such as boxes, used tape, and padding.*
- *Experience.* The movers will know just what to do to transport your precious belongings in good condition.
- *Safety.* The movers do the lifting, which could save you a real injury.

Professional moving contracts typically include the services marked with an asterisk (*). Don't count on something unless you know for sure that the contract covers it, though—it's a good idea to ask your mover a lot of questions and read the contract carefully.

The Cons of Using Pros

- *Administrative chores.* Using professionals requires you to do some up-front work: obtaining estimates, comparing and negotiating prices and move dates, reviewing contracts, and comparing insurance options.
- *Loss of control.* The movers typically take charge of much of the packing and loading process, and you need to adapt to their schedule and procedures.

The Pros of a Self-Move

- *Control.* You pack, so you decide what items get packed together, how they get packed, and in which box they reside.
- *Cost-cutting.* You may save some money. But as you compare costs, be sure to factor in *all* self-move-related moving and travel costs. These include fuel, tolls, mileage charge on the rented truck, food, and lodging. All these costs increase the longer your trip is.

The Cons of a Self-Move

- *Risk to your belongings.* Because of inexperience with packing, loading, and padding heavy and unwieldy boxes and furniture, you or your volunteers may inadvertently damage your property.

MOVING TIP

Save the TV, VCR, kids' videos, and a box of toys to be loaded on the truck last. On arriving at your destination, if you can't find someone to baby-sit, set aside a room in your home where your young children can safely play. Set up the TV and VCR and unpack the kids' videos along with some toys and snacks.

- *Risk to yourself and your friends.* You or your volunteers may injure yourselves or someone else.
- *Responsibility.* Loading and moving day are especially hectic, and you're in charge.
- *Reciprocal obligations.* If you use volunteers, you may be in debt to return the favor.

OTHER THINGS TO KNOW ABOUT PROFESSIONAL MOVING SERVICES

Your moving company may or may not provide the following services, or may charge extra for performing them. Be sure to ask.

- Disassembling beds or other furniture
- Removing window covering hardware (drapery rods, mini-blinds) or other items from the walls or ceiling
- Disconnecting and installing appliances (dryer, washer, automatic ice maker)
- Disconnecting and installing outside fixtures such as a satellite dish, a hose reel, and so on
- Moving furniture or boxes from one room to another

MOVING INSURANCE IN A PROFESSIONAL MOVE

By U.S. law, the mover must cover your possessions at $0.60 per pound. This coverage is free. Consider taking out additional coverage, though, because under this minimal coverage, your three-pound antique Tiffany lamp worth hundreds of dollars at auction fetches exactly $1.80 if the moving company breaks it.

Your homeowner's or renter's insurance provider may be willing to advise you on moving insurance options, and the moving company will offer you a number of insurance options. Be sure you understand each option—what it covers and what it costs you. Ask a lot of questions and read everything carefully. No one wishes for mishaps, but it's best to be prepared and well informed should something break or show up missing.

STORAGE

If you want your moving company to store some or all of your possessions temporarily, inquire about cost and the quality of their facilities:

- Are the facilities heated (or air-conditioned, depending on the time of year that applies to you)?
- Does the moving company own the storage facility or subcontract storage to someone else? If they subcontract, does your contract with the moving company extend to the storage facility company?

Atlanta Storage Companies

A Action Storage & U-Haul
1170 Howell Mill Road
(404) 881-0100

Ark Self Storage
2330 Old Concord Road
Smyrna
(770) 436-0834

Atlanta's Your Extra Attic
4730 Lower Roswell Road
Marietta
(770) 509-0880

Colonial Storage Centers
4141 Snapfinger Woods Drive
Decatur
(404) 284-8242

8457 Roswell Road
Dunwoody
(770) 998-1548

Dunwoody Place Self Storage
8773 Dunwoody Place
(770) 998-6601

Meridian Storage
600 Virginia Avenue
(404) 874-7410

Pinnacle Storage
2489 Cheshire Bridge Road
(404) 248-9600

Public Storage
2080 Briarcliff Road
(404) 321-0224

1067 Memorial Drive
(404) 525-8711

1387 Northside Drive
(404) 351-8415

3391 N. Druid Hills Road
(404) 633-7532

Shurgard Storage Center
4300 Peachtree Road
(404) 814-9999

1210 Clairmont Road
Decatur
(404) 325-2775

Stor-All
4654 Roswell Road
(404) 705-9575

U-Haul Self Storage
300 Peters Street
(404) 681-0502

2951 Northeast Expressway
Access Road
(770) 458-8353

USA Self Storage Centers
1300 Collier Road
(404) 355-1890

CHOOSING A MOVER

- Start by asking around. Chances are your friends, family, or colleagues will have a personal recommendation.
- Take their recommendations and list them in a notebook, each on a separate sheet. Call these companies to request a no-obligation, free written estimate—and take notes on your conversation.
- Find out if the company you're talking to offers the services you need. For example, if you want to ship your car, boat, or powered recreational craft in the van along with your household goods, ask if this service is available.
- Do a little investigating. Ask the company to show you its operating license, and call the Better Business Bureau to ask about complaints and outstanding claims.

GETTING AN ESTIMATE

You need to know what kind of estimate the moving company is giving you. The two most common are "non-binding" and "binding." A *non-binding estimate* (usually free, but potentially less accurate) is one in which the moving company charges you by the hour per worker per truck and quotes you an approximate figure to use in your planning. Depending on circumstances, your final cost could be significantly greater than what shows up in the estimate.

The second type is a *binding estimate,* which you typically pay for. In this type, the professional mover performs a detailed on-site inspection of your belongings and quotes a flat price based on the following:

- The amount of stuff you're moving, whether it is fragile or bulky, and how complicated it is to pack

- Final weight

- Services provided

- Total length of travel

Once you choose a mover, it's a good idea to have a representative visit your home, look at your belongings, and give you a written (binding) estimate. Getting a written estimate may cost you money, but it helps prevent surprises when it comes time to pay the final bill.

You play a big role in making sure that the estimate you receive is accurate. Be sure you show the moving company representative everything you plan to move.

- Remember to take the representative through every closet, out to the garage, into the shed, down to the basement, up into the attic, and to your rented storage facility if you have one.

MOVING TIP

Unless company policy prohibits acceptance of gratuities, it is customary to tip each professional mover. $20 is a good amount; you may want to tip more or less based on the service you receive.

If you move yourself, you might also want to give each of your volunteers a gift. Cash or a gift certificate is a nice gesture. Perhaps one of your volunteers is a plant-lover and will cheerfully accept your houseplants as a thank-you gift. It's also a good idea to supply plenty of soft drinks or water and snacks for them!

- Tell the representative about any item you *don't* plan to move (because you plan to get rid of it before you move). Then be sure to follow through and get rid of it so there are no surprises on moving day.

• Point out any vehicles you want to ship in the van along with your household goods, and ask your representative to include the cost in your estimate.

WHAT MIGHT INCREASE YOUR FINAL BILL

It is reasonable to expect that certain circumstances will unexpectedly increase your final bill, including:

• You do the packing and it's incomplete or done improperly.
• Circumstances unexpectedly increase the time and labor involved in your move. For example:

> You're moving out of or into a high-rise and movers don't have access to an elevator (perhaps it's broken).

> Access at either location is restricted (for example, there is no truck parking close by or the movers have to wait for someone to unlock).

• You change your move destination after you receive your written estimate.
• You require delivery of your belongings to more than one destination.

Researching Your New Area

The section of the Moving Task Time Line that will help you the most at this point is "Decision Making: Weeks 12 to 9," which you'll find at the end of this chapter. Other chapters of this book discuss the details of your destination city. Here are some additional move-related tips and resources.

GENERAL CITY INFORMATION

• Visit your local library and read up on your new area.
• Go online and look for the local newspaper.
• Have a friend or family member mail you a week's worth of newspapers or have a subscription delivered via postal mail.
• Visit *www.monstermoving.com* for easy-to-find city information and links to local services, information, and Web sites.

JOBS, HOUSING, AND COST OF LIVING

Visit *www.monster.com* for career assistance, and visit *www.monster moving.com* for links to apartments for rent, and real estate and other services, as well as free cost-of-living information.

CHOOSING SCHOOLS

Selecting schools is of supreme importance for family members who will attend public or private schools.

Do Your Homework

- Ask your real estate agent to help you find school information and statistics or a list of contacts for home school associations.
- Search the Web.

    Visit *www.2001beyond.com.* There you can compare up to four districts at once. Information on both public and private schools is provided. The extensive twelve-page report provides information on class size, curriculum, interscholastic sports, extracurricular activities, awards, merits, and SAT scores. It also provides the principal's name and phone number for each school in the district. You may need to pay a nominal fee for the twelve-page report (or the cost may be covered by a sponsoring real estate professional, if you don't mind receiving a phone call from an agent).

    Visit *www.monstermoving.com,* which provides links to school information.

Visit Schools

Arrange to visit schools your children might attend, and bring them along. Your children will pick up on subtleties that you will miss. As you talk with your children about changing schools, try to help them differentiate between their feelings about moving to a new school and area and their feelings about that particular school by asking direct but open-ended questions. (An *open-ended* question is one that invites dialogue because it can't be answered with a simple "yes" or "no"— "What was the best or worst thing you saw there?" for example, or "Which electives looked the most interesting?")

PLANNING AND TAKING
A HOUSE—OR APARTMENT—HUNTING TRIP

Preparing and planning in advance will help you make the most of your trip. Ideally, by this point, you will have narrowed your search to two or three neighborhoods or areas.

- Gather documents and information required for completing a rental application:

    Rental history: Landlord name, contact information, dates occupied

    Personal references: Name and contact information for one or two personal references

    Employment information: Current or anticipated employer name and contact info

    Bank account number

- Consider compiling all this information into a "Rental Résumé." Even though most landlords won't accept a rental résumé in lieu of a completed application, spending the time up front could be helpful in a market where rentals are scarce. Handing the landlord a rental résumé lets them know you're serious about finding the right place and are professional and organized in how you conduct your affairs.

- Go prepared to pay an application fee and deposits. Deposit the funds in your account and bring your checkbook. Typically, landlords require first and last month's rent and a flat damage and cleaning deposit.

- Take your Move Planning Notebook. List properties you want to visit, one per notebook page. Clip the classified ad and tape it onto the page. Write notes about the property, rent rate, deposit amount, and terms you discuss with the landlord or property manager.

Planning

Now that you've made pre-move decisions, it's time to plan for the physical move. First, you'll need to organize your moving day. Next, you'll need to prepare to pack.

These are the sections of the Moving Task Timeline that will help you the most at this point:

- "Organizing, Sorting, and Notifying: Weeks 9 to 8"
- "Finalizing Housing Arrangements and Establishing Yourself in Your New Community: Weeks 8 to 6"
- "Making and Confirming Transportation and Travel Plans: Week 6"
- "Uprooting: Weeks 5 to 4"
- "Making and Confirming Moving-Day Plans: Week 3"

You'll find the Moving Task Time Line at the end of this chapter.

PLANNING FOR MOVING DAY

The Professional Move: Some Planning Considerations

- Confirm your move dates and finalize any last contract issues.
- Ask what form of payment movers will accept (check, money order, certified check, traveler's checks) and make necessary arrangements.

The Self-Move: Organizing Volunteers

- Ask friends and relatives to "volunteer" to help you load the truck on moving day.
- Set up shifts, and tactfully let your volunteers know that you are counting on them to arrive on time and stay through their "shift."
- A week or two before moving day, call everyone to remind them.
- Plan on supplying soft drinks and munchies to keep your crew going.

MOVING TIP

Reserve a large place for the moving truck to park on the day you move out. Mark off an area with cones or chairs. If you need to obtain parking permission from your apartment complex manager or the city, do so in advance.

PLANNING CARE FOR YOUR CHILDREN AND PETS

Moving day will be hectic for you and everyone, and possibly danger-ous for your young children. Make plans to take younger children and your pets to someone's home or to a care facility.

PLANNING YOUR MOVING-DAY TRAVEL

Driving

- If you will be renting a truck, be prepared to put down a sizable deposit the day you pick up the truck. Some truck rental compa-nies only accept a credit card for this deposit, so go prepared.
- If you belong to an automobile club such as AAA, contact them to obtain maps, suggested routes, alternate routes, rest-stop information, and a trip packet, if they provide this service.
- Visit an online map site such as *www.mapblast.com,* where you'll find not only a map but also door-to-door driving directions and estimated travel times.
- Find out in advance where you should turn in the truck in your new hometown.

Traveling by Air, Train, or Bus

- Arrange for tickets and boarding passes.
- Speak with the airline to request meals that match dietary restrictions.
- Speak with the airline or the train or bus company to make any special arrangements such as wheelchair accessibility and assistance.
- Plan to dress comfortably.
- If you will be traveling with young children, plan to dress them in bright, distinctive clothing so you can easily identify them in a crowded airport, train station, or bus terminal.

PREPARING TO PACK:
WHAT TO DO WITH THE STUFF YOU HAVE

Moves are complicated, time-consuming, and exhausting. But the process has at least one benefit. A move forces us to consider simplify-ing our lives by reducing the amount of our personal belongings. If we plan to keep it, we also must pack it, load it, move it, unload it, and unpack it. Here are some suggestions for sifting through your belongings as you prepare for packing.

- Start in one area of your home and go through everything before moving to the next area.

- Ask yourself three questions about each item (sentimental value aside):

    Have we used this in the last year?

    Will we use it in the coming year? For example, if you're moving to a more temperate climate, you might not need all your wool socks and sweaters.

    Is there a place for it in the new home? For instance, if your new home has a smaller living room, you might not have room for your big couch or need all your wall decorations.

If you answer "no" to any or all of these questions, you might want to consider selling the item, giving it away, or throwing it out.

Packing

Here are some tips to help you with one of the most difficult stages of your move—packing.

- Follow a plan. Pack one room at a time. You may find yourself leaving one or two boxes in each room open to receive those items you use right up until the last minute.

- On the outside of each box, describe the contents and room destination. Be as specific as you can, to make unpacking easier. However, if you are using a professional

MOVING TIP

A few weeks before you move, start eating the food in your freezer. Also use up canned food, which is bulky and heavy to move.

moving service but doing the packing yourself, consider numbering boxes and creating a separate list of box contents and destinations.

- Put heavy items such as books in small boxes to make them easier to carry.

- Don't put tape on furniture because it may pull off some finish when you remove it.

- As you pack, mark and set aside the items that should go in the truck last (see checklist at the end of this chapter). Mark and set aside your "necessary box" (for a list of items to include in this box, see the checklist at the end of this chapter).

PACKING FRAGILE ITEMS

- When packing breakable dishes and glasses, use boxes and padding made for these items. You may have to pay a little to buy these boxes, but you're apt to save money in the long run because your dishes are more likely to arrive unbroken. Dishes and plates are best packed on edge (not stacked flat atop each other).

- Pad mirrors, pictures, and larger delicate pieces with sheets and blankets.

- Computers fare best if they are packed in their original boxes. If you don't have these, pack your hardware in a large, sturdy box and surround it with plenty of padding such as plastic bubble pack.

- Use plenty of padding around fragile items.

- Mark "FRAGILE" *on the top and all sides* of boxes of breakables so it's easily seen no matter how a box is stacked.

WHAT *NOT* TO PACK

- Don't pack hazardous, flammable, combustible, or explosive materials. Empty your gas grill tank and any kerosene heater fuel as well as gasoline in your power yard tools. These materials are not safe in transit.

- Don't pack valuables such as jewelry, collections, important financial and legal documents, and records for the moving van. Keep these with you in your car trunk or your suitcase.

PACKING AND UNPACKING SAFELY
WITH YOUNG CHILDREN

No matter how well you've kid-proofed your home, that only lasts until the moment you start packing. Then things are in disarray and within reach of youngsters. Here are some tips to keep your toddlers and children safe.

- Items your youngsters have seldom or never seen will pique their curiosity, presenting a potential hazard, so consider what you are packing or unpacking. If you stop packing or unpacking and leave the room even for a moment, take your youngsters with you and close the door or put up a child gate.

- Keep box knives and other tools out of a child's reach.

- As you disassemble or reassemble furniture, keep track of screws, bolts, nuts, and small parts.

- Beware of how and where you temporarily place furniture and other items. (That heavy mirror you just took down off the wall—do you lean it up against the wall until you go get the padding

material, inviting a curious youngster to pull or climb on it?) For the same reason, consider how high you stack boxes.

- On arriving at your destination, if you can't find someone to baby-sit, set aside a room in your home where your young children can safely play. Set up the TV and VCR and unpack the kids' videos, books, coloring books and crayons or markers, and some toys and snacks.

MOVING TIP

Draw up a detailed plan of your new home, including scale drawings of each room that show each piece of furniture you plan to take with you. Label furniture and boxes as to where they go in the new home, and have copies of the plan to put in each room there. This will give you at least a chance that most of the work of moving in will only need to be done once.

- Walk through your new home with children and talk about any potential dangers such as a swimming pool or stairs, establishing your safety rules and boundaries.
- If you have young children who are unaccustomed to having stairs in the home, place a gate at the top and one at the bottom. If your child is walking and over toddler age, walk up and down the stairs together a few times holding the railing until they become accustomed to using the stairs.

Handle with Special Care: Uprooting and Settling the People and Pets in Your Life

The most important advice you can hear is this: Involving children as much as possible will help transform this anxiety-causing, uncertain experience into an exciting adventure. It would take a book to cover this topic comprehensively, but here are some suggestions for making the transition easier:

- *Involve children early.* Ask for their input on decisions and give them age-appropriate tasks such as packing their own belongings and assembling an activity bag to keep them busy while traveling.
- *Don't make empty promises.* Kids can hear the hollow ring when you say, "It'll be just like here. Just give it time," or "You can stay friends with your friends here." That's true, but you know it's not true in the same way, if you're moving a long distance.
- *Deal with fear of the unknown.* If possible, take children with you to look at potential neighborhoods, homes or apartments, and schools. It may be more expensive and require extra effort, but it will ease the transition and help children begin to make the adjustment.
- *Provide as much information as you can.* If it's not possible to take children with you when you visit new neighborhoods, homes or apartments, and schools, take a camera or video recorder. Your children will appreciate the pictures, and the preview will help them begin the transition. You can also use a map to help them understand the new area and the route you will take to get there.

- *Make time to talk with your children about the move.* Especially listen for—and talk about—the anxieties your children feel. By doing so, you will help them through the move (your primary goal)—and you'll deepen your relationship at the same time, which may be more important in the long run.

- *Share your own anxieties with your children—but be sure to keep an overall positive outlook about the move.* Because most aspects of a move are downers, a negative outlook on your part may shed gloom over the whole experience—including its good aspects. On the other hand, a positive outlook on your part may counteract some of your child's emotional turmoil, uncertainty, and fear.

- *Make it fun.* Give older children a disposable camera and ask them to photograph your move. Once you arrive and are settled in, make time together to create the "moving" chapter of your family photo album.

HELPING FAMILY MEMBERS MAINTAIN FRIENDSHIPS

Moving doesn't have to end a friendship.

- Give each child a personal address book and have them write the e-mail address, phone number, and postal mail address for each of their friends.

- Stay in touch. E-mail is an easy way. Establish an e-mail address for every family member (if they don't already have one) before you move so they can give it out to friends. Many Web mail services are free and can be accessed from anywhere you can access the Internet. Examples include *www.msn.com, www.usa.net,* and *www.yahoo.com.*

- Make (and follow through with) plans to visit your old hometown within the first year following your move. Visit friends and drive by your old home, through neighborhoods, and past landmarks. This reconnection with dear friends and fond memories will help your family bring finality to the move.

TRAVELING WITH YOUR PET

- Keep a picture of your pet on your person or in your wallet just in case you get separated from Fido or Fluffy during the move.
- Place identification tags on your pet's collar and pet carrier.
- Take your pet to the vet for an examination just before you move. Ask for advice on moving your particular pet. Specifically ask for advice on how you can help your pet through the move—what you can do before, during, and after the move to help your pet make the transition smoothly.
- Find out if you will need any health certificates for your pet to comply with local regulations in your new home, and obtain them when you visit the vet.
- If your pet is prone to motion sickness or tends to become nervous in reaction to excitement and unfamiliar surroundings, tell your veterinarian, who may prescribe medication for your pet.
- Ask for your pet's health records so you can take them to your new vet.
- If your pet is unusual—say, a ferret or a snake or other reptile—there might be laws in your new city or state regarding the transportation or housing of such an animal. Contact the department of agriculture or a local veterinarian to find out.
- Cats: It's wise to keep your cat indoors for the first two weeks until it recognizes its new surroundings as home.
- Dogs: If appropriate, walk your dog on a leash around your neighborhood to help it become familiar with its new surroundings and learn its way back home.
- If your pet will travel by plane, check with your airline regarding fees and any specific rules and regulations regarding pet transport.
- Your pet will need to travel in an approved carrier (check with your airline regarding acceptable types and sizes).
- Your airline may require a signed certificate of health dated within a certain number of days of the flight. Only your vet can produce this document.

Move Budget-Planning Guide

Housing

Home repairs $ _____

Cleaning supplies and services $ _____

Rental expenses in new city

    Application fees
    (varies—figure $15 to $35 per application) $ _____

    First and last month's rent $ _____

    Damage and security deposit $ _____

    Pet deposit $ _____

    Utility deposits $ _____

    Storage unit rental $ _____

Total...................................**$** _____

Moving

Professional moving services or truck rental $ _____

Moving supplies $ _____

Food and beverage for volunteers $ _____

Tips for professional movers; gifts for volunteers $ _____

Moving travel:

    Airline tickets $ _____

    Fuel $ _____

    Tolls $ _____

    Meals: per meal $_____ × _____ meals $ _____

    Hotels: per night $_____ × _____ nights $ _____

Total...................................**$** _____

(continues on next page)

(continued from previous page)

Other Expenses

_____	$ _____
_____	$ _____
_____	$ _____
_____	$ _____
_____	$ _____
_____	$ _____
_____	$ _____

Total. . . . . $ _____

GRAND TOTAL. . . . . $ _____

Utilities to Cancel

Utility	Provider name and phone	Cancel date[1]
Water and sewer		
Electricity		
Gas		
Phone		
Garbage		
Cable		
Alarm service		

1. If you are selling your home, the shutoff of essential services (water, electricity, gas) will depend on the final closing and walk-through. Coordinate with your real estate agent.

Utilities to Connect

Utility	Provider name and phone	Service start date	Deposit amount required
Water and sewer			
Electricity			
Gas			
Phone			
Garbage			
Cable			
Alarm service			

Other Services to Cancel, Transfer, or Restart

Service	Provider name and phone	Service end date[1]	Service start date[1]
Subscriptions and Memberships			
Newspaper			
Memberships (health club and so on)			
Internet Service Provider			

1. If applicable

(continues on next page)

(continued from previous page)

Other Services to Cancel, Transfer, or Restart			
Service	**Provider name and phone**	**Service end date**[1]	**Service start date**[1]
Government and School			
Postal mail change of address			
School records			
Voter registration			
Vehicle registration			
Financial			
Bank account[2]			
Direct deposits and withdrawals			
Safe deposit box			
Professional			
Health care (transfer doctors' and dentists' records for each family member)			
Veterinarian (transfer records)			
Cleaners (pick up your clothes)			

1. If applicable; 2. Open an account in your new town before closing your existing account.

Checklists

MOVING SUPPLIES

Packing and Unpacking

_____ Tape and tape dispenser. (The slightly more expensive gun-style dispenser is a worthwhile investment because its one-handed operation means you don't need a second person to help you hold the box closed while you do the taping.)

_____ Boxes. (It's worth it to obtain specialty boxes for your dinnerware, china set, and glasses. Specialty wardrobe boxes that allow your hanging clothes to hang during transport are another big help.)

_____ Padding such as bubble wrap.

_____ Markers.

_____ Scissors or a knife.

_____ Big plastic bags.

_____ Inventory list and clipboard.

_____ Box knife with retractable blade. (Get one for each adult.)

Loading and Moving

_____ Rope. (If nothing else, you'll need it to secure heavy items to the inside wall of the truck.)

_____ Padding blankets. (If you use your own, they may get dirty and you'll need bedding when you arrive. Padding is available for rent at most truck rental agencies.)

_____ Hand truck or appliance dolly. (Most truck rental agencies have them available for rent.)

_____ Padlock for the cargo door.

THE "NECESSARY BOX"

Eating

_____ Snacks or food. (Pack enough durable items for right before you depart, your travel, and the first day in your new home—and disposable utensils, plates, cups.)

_____ Instant coffee, tea bags, and so on.

_____ Roll of paper towels and moistened towelettes.

_____ Garbage bags.

Bathing

_____ A towel for each person.

_____ Soap, shampoo, toothpaste, and any other toiletries.

_____ Toilet paper.

Health Items

_____ First aid kit including pain relievers.

_____ Prescription medicines.

Handy to Have

_____ List of contact information. (Make sure you can reach relatives, the moving company, the truck driver's cell phone, and so on.)

_____ Small tool kit. (You need to be able to take apart and reassemble items that can't be moved whole.)

_____ Reclosable plastic bags to hold small parts, screws, bolts.

_____ Spare lightbulbs. (Some bulbs in your new home might be burned out or missing.)

_____ Nightlight and flashlight.

OVERNIGHT BAG

_____ Enough clothes for the journey plus the first day or two in your new home.

_____ Personal toiletries.

ITEMS FOR KIDS

_____ Activities for the trip.

_____ Favorite toys and anything else that will help children feel immediately at home in their new room.

Pet Checklist

_____ Food.

_____ A bottle of the water your pet is used to drinking.

_____ Dishes for food and water.

_____ Leash, collar, identification tags.

_____ Favorite toy.

_____ Medicines.

_____ Bed or blanket.

_____ Carrier.

_____ Paper towels in case of accidents.

_____ Plastic bags and a scooper.

_____ Litter and litter box for your cat or rabbit.

Last Items on the Truck

CLEANING

_____ Vacuum cleaner.

_____ Cleaning supplies.

GENERAL

_____ Necessary box.

_____ Setup for kids' temporary playroom.

_____ Other items you'll need the moment you arrive.

New Home Safety Checklist

GENERAL

_____ Watch out for tripping hazards. They will be plentiful until you get everything unpacked and put away, so be careful, and keep a path clear at all times.

HEAT, FIRE, ELECTRICAL

_____ Be sure nothing gets placed too close to heaters.

_____ Test smoke, heat, and carbon monoxide detectors. Find out your fire department's recommendations regarding how many of these devices you should have and where you should place them. If you need more, go buy them (remember to buy batteries) and install them.

_____ Find the fuse or breaker box before you need to shut off or reset a circuit.

WATER

_____ Check the temperature setting on your water heater. For child safety and fuel conservation, experts recommend 120 degrees Fahrenheit.

_____ Locate the water shutoff valve in case of a plumbing problem.

Moving Task Time Line

DECISION MAKING: WEEKS 12 TO 9

_____ Consider your moving options (professional versus self-move) and get quotes.

_____ If you are being relocated by your company, find out what your company covers and what you will be responsible for doing and paying.

_____ Set a move date.

_____ Choose your moving company or truck rental agency and reserve the dates.

If You Own Your Home

_____ Decide whether you want to sell or rent it out.

_____ If you decide to sell, choose a real estate agent and put your home on the market or look into, and begin planning for, selling it yourself.

_____ If you decide to rent out your home, decide whether you want to hire a property management agency or manage the property yourself.

_____ Perform (or hire contractors to perform) home repairs.

If You Currently Rent

_____ Notify your landlord of your plans to vacate.

_____ Check into cleaning obligations and options.

Tour Your New City or Town

_____ Research your new area at the library or online at *www.mon-stermoving.com*.

_____ Contact a real estate agent or property management agency to help you in your search for new lodgings.

_____ Go on a school-hunting and house- or apartment-hunting trip to your new town or city.

Additional items:

_____

_____

_____

_____

_____

_____

_____

_____

_____

_____

_____

_____

_____

_____

_____

_____

_____

_____

_____

_____

_____

_____

_____

_____

ORGANIZING, SORTING, AND NOTIFYING: WEEKS 9 TO 8

_____ Obtain the post office's change of address kit by calling 1-800-ASK-USPS or visiting your local post office or *www.usps.gov/moversnet/* (where you'll find the form and helpful lists of questions and answers).

_____ Complete and send the form.

_____ List and notify people, businesses, and organizations who need to know about your move. You may not think of everyone at once, but keep a running list and add people to your list and notify them as you remember them. As you notify them, check them off your list.

_____ Start sorting through your belongings to decide what to keep. Make plans to rid yourself of what you don't want: pick a date for a garage sale; call your favorite charity and set a date for them to come pick up donations; call your recycling company to find out what they will accept.

_____ For moving insurance purposes, make an inventory of your possessions with their estimated replacement value.

_____ If you have high-value items (such as antiques) that you expect to send with the moving company or ship separately, obtain an appraisal.

Additional items:

_____

_____

_____

_____

_____

_____

_____

_____

_____

FINALIZING HOUSING ARRANGEMENTS
AND ESTABLISHING YOURSELF
IN YOUR NEW COMMUNITY: WEEKS 8 TO 6

_____ **Home.** Select your new home and arrange financing; establish a tentative closing date or finalize rental housing arrangements.

_____ **Schools.** Find out school calendars and enrollment and immunization requirements.

_____ **Insurance.** Contact an agent regarding coverage on your new home and its contents as well as on your automobile.

_____ **Finances.** Select a bank, open accounts, and obtain a safe deposit box.

_____ **New Home Layout.** Sketch a floor plan of your new home and include room measurements. Determine how your present furniture, appliances, and decor will fit.

_____ **Mail.** If you haven't found a new home, rent a post office box for mail forwarding.

_____ **Services.** Find out the names and phone numbers of utility providers and what they require from you before they will start service (for example, a deposit, a local reference). (You can list your providers and service start dates on the checklist provided in this chapter.) Schedule service to start a few days before you arrive.

Additional items:

_____

_____

_____

_____

_____

_____

_____

MAKING AND CONFIRMING TRANSPORTATION AND TRAVEL PLANS: WEEK 6

_____ Schedule pick-up and delivery dates with your mover.

_____ Make arrangements with your professional car mover.

_____ If you need storage, make the arrangements.

_____ Confirm your departure date with your real estate agent or landlord.

_____ Make your travel arrangements. If you will be flying, book early for cheaper fares.

_____ Map your driving trip using *www.mapblast.com* or ask your automobile club for assistance with route and accommodation information.

Additional items:

_____

_____

_____

_____

_____

_____

_____

_____

_____

_____

_____

_____

_____

_____

_____

_____

_____

_____

_____

UPROOTING: WEEKS 5 TO 4

_____ Hold your garage sale, or donate items to charity.

_____ Gather personal records from all health care providers, your veterinarian, lawyers, accountants, and schools.

_____ Notify current utility providers of your disconnect dates and your forwarding address. (You can list your providers and service end dates on the checklist provided in this chapter.)

Additional items:

_____

_____

_____

_____

_____

_____

_____

_____

_____

_____

_____

_____

_____

_____

_____

_____

_____

_____

_____

_____

_____

_____

_____

_____

_____

MAKING AND CONFIRMING MOVING-DAY PLANS: WEEK 3

_____   Make arrangements for a sitter for kids and pets on moving day.

_____   Call moving-day volunteers to confirm move date and their arrival time.

_____   Obtain travelers' checks for trip expenses and cashiers' or certified check for payment to mover.

_____   Have your car serviced if you are driving a long distance.

Additional items:

_____

_____

_____

_____

_____

_____

_____

_____

_____

_____

_____

_____

_____

_____

_____

_____

_____

_____

_____

_____

_____

_____

_____ If you have a pet, take it to the vet for a checkup. For more pet-moving tips, see the section earlier in this chapter on moving with pets.

_____ Arrange for transportation of your pet.

_____ If you are moving into or out of a high-rise building, contact the property manager and reserve the elevator for moving day.

_____ Reserve parking space for the professional moving van or your rental truck. You may need to obtain permission from your rental property manager or from the city.

_____ Drain oil and gas from all your power equipment and kerosene from portable heaters.

Additional items:

_____

_____

_____

_____

_____

_____

_____

_____

_____

_____

_____

_____

_____

_____

_____

_____

_____

_____

_____

_____

_____

MOVING WEEK

_____ Defrost the freezer.

_____ Give away any plants you can't take with you.

_____ Pack your luggage and your necessary box for the trip (see the list provided in this chapter).

_____ Get everything but the day-to-day essentials packed and ready to go.

Additional items:

_____

_____

_____

_____

_____

_____

_____

_____

_____

_____

_____

_____

_____

_____

_____

_____

_____

_____

_____

MOVING DAY

_____ Mark off parking space for the moving van using cones or chairs.

_____ See "Moving Day" section of chapter 5 for further to-do items.

Getting from Here to There: Moving Day and Beyond

This chapter guides you through the next stage in your move: moving day, arriving, unpacking, and settling in. Here you'll find important travel tips for both the self-move and the professional move, information related to a professional car move, and pointers for your first days and weeks in your new home.

The Professional Move

Early on moving day, reserve a large place for the moving truck to park. Mark off an area with cones or chairs. If you need to obtain parking permission from your apartment complex manager or the local government, do so in advance.

GUIDE THE MOVERS

Before work starts, walk through the house with the movers and describe the loading order. Show them the items you plan to transport yourself. (It's best if these are piled in one area and clearly marked, maybe even covered with a sheet or blanket until you're ready to pack them in your car.)

Remain on-site to answer the movers' questions and to provide special instructions.

BEFORE YOU DEPART

Before you hit the road, you will need to take care of some last-minute details:

- Walk through your home to make sure everything was loaded.
- Sign the bill of lading. But first, read it carefully and ask any questions. The bill of lading is a document the government requires movers to complete for the transportation of supplies, materials, and personal property. The mover is required to have a signed copy on hand, and you should keep your copy until the move is complete and any claims are settled.
- Follow the movers to the weigh station. Your bill will be partly based on the weight of your property moved.

UNLOADING AND MOVING IN

Be sure to take care of these details once the movers arrive at your new home:

- Have your money ready. (Professional movers expect payment in full before your goods are unloaded.)
- Check for damage as items are unpacked and report it right away.
- Unless the company's policy prohibits the acceptance of gratuities, it is customary to tip each mover. $20 is a good amount; you may want to tip more or less based on the service you receive.

The Self-Move

The following tips should help you organize and guide your help, as well as make the moving day run more smoothly:

- The day before your move, create a task list. Besides the obvious (loading the truck), this list will include tasks such as disconnecting the washer and dryer and taking apart furniture that can't be moved whole.

- Plan to provide beverages and food for your volunteers. Make it easy on yourself and provide popular options such as pizza or sub sandwiches (delivered), chilled soda pop and bottled water (in an ice chest, especially if you're defrosting and cleaning the refrigerator).

MOVING TIP

Most storage facilities base their costs on size. Don't pay to stash items you don't really need or want.

- On moving day, remember, you are only one person. So if you need to defrost the freezer or pack last-minute items, choose and appoint someone who knows your plan to oversee the volunteers and answer questions.

- Be sure you have almost everything packed before your help arrives. Last-minute packing creates even more chaos and it's likely that hastily packed items will be damaged during loading or transit.

- If you end up with an even number of people, it's natural for people to work in pairs because they can carry the items that require two people. If you have an odd number of people, the extra person can rotate in to provide for breaks, carry light items alone, or work on tasks you assign.

- Be sure to match a person's physical ability and health with the tasks you assign.

- Appoint the early shift to start on tasks such as disconnecting the washer and dryer and taking apart furniture (such as bed frames) that can't be moved whole.

- Before work starts, walk through the house with your volunteers and describe your loading plan.

- Know your moving truck and how it should be packed for safe handling on the road (ask the truck rental company for directions).

- Load the truck according to the directions your truck rental agency gave you. Tie furniture items (especially tall ones) to the inside wall of the truck. Pack everything together as tightly as possible, realizing that items will still shift somewhat as you travel.

Move Travel

DIRECTIONS TO ATLANTA

Atlanta is easily reached by three major interstates. In Richmond, I-95 from the northeast splits and continues to Georgia's east coast and Florida; the opposite fork becomes I-85 through the Carolinas and the heart of Atlanta.

I-75 enters Georgia in the state's northwest quadrant, travels through downtown and continues south through Macon to Florida.

I-75 and I-85 converge in the middle of town, on a stretch known as the Downtown Connector.

I-20 is the state's main east-west highway. Travelers heading east from Birmingham, Alabama, drive through Atlanta's downtown district en route to Augusta and South Carolina.

The three interstates through the metropolitan area are bypassed by the ring road I-285, also known as the Perimeter.

SELF-MOVE—DRIVING A TRUCK

- A loaded moving truck handles far differently from the typical car. Allow extra space between you and the vehicle you're following. Drive more slowly and decelerate and brake sooner—there's a lot of weight sitting behind you.
- Realize that no one likes to follow a truck. Other drivers may make risky moves to get ahead of you, so watch out for people passing when it's not safe.
- Know your truck's height and look out for low overhangs and tree branches. Especially be aware of filling station overhang height.
- Most accidents in large vehicles occur when backing. Before you back, get out, walk around, and check for obstacles. Allow plenty

of maneuvering room and ask someone to help you back. Ask them to stay within sight of your sideview mirror—and talk over the hand signals they should use as they guide you.

- Stop and rest at least every two hours.
- At every stop, do a walk-around inspection of the truck. Check tires, lights, and the cargo door. (If you're towing a trailer, check trailer tires, door, hitch, and hitch security chain.) Ask your truck rental representative how often you should check the engine oil level.
- At overnight stops, park in a well-lighted area and lock the truck cab. Lock the cargo door with a padlock.

IF YOU'RE FLYING OR TRAVELING BY TRAIN OR BUS

- Coordinate with the moving van driver so that you arrive at about the same time.
- Plan for the unexpected, such as delays, cancellations, or missed connections.
- Keep in touch with the truck driver (by cell phone, if possible), who may also experience delays for any number of reasons: mechanical problems, road construction, storms, or illness.
- Dress comfortably.
- If you are traveling with young children, dress them in bright, distinctive clothing so you can easily identify them in a crowded airport, train station, or bus terminal.

MOVING TIP

While living in an apartment or temporary quarters, it's a good idea to have contents insurance on the valuable items you've placed in storage.

PROFESSIONAL MOVERS MAY NEED HELP, TOO

Make sure the movers have directions to your new home. Plan your travel so that you will be there to greet them and unlock. Have a backup plan in case one of you gets delayed. It is also a good idea to exchange cell phone numbers with the driver so you can stay in touch in case one of you is delayed.

TIPS FOR A PROFESSIONAL CAR MOVE

A professional car carrier company can ship your car. Alternatively, your moving company may be able to ship it in the van along with your household goods. Ask around and compare prices.

- Be sure that the gas tanks are no more than one-quarter full.
- It's not wise to pack personal belongings in your transported auto, because insurance typically won't cover those items.
- If your car is damaged in transport, report the damage to the driver or move manager and note it on the inventory sheet. If you don't, the damage won't be eligible for insurance coverage.

Unpacking and Getting Settled

You made it. Welcome home! With all the boxes and bare walls, it may not feel like home just yet, but it soon will. You're well on your way to getting settled and having life return to normal. As you unpack boxes, arrange the furniture, and hang the pictures, here are a few things to keep in mind:

- Approach unpacking realistically. It's not necessary (and probably not possible) to unpack and arrange everything on the first day.
- Find your cleaning supplies and do any necessary cleaning.
- Consider your family's basic needs (food, rest, bathing) and unpack accordingly:

  Kitchen: Start with the basics; keep less frequently used items in boxes until you decide your room and storage arrangements.

  Bedrooms: Unpack bedding and set up and make beds.

  Bathroom: Because this tends to be a small room with little space for boxes, unpack the basics early and find a place to store the still-packed boxes until you have a chance to finish.

MAINTAINING NORMALCY . . . STARTING FRESH

During the move and the days following, it's good to keep things feeling as normal as possible. But this can also be a fresh starting point: a time to establish (or reestablish) family rituals and traditions. Beyond the family, this is a time to meet and connect with new neighbors, schoolmates, and your religious or other community.

MOVING TIP

Before you leave, measure your current home and draw a sketch plan, showing room measurements and furniture placement. Take the plan with you, along with a tape measure and notebook, and draw up similar plans for the house or rental unit you're thinking of choosing. Sketches needn't be very detailed at this stage to help you avoid unpleasant surprises—no point in dragging that California King bed across country if it won't fit in the bedroom.

- Keep regular bedtimes and wake-up times (naps for kids if appropriate).
- If you typically eat dinner together, continue to do this, despite the chaos.
- If you typically have a regular family time—an activity or outing—don't feel bad if you must skip it one week due to move-related chores, but restart this ritual as soon as you can. In fact, your family may appreciate this special time even more in the midst of the upheaval and change.

Rome wasn't built in a day, and neither are friendships. If your move means you have to start over, take heart: persistence and work will pay off over time. Here are a few suggestions for making your first connections with people—individuals and communities of people—in your new area.

- Encourage family members who need encouragement in making new friends.

- Provide opportunities for building friendships from day one. Take a break from unpacking and knock on doors to meet neighbors. (It's not a good idea to start a friendship by asking for help unloading, though!)
- Get involved in activities your family enjoys and make time in your schedule for people, even though moving and resettling is a hectic and busy time.
- Meet and connect with your religious or other community.

DISCOVERING YOUR COMMUNITY

Here you'll find suggestions for getting settled in your new surroundings:

- Be sure every family member gets a feel for the neighborhood and main streets; memorizes your new address; learns (or carries) new home, office, and mobile phone numbers; and knows how to contact local emergency personnel including police, fire, and ambulance.
- Go exploring on foot, bike, mass transit, or by car (turn it into a fun outing) and start learning your way around.
- Locate your local post office and police and fire stations, as well as hospitals and gas stations near your home.
- Scout your new neighborhood for shopping areas.
- Register to vote.
- If you have moved to a new state, visit the Department of Motor Vehicles to obtain your driver's license and register your vehicle (see below).
- If you haven't already done so, transfer insurance policies to an agent in your new community.

IMPORTANT NUMBERS TO KNOW

Atlanta

Electric: Georgia Power, (888) 660-5890

Gas: For a list of gas suppliers, visit *www.aglc.com* or call (877) 427-2464

Phones: BellSouth, (800) 945-6500

Water: (404) 330-6075

Fire: (404) 8853-7000

Police: (404) 853-3434

Suburban

Clayton

Electric: Georgia Power
Company,
(888) 660-5890

Gas: For a list of gas suppliers,
visit *www.aglc.com* or call
(877) 427-2464

Phones: BellSouth,
(800) 945-6500

Water: (770) 961-2130

Fire: (770) 473-7833

Police: (770) 477-3747

Cobb

Electric: Cobb Electric
Membership
Corporation,
(770) 429-2100; Georgia
Power Company,
(888) 660-5890

Gas: For a list of gas suppliers,
visit *www.aglc.com* or call
(877) 427-2464

Phones: BellSouth,
(800) 945-6500

Water: (770) 423-1000

Fire: (770) 528-8000

Police: (770) 499-3900

MOVING TIP

Movers usually won't hook up appliances, such as the ice maker on the refrigerator or the gas line for the dryer. Ask your real estate agent for a list of recommended local handymen who can do the job.

DeKalb

Electric: Oglethorpe Power
Corporation,
(770) 745-9719; Georgia
Power Company,
(888) 660-5890

Gas: For a list of gas suppliers,
visit *www.aglc.com* or call
(877) 427-2464

Phones: BellSouth,
(800) 945-6500

Water: (404) 378-4475

Fire: (404) 294-2345

Police: (404) 294-2000

Douglas

Electric: Georgia Power Company, (888) 660-5890

Gas: For a list of gas suppliers, visit *www.aglc.com* or call (877) 427-2464

Phones: BellSouth, (800) 945-6500

Water: (770) 949-7617

Fire: (770) 942-8626

Police: (770) 942-2121

Fayette

Electric: Coweta-Fayette Electric Membership Corporation, (770) 502-0226; Georgia Power Company, (888) 660-5890

Gas: For a list of gas suppliers, visit *www.aglc.com* or call (877) 427-2464

Phones: BellSouth, (800) 945-6500

Water: (770) 461-1146

Fire: (770) 460-5370

Police: (770) 461-6353

Fulton

Electric: Georgia Power Company, (888) 660-5890

Gas: For a list of gas suppliers, visit *www.aglc.com* or call (877) 427-2464

Phones: BellSouth, (800) 945-6500

Water: (404) 730-6830

Fire: (404) 768-8200

Police: (404) 730-5100

Gwinnett

Electric: Walton Electric Membership Corporation, (770) 972-2917; Georgia Power Company, (888) 660-5890

Gas: For a list of gas suppliers, visit *www.aglc.com* or call (877) 427-2464

Phones: BellSouth, (800) 945-6500

Water: (770) 822-7399

Fire: (770) 513-5500

Police: (770) 513-5100

Henry

Electric: Georgia Power
Company,
(888) 660-5890

Gas: For a list of gas suppliers,
visit *www.aglc.com* or call
(877) 427-2464

Phones: BellSouth,
(800) 945-6500

Water: (770) 957-6659

Fire: (770) 954-2280

Police: (770) 954-2900

Cherokee

Electric: Georgia Power
Company,
(888) 660-5890

Gas: For a list of gas suppliers,
visit *www.aglc.com* or call
(877) 427-2464

Phones: BellSouth,
(800) 945-6500

Water: (770) 479-1813

Fire: (770) 720-6346

Police: (770) 345-3305

Exurban

Bartow

Electric: Georgia Power
Company,
(888) 660-5890

Gas: For a list of gas suppliers,
visit *www.aglc.com* or call
(877) 427-2464

Phones: BellSouth,
(800) 945-6500

Water: (770) 387-5170

Fire: (770) 387-5151

Police: (770) 382-5011

MOVING TIP

If you're storing items while you scout around for a place to live, it's best to select a storage facility where the units can be secured with your own padlock and key. And making a copy of that key is a great idea.

Coweta

Electric: Coweta-Fayette Electric
Membership
Corporation,
(770) 502-0226; Georgia
Power Company,
(888) 660-5890

Gas: For a list of gas suppliers,
visit *www.aglc.com* or call
(877) 427-2464

Phones: BellSouth,
(800) 945-6500

Water: (770) 254-3710

Fire: (770) 254-3900

Police: (770) 253-1502

Forsyth

Electric: Sawnee Electric
Membership
Corporation,
(770) 887-2363; Georgia
Power Company,
(888) 660-5890

Gas: For a list of gas suppliers,
visit *www.aglc.com* or call
(877) 427-2464

Phones: BellSouth,
(800) 945-6500

Water: (770) 781-2160

Fire: (770) 781-2180

Police: (770) 781-2222

Paulding

Electric: Georgia Power
Company, (888) 660-
5890

Gas: For a list of gas suppliers,
visit *www.aglc.com* or call
(877) 427-2464

Phones: BellSouth,
(800) 945-6500

Water: (770) 445-2761

Fire: (770) 443-7545

Police: (770) 443-3010

Rockdale

Electric: Georgia Power
Company,
(888) 660-5890

Gas: For a list of gas suppliers,
visit *www.aglc.com* or call
(877) 427-2464

Phones: BellSouth,
(800) 945-6500

Water: (770) 918-6512

Fire: (770) 929-1150

Police: (770) 918-6700

VEHICLE REGISTRATION
AND DRIVER'S LICENSE LAWS

Georgia Department of Public Safety

Driver Service Division
(404) 657-9300

www.ganet.org/dps

When you move to Georgia, you have thirty days to register your vehicle and receive a Georgia tag. Registrations are recorded in the county where you live; check with the state Department of Public Safety or call the county for a list of area offices.

The state collects an annual ad valorem tax based on the vehicle's current fair market value. To determine if any taxes are due on your vehicle, the state requires that you present proof of when you moved to Georgia. Acceptable proof includes a movers' bill or a final pay stub from your out-of-state employer.

New residents with a valid driver's license from another state must pass an eye test and surrender their old license to obtain a Georgia license. New residents with expired out-of-state licenses must pass eye, road rules, road signs, and driving tests. The same exams are required of new residents under eighteen years old, even if they possess a valid out-of-state license.

In addition to a current out-of-state license, you'll need to show a birth certificate or passport, as well as proof of Georgia residency (a lease agreement, bank statement, or utility bill). The $15 fee is payable in cash only.

TAKING CARE OF
THE FINANCIAL IMPLICATIONS OF YOUR MOVE

Now that you have arrived, you can take care of some of the financial and tax implications of your move. Here are some things to think about (it's also wise to consult an accountant):

- Some of your moving expenses may be tax-deductible. Prepare for tax filing by collecting receipts from your move. Also contact the Internal Revenue Service to obtain the publication and form you need. Visit *www.irs.gov* or call (800) 829-3676.

- State income tax. If your new state collects income tax, you'll need to file a state income tax form. For help with your relocation-related taxes, visit *www.monstermoving.com* and check out the "Relocation Tax Advisor."

- Other income sources may have tax implications. As you prepare to file, you'll want to consider any other sources of income and whether your new state will tax you on this income. For example, if you are paying federal income tax on an IRA that you rolled over into a Roth IRA and your new state collects income tax, you may also have to pay state income tax on your rollover IRA.

Home at Last

Once the truck is unloaded, the boxes are unpacked, and the pictures are hung, once you're sleeping in a *bed*—instead of on a loose mattress—you'll dream sweet dreams. Tomorrow, with the stress of this move slipping away behind you and the next move not even a faint glimmer on the horizon of your mind, you'll begin to discover the opportunities and savor the possibilities of your new city, new job, new school—your new home.

Getting to Know Your Town

CHAPTER 6

What's Around Town

One of the most enjoyable aspects of relocating to a new city is learning about the area's culture and history. It's also fun finding out what people do for fun. As an Atlanta newcomer, you'll discover plenty to see and savor, as well as a plethora of activities that afford a nice break from unpacking boxes.

Whether your passion is art, music, history, sports, or shopping, you're sure to find an assortment of venues that cater to your interests within the metro Atlanta area. And in most cases, you'll find them in a range of sizes. For instance, the city is home to the internationally acclaimed Atlanta Symphony Orchestra. But there are also several very good community orchestras that perform in various locales in the suburbs. Theaters abound, from the renowned Alliance Theatre in Midtown (which held the world premiere of Sir Elton John's *Aida*) and the historic Fox Theatre to the intimate stages of the 14th Street Playhouse and Marietta's Theatre in the Square.

No matter what part of the metro area you traverse, it's hard to escape Atlanta's historic importance. Preserved battlefields, monuments, and markers are visual reminders of the strategic role the city played during the Civil War. From the Cyclorama, a gigantic depiction of the Battle of Atlanta, to Stone Mountain, where the Confederacy's leaders are carved for posterity, Atlanta makes it easy for newcomers to trace the path of the conflict.

Sports fans will find a professional team for every major game, including ice hockey since the Thrashers came to town in 1999. College football and basketball are also big draws. But those who prefer to do it themselves aren't left out either; Atlanta has amateur clubs dedicated to a variety of sports that always welcome new members.

MOVING TIP

Use towels, T-shirts, and socks as wrapping for delicate items. This cuts down on pricey bubble wrap, and you won't have to pack them separately.

After in-line skating in Piedmont Park or tubing down the Chattahoochee, there's still plenty to do in an Atlanta day. Restaurants and nightclubs, particularly in Midtown and Buckhead, offer a myriad of entertainment choices long after the sun goes down.

Here's a look at some of the options for amusement in Atlanta.

Amusement Parks

American Adventures Amusement Park

250 Cobb Parkway
Marietta
(770) 424-9283

Open weekends in winter; daily, Memorial Day through Labor Day. Admission $15, ages 4–17; $4 parents; à la carte prices for individual attractions.

Geared toward families, American Adventures features rides suitable for toddlers, as well as ones older kids will enjoy. It offers a giant carousel, the Foam Factory Funhouse, miniature golf, and go-carts.

Six Flags over Georgia

7561 Six Flags Road
Mableton
(770) 948-9290

Open weekends in spring and fall, daily May through September. Admission $37 adults, half price for children under four feet tall.

More than eight-five acres of fun await visitors to Georgia's premier amusement park, where the Great American Scream Machine, the Mind Bender, the Ninja, and the Georgia Cyclone roller coasters are the chief thrills. Water rides, stunt shows, a music hall, amphitheater, and several places to purchase food are all part of the package.

White Water Theme Park
250 Cobb Parkway
Marietta
(770) 424-WAVE

Open weekends in May; daily, Memorial Day through Labor Day. Admission $24 for those taller than four feet, $16 for those under four feet, free for children under two years old.

More than fifty wet rides are in this cool park. Grab an inner tube and dive into the wave pool, ride down a flume, or float under a waterfall. A water playground and wading pool is set aside for the kiddies, while adults will thrill to the ninety-foot water free-fall and the enclosed white-water raft ride, Runaway River.

Athletic Clubs

Athletic Club Northeast
1515 Sheridan Road
(404) 325-2700

Monday–Friday, 5:30 A.M.–10 P.M. Saturday and Sunday, 8 A.M.–8 P.M. Initiation fee $200; monthly dues $66 to $184.

Month-to-month memberships allow use of eight racquetball courts, eight tennis courts, indoor lap and outdoor swimming pools, basketball and volleyball gym, indoor track, aerobic studios, weight training, steam room, sauna, and whirlpool.

Australian Body Works
3872 Roswell Road
(404) 365-9696

11 Piedmont Center
(404) 816-5209

1197 Peachtree Street
(404) 897-1550

Hours vary by location. Initiation fees from $49 to $149; monthly dues $30 to $50.

Multiple locations offer strength and cardiovascular equipment, group exercise classes, kickboxing, yoga, child care, "smoothie" bars, saunas, and steam rooms.

Buckhead Athletic Club

3353 Peachtree Road
(404) 364-2222

Monday and Wednesday, 6 A.M.–9 P.M.; Tuesday, Thursday, Friday, 6 A.M.–8 P.M.; Saturday, 10 A.M.–4 P.M. Initiation fees, $50 to $100; monthly dues $55 to $75.

Tucked into the Atlanta Financial Center, this state-of-the-art facility features Nautilus and Paramount resistance training, swimming pools, whirlpool, steam room, sauna, aerobic classes, fitness testing, and personal trainers.

Buckhead YMCA

1160 Moores Mill Road
(404) 350-9292

Monday–Thursday, 5:30 A.M.–9:30 P.M.; Friday, 5:30 A.M.–9 P.M.; Saturday, 8 A.M.–6 P.M.; Sunday, 8:30 A.M.–6 P.M. Initiation fees start around $125; monthly fees range from $43 to $65.

Opened in January 2000, this state-of-the-art facility features aerobics, gym, indoor and outdoor pool, nine tennis courts, fitness room with cardio and strength training, and child care.

Crunch

3340 Peachtree Road
(404) 262-2120

Monday–Friday, 5:30 A.M.–11 P.M.; Saturday and Sunday, 8 A.M.–8 P.M. Initiation fees go as high as $300, but are sometimes waived during special promotions; monthly dues $38 to $100.

A boxing ring, yoga, personal training, racquetball, and hip aerobics classes that do "gospel moves" are part of this Buckhead facility.

DeKalb Medical Center Wellness Center

2665 North Decatur Road
Decatur
(404) 501-2222

Monday–Friday, 5:30 A.M.–9 P.M.; Saturday, 8 A.M.–4 P.M.; Sunday, 11 A.M.–5 P.M. No initiation fee, monthly dues from $38, annual dues, $296 to $365.

Membership includes unlimited aerobics, free weights, cardiovascular equipment, indoor track, strength training, water aerobics, and swimming.

Jeanne's Body Tech

3165 Peachtree Road
(404) 261-0227

Monday–Thursday, 5:30 A.M.–10 P.M.; Friday, 5:30 A.M.–9 P.M.; Saturday, 7 A.M.–8 P.M.; Sunday, 8 A.M.–8 P.M. Memberships are $59 per month, $449 per year, classes are $10 each.

More than 135 individual strength training units, 115 cardio units, and classes that concentrate on sculpting, toning, stepping, and yoga are part of the program at Jeanne's.

Perimeter Summit Health Club

4000 Summit Boulevard
Atlanta
(404) 256-6527

Monday–Friday, 6 A.M.–8 P.M.; Saturday, 10 A.M.–2 P.M. Initiation fee $60; monthly memberships from $30 to $50.

Circuit weight training, free weight area, aerobics, sauna, and a fitness assessment are offered at this facility just north of Atlanta.

The Sporting Club at Windy Hill
135 Interstate North Parkway
Atlanta
(770) 953-1100

Monday–Friday, 5:30 A.M.–10 P.M.; Saturday and Sunday, 8 A.M.–8 P.M. Initiation fees vary month to month; monthly dues range between $46 and $128.

Tennis, squash, and racquetball courts, cardio and weight centers, indoor and outdoor pools, indoor running track, basketball and volleyball courts, fifty-foot rock climbing wall, and more are part of this high-tech facility.

Wellstar Health Place
65 S. Medical Drive
Marietta
(770) 793-7300

Monday–Friday, 5:30 A.M.–10 P.M.; Saturday, 8 A.M.–6 P.M.; Sunday, 1 P.M.–6 P.M. Initiation fees, $119 to $169; monthly fees, $54 to $73.

Located on a corner of the Kennstone Hospital campus, the Health Place focuses on lifelong total fitness. Along with an indoor track, outdoor jogging trail, free weight room, swimming pool, and racquetball courts, the center offers classes on nutrition, health, and safety.

Attractions

Atlanta Botanical Garden
1345 Piedmont Avenue
(404) 876-5859

Tuesday–Sunday, 9 A.M.–6 P.M. Admission $7 adults, $5 seniors, $4 students, free for children three and younger; free for everyone Thursday after 3 P.M.

A children's garden, an enormous greenhouse, and more than 3,000 plantings are part of the attractions at this fifteen-acre garden.

Atlanta Preservation Center

537 Peachtree Street
(404) 876-2041

Times and tours vary; call ahead for a current schedule. Tours are $5 adults, $4 seniors, $3 students.

A nonprofit organization, the APC is housed in the historic Rufus Rose House, one of the last remaining residences along Peachtree. The center hosts year-round tours of the city's historic districts, including the Martin Luther King Jr. district, Piedmont Park, downtown, the Fox Theatre, and the Inman Park, Druid Hills, and Ansley Park neighborhoods.

Bulloch Hall

180 Bulloch Avenue
Roswell
(770) 992-1731

Monday–Saturday, 10 A.M.–4 P.M.; Sunday, 1 P.M.–4 P.M. Admission $5 adults, $3 children six through sixteen.

Built in 1840, this mansion was the childhood home of Martha Bulloch, the mother of Theodore Roosevelt. It frequently hosts teas, art exhibits, and craft shows.

CITY FACT

Fulton County registers the highest per-capita income of the metro area, with an average of $32,536.

CNN Center

Marietta and Techwood Drive
(404) 827-2491

Food court daily, 7:30 A.M.–9:30 P.M.; stores 10 A.M.–6 P.M. Monday–Sunday. Free admission. CNN studio tours in sixteen languages are conducted daily from 9 A.M. to 6 P.M.; tickets are $7 adults, $5 seniors, $4.50 children six through twelve (children under six not permitted).

Global headquarters of the Turner Broadcasting System, CNN studios and newsrooms, a food court, boutiques of Braves and Turner merchandise, specialty shops, and a multi-screen theater are under one roof at this downtown building. The public is invited to be part of the audience for CNN's *TalkBack Live* by calling (800) 410-4CNN for show topics and reservations.

Georgia State Capitol

106 Washington Street
(404) 656-2844

Monday–Friday, 8 A.M.–5 P.M.; tours at 9:30 A.M., 10:30 A.M., 1 P.M. and 2 P.M. Free admission.

A gold-coated dome tops the state capitol, built in 1889. Recently restored legislative chambers, a Hall of Flags, natural science displays, and a Hall of Fame are inside.

Governor's Mansion

391 West Paces Ferry Road
(404) 261-1776

Tuesday–Thursday, 10 A.M.–11:30 A.M. Free admission.

The white-columned Greek Revival mansion is home to the state's First Family. Tours admit visitors to the public rooms, decorated with Federal period furnishings and antiques.

Martin Luther King Jr. National Historic Site

450 Auburn Avenue
(404) 331-5190

Open daily, 9 A.M.–5 P.M. Free admission.

The birthplace, home, and tomb of the renowned Civil Rights leader are part of the historic district. Museum exhibits depict the story of the Civil Rights movement. Also in the vicinity is Ebenezer Baptist Church, where King preached.

Oakland Cemetery

248 Oakland Avenue
(404) 688-2107

Open daily dawn to dusk, visitors center, 9 A.M.–5 P.M. Free admission.

Some of Atlanta's most prominent citizens are laid to rest in this Victorian cemetery, noted for its detailed statuary and architecture. A free map directs visitors to several important sites, including the graves of Margaret Mitchell and golf-great Bobby Jones.

Rhodes Hall

1516 Peachtree Street
(404) 885-7800

Monday–Friday, 11 A.M.–4 P.M.; Sunday, noon–3 P.M. Admission $5 all ages.

Built in the early 1900s, when elegant homes lined Peachtree Street, this Romanesque Revival mansion resembles a castle on the Rhine. Check out the Southern heroes captured in the stairwell's stained-glass windows.

SciTrek

395 Piedmont Avenue
(404) 522-5500

Monday–Saturday, 10 A.M.–5 P.M.; Sunday, noon–5 P.M. Admission $6 ages three through seventeen, $7.50 adults, free for children under three.

A hands-on science and technology center, SciTrek delights and entertains all ages with simple machines, simulated Martian landscapes, and a forty-foot replica of the Eiffel Tower made of Erector set pieces. Plenty of do-it-yourself activities keep the kids busy with paint, music, and simple science experiments.

Smith Plantation Home

935 Alpharetta Street
Roswell
(770) 641-3978

Tours at 11 A.M. and 2 P.M. Monday–Friday; 11 A.M., noon, and 1 P.M. Sunday. Admission $5 adults, $3 children.

Along with the elegant home, the outbuildings of this 1845 plantation offer a glimpse into everyday farm life in the antebellum South.

World of Coca-Cola Atlanta
55 Martin Luther King Jr. Drive
(404) 676-5151

Monday–Saturday, 9 A.M.–5 P.M.; Sunday, noon–6 P.M. Admission $6 adults, $4 seniors, $3 children six through eleven, free for children under five.

Exhibits, memorabilia, a retrospective of TV ads, and a taste-testing tell the story of Atlanta's most famous soft drink.

Yellow River Game Ranch
4525 Highway 78
Lilburn
(770) 972-6643

Open daily 9:30 A.M.–6 P.M. Admission $6 adults, $5 ages three through eleven, free for kids under three.

Follow the winding trails through the woods and visit with a variety of people-friendly animals that love to be petted. The ranch is home to General Beauregard Lee, the weather-predicting groundhog.

Zoo Atlanta
800 Cherokee Avenue
(404) 624-5600

Open daily 9:30 A.M.–4:30 P.M. Admission $12 adults, $10 seniors, $8 children ages three through eleven.

Visit the petting zoo, sneak up on the giant pandas, squeal over the snakes, and check out the gorillas at the Zoo, where natural habitats have been recreated to house more than 250 species from around the world.

Cinemas

Movie complexes abound across the metro area, with anywhere from a single screen up to twenty-four screens. In the past few years, several new centers have opened with stadium seating, love seats, and reclining seats for the max in viewing comfort. Many theaters sell tickets in advance; call ahead for specific film times. Also, be aware that theaters strictly enforce the policy of not selling tickets to children under 17 for any R-rated movies, unless they are with an adult.

Atlanta AMC Theatres

Buckhead and various metro area locations
(404) 816-4262

Multiple locations around the metro area offer matinees and twilight discounts. Evening performances average $7. Call for directions and prices.

Garden Hills Cinema

2835 Peachtree Road
(404) 266-2202

Before 6 P.M. $5; after 6 P.M. $7 adults, $5 children and seniors. Independent and foreign films featured.

General Cinema Sandy Springs

5920 Roswell Road
Sandy Springs
(404) 851-1890

Before 4 P.M. $5; after 4 P.M. $7.50 adults, $5 children and seniors.

Magic Johnson Theatres

2841 Greenbriar Parkway
(404) 629-0000

Before 6 P.M. $4.25; after 6 P.M. $6.25 adults, $4.25 children.

North Springs Cinema Grill

7270 Roswell Road
Sandy Springs
(770) 395-0724

Before 6 P.M., $1.50 adults; after 6 P.M., $3. Beer and wine and a casual menu served; entrees average $7.

United Artists Cinema CNN Center

247 CNN Center
(404) 827-4000

www.uatc.com

Before 6 P.M. $4; after 6 P.M. $6.75 adults, $4 children and seniors. Validated parking across the street.

United Artists Tara Cinema

2345 Cheshire Bridge Road
(404) 634-6288

www.uatc.com

Before 6 P.M. $4.50; after 6 P.M., $7.50 adults, $4.50 children and seniors.

Concert Halls

Atlanta Civic Center
395 Piedmont Avenue
(404) 658-7159

The center's big stage has hosted visiting Broadway spectacles such as *Miss Saigon* and *The King and I*, as well as concerts from *Riverdance* to rock 'n roll. With 4,600 seats, it's one of the city's most spacious venues.

Callanwolde Fine Arts Center
980 Briarcliff Road
(404) 872-5338

Built by a Coca-Cola founder, this Tudor estate has been turned into an arts venue, where intimate recitals are offered in the grand foyer and salon. The Center also hosts art exhibits and offers classes, and is a favorite site for weddings in the spring.

Chastain Park Amphitheater
4469 Stella Drive
(404) 733-4900

This open-air venue is an Atlanta summer tradition. Up to six thousand concert-goers pack elegant picnics and settle into their seats to hear the Atlanta Symphony or international performing artists under the stars.

The Coca-Cola Lakewood Amphitheater
2002 Lakewood Way
(404) 627-9704

www.lakewoodamp.com

Located on the city's southside, Lakewood is one of the area's premier outdoor venues. Musical stars of rock, country, and blues have packed the property during the warmer months. Extensive fairgrounds host a monthly antiques fair.

The Coca-Cola Roxy
3110 Roswell Road
(404) 233-ROXY

This intimate theater in the heart of Buckhead hosts concerts and plays as well as boxing matches.

Conant Performing Arts Center
4484 Peachtree Road
(404) 264-0020

www.gashakespeare.org

Home of the Georgia Shakespeare Festival, this state-of-the-art theater on the campus of Oglethorpe University has an amazing feature: In warm weather, the walls retract, recreating a sense of the Bard's open-air theater. It's one of the area's newest venues, built in 1997 with 509 seats.

Glenn Memorial Auditorium

1652 North Decatur Road
Decatur
(404) 727-5050

Music lovers pack the pews of this former church on the campus of Emory University for choral, chamber, and small-group performances throughout the year.

Rialto Center for the Performing Arts

80 Forsyth Street
(404) 651-4727

www.rialtocenter.org

Georgia State University restored an old movie theater and turned it into a premier venue for concerts, dance, theater, and film.

Robert Ferst Center for the Arts

349 Ferst Drive
(404) 894-9600

www.aux.gatech.edu

The arts center of Georgia Tech hosts classical concerts, plays, and dance performances, as well as local theater productions, in this 1,200-seat theater.

Spivey Hall

5900 North Lee Street
Morrow
(770) 961-3683

South of town, on the campus of Clayton State College, stands this 400-seat concert hall, considered one of the most acoustically perfect venues around. The hall includes a 4,413-pipe organ that is regularly featured in the hall's classical concert lineup.

The Tabernacle

152 Luckie Street
(404) 659-9022

In 1998, this former Baptist church was transformed into a concert hall that holds 2,500. The cellar of the building is home to the Cotton Club, a nightclub that features up-and-coming musical acts.

Woodruff Arts Center

1280 Peachtree Street
(404) 733-4200

One of the city's premier venues, the Woodruff is home to the Atlanta Symphony Orchestra, the Alliance Theatre Company, the High Museum of Art, and the Atlanta College of Art. The multipurpose facility includes a concert hall, a theater, and a private reception area.

Libraries

Atlanta-Fulton County Public Library

1 Margaret Mitchell Square
(404) 730-1700

www.af.public.lib.ga.us

Monday, Friday, and Saturday, 9 A.M.–6 P.M.; Tuesday, Wednesday, Thursday, 9 A.M.–8 P.M.; Sunday, 2 P.M.–6 P.M.; call for branch locations and hours. Free to Atlanta City and Fulton County residents.

The Atlanta-Fulton library has books, audiotapes, CDs, videos, and Internet access at each of its thirty-five branches. Patrons may also check book availability and put in reserves on the library's Web site. The system's Auburn Avenue Research Library is the only one in the Southeast dedicated to African-American culture and history. And if you need a question answered quickly, dial the reference line at (404) 730-4636.

Clayton County Public Library

865 Battle Creek Road
Jonesboro
(770) 473-3850

www.clayton.public.lib.ga.us

Monday–Thursday, 9 A.M.–9 P.M.; Friday, 9 A.M.–6 P.M.; Saturday, 9 A.M.–5 P.M.; Sunday, 1:30 P.M.–5:30 P.M. during the school year; call for branch locations and times. Free to residents of Clayton County.

Headquartered in Jonesboro, this five-branch system provides books, audiotapes, videos, and Internet access. Morrow and Riverdale locations have free word processors. Books can be renewed over the phone at any branch.

Cobb County Public Library

266 Roswell Road
(770) 528-2318

www.cobbcat.org

Monday–Thursday, 9 A.M.–9:30 P.M.; Friday and Saturday, 9 A.M.–6 P.M.; Sunday, 1 P.M.–5 P.M.; call for branch locations and times. Services are free to Cobb residents; others may purchase a two-year library card for $20.

Books, CDs, videos, audiotapes, magazines, Internet resources are available at Cobb's fifteen branches. Patrons may also reserve and renew books through the online catalog.

DeKalb County Public Library

215 Sycamore Street
Decatur
(404) 370-3070

www.dekalb.lib.ga.us

Monday–Thursday, 9 A.M.–9 P.M.; Friday, and Saturday, 9 A.M.–5 P.M.; Sunday, 1 P.M.–5 P.M.; call for branch locations and times. Free.

DeKalb's twenty-three-branch system has books, videos, audiotapes, Internet access; some locations feature foreign-language collections and homework centers.

Gwinnett County Public Library

Lawrenceville
(770) 822-4522

www.gwinnett.public.library.ga.us

Monday–Thursday, 10 A.M.–8:30 P.M.; Friday and Saturday, 10 A.M.–5:30 P.M.; call for branch locations and times. Free to all county residents.

Gwinnett's ten-branch library system has books, magazines, newspapers, audiotapes, videos, CDs, and 167 terminals that provide free Internet access.

Henry County Library System

99 Sims Street
McDonough
(770) 954-2806

Monday–Thursday, 9:30 A.M.–8 P.M.; Friday, 9:30 A.M.–6 P.M.; Saturday, 9 A.M.–5 P.M.; call for branch locations and times.

Books, videos, audiotapes, and Internet access are available at Henry's four public libraries. The system recently joined PINES (Public Information Network for Electronic Services), a network of twenty-six libraries around the state that share materials for free.

Museums

APEX Museum

135 Auburn Avenue
(404) 523-APEX

Tuesday–Saturday, 10 A.M.–5 P.M. Admission $3 adults, $2 students and seniors, free children under four.

The African-American Panoramic Experience (APEX) features art and historical exhibits of black history.

Atlanta Cyclorama and Civil War Museum
800 Cherokee Avenue
(404) 624-1071

Open daily, 9:20 A.M.–4:30 P.M. Admission $5 adults, $4 seniors, $3 children six through twelve, under six free.

It's always a steamy July day in 1864 at this immense mural depicting the Battle of Atlanta. Soaring 358 feet, the canvas is believed to be one of the biggest in the world. The painting revolves around visitors, who are challenged to pick out the Clark Gable look-alike as well as Atlanta landmarks. The building also houses Civil War memorabilia and a period locomotive engine.

Atlanta History Center
130 West Paces Ferry Road
(404) 814-4000

www.atlantahistory.net

Open Monday–Saturday, 10 A.M.–5:30 P.M.; Sunday, noon–5:30 P.M. Admission $10 adults, $8 students and seniors, $4 ages six through seventeen, free for children five and younger.

Nestled in the heart of Buckhead, the History Center features permanent exhibits on the Civil War, golf-great Bobby Jones, Southern folk arts, and Atlanta's story from its days as a crossroads to its glory as an Olympic city. The grounds include the Swan House (a magnificent 1928 mansion), the Tullie Smith working farmhouse, and thirty-three acres of gardens. The Swan House coach house has been transformed into a gift shop and art gallery, as well as an elegant lunch spot where chicken salad is the perennial favorite.

Atlanta International Museum of Art and Design
285 Peachtree Center Avenue
(404) 688-2467

Open Tuesday–Friday, 11 A.M.–5 P.M.; Saturday, 11 A.M.–4 P.M. Admission $3 all ages, free on Wednesdays.

Exhibits of art and artifacts from around the world are showcased in this downtown space.

Fernbank Museum of Natural History

767 Clifton Road
(404) 378-0127

www.fernbank.edu/museum

Monday–Saturday, 10 A.M.–5 P.M.; Sunday, noon–5 P.M. Admission $8.95 adults, $7.95 students and seniors, $6.95 children twelve and under.

IMAX movies, children's discovery rooms, and a walk through Georgia's evolving landscape are part of the permanent displays.

High Museum of Art

1280 Peachtree Street
(404) 733-4444

Open Monday–Wednesday, Saturday, and Sunday, 10 A.M.–5 P.M.; Thursday and Friday, 10 A.M.–7:30 P.M. Admission $13 ($15 on weekends) for adults, $10 ($12 on weekends) for children ages six through seventeen and seniors.

The 135,000-square-foot museum, part of the Woodruff Arts Center complex, houses a 10,000-piece permanent collection. In addition, it welcomes renowned traveling exhibits from around the world.

Herndon Home

587 University Place
(404) 581-9813

Open Tuesday–Saturday, 10 A.M.–3 P.M. Free admission, $3.50 for group tours.

This 1910 mansion is now an African-American museum that showcases the life of an upscale black family. The home was built by Alonzo Herndon, founder of the Atlanta Life Insurance Company.

Jimmy Carter Presidential Library and Museum

453 Freedom Parkway
(404) 331-0296

Open Monday–Saturday, 9 A.M.–4:45 P.M.; Sunday, noon–4:45 P.M.
Admission $5 adults, $4 seniors, sixteen and under free.

Learn about the legacy of the president from Georgia and view a variety of traveling exhibits at the only presidential library in the Southeast. Along with a gift shop, gardens, and a café, the museum boasts one of the best views of the Atlanta skyline.

Margaret Mitchell House & Museum

Peachtree and 10th Streets
(404) 249-7015

Open daily, 9 A.M.–4 P.M. Admission $10 adults, $8 seniors and children.

She called it "The Dump," but visitors will be charmed by the tiny apartment where Margaret Mitchell penned her classic tale of the Civil War. Also on the grounds is an art gallery with rotating exhibits and the *Gone With the Wind* Museum, packed with memorabilia from the movie and photos of the Atlanta premiere.

Marietta/Cobb Museum of Art

30 Atlanta Street
(770) 528-1444

Open Tuesday–Saturday, 11 A.M.–5 P.M.; Sunday, 1 P.M.–5 P.M.
Admission $5 adults, $3 seniors and students, children under six free.

An ambitious collection of American and European art is housed in the modest turn-of-the-century post office building.

Michael C. Carlos Museum at Emory University

571 South Kilgo Street
(404) 727-4282

www.cc.emory.edu/CARLOS/

Open Monday–Saturday, 10 A.M.–5 P.M.; Sunday, noon–5 P.M.
Admission $3 (suggested donation).

Permanent collections include 16,000 objects from Egypt, Greece, Rome, Asia, and Africa, and artworks from the Middle Ages to the twentieth century. Special national and international exhibitions are also welcomed.

William Breman Jewish Heritage Museum

1440 Spring Street
(404) 873-1661

Open Monday–Thursday, 10 A.M.–5 P.M.; Friday, 10 A.M.–3 P.M.; Sunday, 1 P.M.–5 P.M. Admission $5 adults, $3 seniors and students, children under six free.

Atlanta's Jewish heritage and the Holocaust are explored at this museum, which also hosts traveling exhibits and several hands-on projects for kids.

Recreation Centers and Parks

The city's Bureau of Parks and Recreation provides information about area parks and centers. Most of the parks are free, but there may be a charge for attractions located within the park boundaries (as with Zoo Atlanta in Grant Park) or to reserve picnic pavilions. To reach the Parks Bureau, call (404) 817-6744. City parks are open daily, 6 A.M.–11 P.M.

Centennial Olympic Park

Techwood Drive and Spring Street

Built during the 1996 Centennial Olympic Games, this downtown oasis is lined with commemorative bricks purchased by supporters from around the country. The open fountains are a favorite place for kids of all ages to romp during hot summer months. At night, the tall decorative columns are lit with hundreds of tiny lights.

Chastain Memorial Park

235 West Wieuca Road

Jogging trails, a gym, ball fields, picnic areas, a playground, swimming pool, tennis courts, riding stables, and a public golf course are part of this Buckhead greenspace. Chastain is also the summer home of the Atlanta Symphony Orchestra, which plays in the amphitheater on the park grounds.

Chattahoochee River National Recreation Area

Island Ford Parkway
Dunwoody
(770) 399-8070

Open daily, 10 A.M.–4 P.M. Parking fee, $2.

The banks of the river from Gwinnett to Cobb Counties are bordered by hiking and walking trails. There are also picnic areas, fishing spots, and several areas where rafters slide their inflatables into the water for a leisurely float.

Grant Park

Georgia and Cherokee Avenues

Athletic fields, picnic pavilions, and the nearby attractions of the Cyclorama and Zoo Atlanta make this intown park a popular spot for area residents as well as out-of-town visitors.

Kennesaw National Battlefield Park

905 Kennesaw Mountain Drive
Marietta
(770) 427-4686

Open daily 7:30 A.M.–dusk.

Hiking and horse trails wind through historic battlefields where visitors can view earthworks and fortifications built during the 1864 Atlanta Campaign of the Civil War. A visitors' center features exhibits and a twenty-minute film about the fighting. Ambitious hikers can climb to the peak, 1,808 feet up; the weak-kneed may prefer to wait until Saturday or Sunday, when they can board a free shuttle to the summit. Buses leave every half hour beginning at 9:30 A.M. from the visitors center. Picnic areas and grills are on the grounds.

Piedmont Park

Piedmont Avenue and 14th Street

Atlanta's biggest green space was designed to host the 1895 Cotton States and International Exposition. The city purchased the property for a park in 1904. A playground, walking trails, and a paved four-mile loop are crowded on the weekends with joggers, in-line skaters, and people pushing baby strollers.

Stone Mountain Park

U.S. Highway 78
Stone Mountain
(770) 498-5690

Open daily, 6 A.M.–midnight. Admission to the park is free, but there is a $5 admission charge for the beach and water park, paddleboat rides, scenic railroad, sky lift, wildlife preserve, antebellum mansion, and museums; $6 parking permit required. There are also some fees for special events and exhibits.

With its lakeside beach, paddle wheel boat, nineteen antebellum structures, restaurant, and summer laser show, there's more to this 3,200-acre park than you can pack into one day. A favorite with hikers, the 825-foot mountain is one of the world's largest granite masses, and is crisscrossed with paths to the summit. Less athletic sightseers can hop on the skylift to the top, where the vistas are majestic. A steam engine chugs around the base of the granite, on which are carved the likenesses of Robert E. Lee and other Confederate leaders. In addition, there's boating, miniature golf, tennis, swimming, and golfing.

Symphonies

Atlanta Symphony Orchestra

1280 Peachtree Street
(404) 733-5000

www.atlantasymphony.org

Premier classical musicians from around the world perform with the internationally acclaimed orchestra housed in Symphony Hall at the Woodruff Arts Center.

Cobb Symphony
1000 Chastain Road
Kennesaw
(770) 423-6650

Adults, $20, students and children $13.

Since 1951, this eighty-member orchestra of paid professionals and volunteers has performed at the Cobb Civic Center and venues in the northwest part of town. Along with free children's and summer concerts, the orchestra books a solid season of music into its home theater at Kennesaw State University.

Orchestra Atlanta
30 Mansell Road
Roswell
(770) 992-2559

Tickets $20–$30.

This fifty-five-member all-volunteer orchestra has been performing classical works since 1985. In recent years, its home stage has been the Roswell Cultural Arts Center.

Theaters

Atlanta has a wealth of theaters, and even more theater companies. Many small troupes rent main stages at various locations around town. For particular productions, times, and prices, it's always best to check ahead with the individual theater.

Actor's Express
887 West Marietta Street
(404) 607-7469

Tucked into the King Plow Arts Center, this cutting-edge theater has won raves for its comedic and dramatic productions.

Agatha's, A Taste of Mystery
693 Peachtree Street
(404) 875-1610

Like a little mayhem with your meal? The devilishly creative owners of this Midtown spot serve up original, satirical whodunits with the five-course dinners. Audience participation is encouraged, and always hilarious.

Alliance Theater Company

1280 Peachtree Street
(404) 733-5000

Noted for premiering works from Elton John's *Aida* to Alfred Uhry's *Driving Miss Daisy,* the Alliance is one of the city's premier theater groups. It's part of the Woodruff Arts Center complex, home to the High Museum and the Atlanta Symphony.

14th Street Playhouse

173 14th Street
(404) 733-4750

Throughout the year, various troupes take over this cozy theater in Midtown, with its three stages and art gallery. But it's home to Theatre Gael, a group dedicated to productions of Celtic origins; Jomandi Productions, one of the Southeast's oldest African-American companies; and Abracadabra Children's Theatre.

The Fox Theatre

660 Peachtree Street
(404) 817-8700

Built in 1929, this National Register historic property resembles a Moorish castle, with its turrets and twinkling lights (stars) in the ceiling. As the city's premier stage, the Fox hosts Broadway road shows as well as concerts and comedy acts.

Horizon Theatre Company

1083 Austin Avenue
(404) 584-7450

The Horizon's intimate black box, housed in one wing of a former school building, has long been a launching pad for the city's budding performers and playwrights. Teen and senior citizen ensembles bring a range of ages into the theater.

New American Shakespeare Tavern

499 Peachtree Street
(404) 874-5299

Beyond the unassuming facade of the Tavern's doors lies a replica of Shakespeare's Globe Theatre. No turkey legs, but you can grab a beer and a plate of bar food to enjoy during classic productions, from Shakespeare and beyond.

7 Stages

1105 Euclid Avenue
(404) 522-0911

www.7stages.org

One of the city's cutting-edge companies, 7 Stages presents works by local and national artists to the Little Five Points neighborhood.

Theatrical Outfit

70 Fairlie Street
(404) 651-4727

Classic plays as well as new works that reflect Southern culture are the focus of this fast-growing professional troupe, which performs at the Rialto Center for the Performing Arts.

Restaurants

Stars indicate the price range of a dinner entree:

★ = less than $10

★★ = $11–$20

★★★ = $21–$30

★★★★ = $31 and up

The Abbey ★★★

163 Ponce de Leon Avenue
(404) 876-8532

Daily, 6 P.M.–10 P.M.

Built as a church in 1915, the Abbey retains its stained-glass windows and soaring ceilings. Waiters dressed as monks serve veal, seafood, lamb, duck, and steak.

Agnes & Muriel's ★★

1514 Monroe Drive
(404) 885-1000

Daily, 11 A.M.–11 P.M.

This converted bungalow is a restaurant named for the owners' mothers, and you almost expect Mom to come out of the kitchen and make you clean your plate. Pork chops, T-bones, meatloaf, and pot pies feature on the home-cooked menu.

Anis ★★

2974 Grandview Avenue
(404) 233-9889

Lunch daily 11:30 A.M.–2:30 P.M.; dinner, Sunday–Thursday, 6 P.M.–10 P.M.; Friday and Saturday, 6 P.M.–10:30 P.M.

Tables in this cottage-turned-eatery are laden with Italian and French selections, from mussels mariniere to risotto, lamb, chicken, beef, and seafood.

Anthony's ★★★

3109 Piedmont Road
(404) 262-7379

www.anthonysfinedining.com

Monday–Saturday, 6 P.M.–10:30 P.M.

It's hard to believe you're still in Buckhead by the time you reach the end of the winding, tree-lined drive and find this restored 1797 plantation house. Generous portions of pasta, steak, seafood, pheasant, lamb, and chateaubriand for two are served elegantly in the home's several dining rooms.

Antica Posta ★★★

519 East Paces Ferry Road
(404) 262-7112

Dinner daily, 5:30 P.M.–10:30 P.M.

Specialties from Tuscany star at this Buckhead favorite. Classics from ossobuco to tiramisu are favorites, along with filet mignon, rack of lamb, veal scaloppini, and several seafood selections.

Atlanta Fish Market ★★

265 Pharr Road
(404) 262-3165

Lunch, Monday–Saturday, 11:30 P.M.–2:30 P.M.; dinner, Monday–Thursday, 5 P.M.–11 P.M.; Friday and Saturday, 5 P.M.–midnight; Sunday, 5 P.M.–10 P.M.

A gigantic copper-scaled fish greets visitors to this seafood extravaganza that specializes in the freshest seafood in a Savannah-style dining room.

Atlanta Grill ★★★

181 Peachtree Street—in the Ritz-Carlton Atlanta
(404) 659-0400

Breakfast, lunch, and dinner daily, 6:30 A.M.–11 P.M.

A newcomer on the downtown restaurant scene, the Atlanta Grill features regional Southern dishes from fried green tomatoes to a luscious honey pecan tart. The Grill's most striking feature, though, is its verandah, hovering two stories above Peachtree Street.

Bone's ★★★

3130 Piedmont Road
(404) 237-2663

Lunch, Monday–Friday, 11:30 A.M.–2:30 P.M.; dinner, Sunday–Thursday, 5:30 P.M.–10:30 P.M.; Friday, and Saturday, 5:30 P.M.–11 P.M.

One of the city's first upscale steakhouses, Bone's boasts the style of a private New York supper club. Rich woods, glass, and brass abound. Prime steaks and seafood have made the eatery a favorite for both business and special-occasion dinners.

Brasserie Le Coze ★★

3393 Peachtree Road
(404) 266-1440

Lunch, Monday–Saturday, 11:30 A.M.–2:30 P.M.; dinner, Monday–Thursday, 5:30 P.M.–10 P.M.; Friday and Saturday, 5:30 P.M.–10:30 P.M.

The owners split their time between this Lenox Square bistro and their award-winning New York restaurant. From their family cookbooks, they whip up French specialties such as coq au vin, pork tenderloin, and cod in a truffle vinaigrette.

Buckhead Diner ★★

3073 Piedmont Road
(404) 262-3336

Daily, Monday–Saturday, 11 A.M.–midnight; Sunday, 10 A.M.–10 P.M.

Don't let the name fool you; this is the furthest you can get from a greasy-spoon diner. Specialties include veal and wild mushroom meatloaf, sweet-and-sour calamari, homemade potato chips drizzled with blue cheese, and, for dessert, white chocolate banana cream pie.

The Cabin ★★

2678 Buford Highway
(404) 315-7676

Lunch, Monday–Friday, 11:30 A.M.–2:30 P.M.; dinner, Monday–Thursday, 5:30 P.M.–10 P.M.; Friday and Saturday, 5:30 P.M.–11 P.M.

A rustic log cabin gives this local favorite a feel of the country, though it's only minutes from Buckhead. Beef, wild game, and seafood are featured.

Café Tu Tu Tango ★

220 Pharr Road
(404) 841-6222

Sunday–Tuesday, 11:30 A.M.–11 P.M.; Wednesday, 11:30 A.M.–midnight; Thursday, 11:30 A.M.–1 A.M.; Friday and Saturday, 11:30 A.M.–2 A.M.

Watch local artists ply their trade while you sample from the café's extensive tapas and pizza menu.

Canoe ★★

4199 Paces Ferry Road
(770) 432-2663

Lunch, Monday–Friday, 11:30 A.M.–2:30 P.M.; dinner, Sunday–Saturday, 5:30 P.M.–10:00 P.M.

Seasonal specialties keep Canoe's menu fresh, but you can always count on an array of seafood, beef, and veal dishes. Most of the seats afford a relaxing view of the Chattahoochee River at the edge of the garden.

Champps Americana ★★

7955 North Point Parkway
Alpharetta
(770) 642-1933

Monday–Thursday, 11 A.M.–1 A.M.; Friday and Saturday, 11 A.M.–2 A.M.; Sunday, 10 A.M.–midnight.

Big portions of chicken, seafood, and steak—and big TVs—are the chief attractions at this sports-oriented eatery. Weeknight diners vie for prizes in video horse races and karaoke contests; Sunday brunch features a Bloody Mary bar with ten varieties of vodka and beer chasers.

Chequers Seafood Grill ★★

3424 Peachtree Road
(404) 842-9997

Lunch, Monday–Friday, 11:30 A.M.–2:30 P.M.; dinner, Monday–Friday, 5:30 P.M.–10 P.M.; Saturday, 5 P.M.–10 P.M.; Sunday, 5 P.M.–9:30 P.M.; Sunday, brunch 10:30 A.M.–2 P.M.

Tucked away behind the Ritz-Carlton, Chequers isn't easy to find, but the jumbo crab cakes, Australian lobster tails, and an extensive Sunday brunch buffet make it well worth the search.

Chops and the Lobster Bar ★★★

70 West Paces Ferry Road
(404) 262-2675

Lunch Monday–Friday, 11:30 A.M.–2:30 P.M.; dinner, Monday–Thursday, 5:30 P.M.–11 P.M.; Friday and Saturday, 5:30 P.M.–midnight; Sunday, 5:30 P.M.–10 P.M.

One of the city's best steakhouses, serving USDA prime aged beef as well as seafood, fills the restaurant's first level. Ride the elevator down to the Lobster Bar, where a raw bar and a menu of fresh seafood awaits.

Chopstix ★★

4279 Roswell Road
(404) 255-4868

Lunch, Monday–Friday, 11:30 A.M.–2:30 P.M.; dinner, Sunday–Saturday, 6 P.M.–11 P.M.

Live piano music accompanies Szechwan chicken, Peking duck, and stir-fried lobster tail at this upscale Chinese eatery.

Cipollini ★★

1529 Piedmont Avenue
(404) 875-5001

Lunch, Monday–Friday, 11:30 A.M.–2 P.M.; dinner, Monday–Saturday, 5:30 P.M.–11 P.M.

CITY FACT

Not all of Atlanta's treasures are in museums. You'll find an array of outdoor artworks across the city, including many that were erected during the 1996 Olympic Games. MARTA is one of the area's biggest art collectors, with works adorning many train stations. An assortment of works also decorates Hartsfield Atlanta International Airport.

You don't have speak Italian to love Cipollini's intimate dining room and classic cooking. The menu comes with translations for each dish, from "Osso Buco Milanese" (braised veal shank) to "Tonno alla Mediterraneo" (grilled tuna).

City Grill ★★★

50 Hurt Plaza
(404) 524-2489

Lunch, Monday–Friday, 11:30 A.M.–2:30 P.M.; dinner, Monday–Saturday, 5:30 P.M.–10 P.M.

One of Atlanta's most elegant dining rooms occupies the second floor of this classic downtown building. Beneath the giant windows, chandeliers, and ornate moldings, attentive waitstaff will serve you crab cakes, roasted rack of pork, grilled duck, and game hen.

dick and harry's ★★

1570 Holcomb Bridge Road
Roswell
(770) 641-8757

Lunch, Monday–Friday, 11:30 A.M.–2:30 P.M.; dinner, Monday–Thursday, 5:30 P.M.–10 P.M.; Friday and Saturday, 5:30 P.M.–11 P.M.

The brother-owners have made their mark on the northside with lamb, beef, seafood, and salads.

The Dining Room ★★★★

3434 Peachtree Road—in the Ritz-Carlton Buckhead
(770) 240-7035

Select from a three- or five-course menu, with or without wine selections, at one of the city's poshest dining spots—and the state's only Mobil Five Star and AAA Five Diamond restaurant. Look for twists on French and Mediterranean specialties with Thai influences. The lighting is dim, the seating intimate, and the service supreme. Three-course dinners are $68 per person; five courses are $82; five courses with wine are $130.

1848 House ★★★

780 South Cobb Drive
Marietta
(770) 428-1848
www.1848House.com

Tuesday–Saturday, 6 P.M.–9:30 P.M.; Sunday, 5:30 P.M.–8 P.M.; Sunday brunch, 10:30 A.M.–2:30 P.M.

Built in 1848, this white-columned mansion has won rave reviews for its contemporary Southern cuisine, which includes rock shrimp cakes with Vidalia onions, chili-rubbed pork tenderloin, and smoked chicken with wild rice. Each room of the house, as well as a restored stone kitchen next to the herb garden, offers a different intimate setting for a memorable evening.

Einstein's ★

1077 Juniper Street
(404) 876-7925

Service continuously from 11 A.M. during the week (10:30 A.M. Saturday and Sunday) to 11 P.M.

Best noted for its enormous street-side patio, Einstein's is packed with people-watching diners for lunch, dinner, and late-night snacks. Expect to wait for a table under the trees on Sundays, when the brunch and Bloody Mary specials are in full swing.

Eno ★★

800 Peachtree Street
(404) 892-8313

Lunch, Monday–Friday, 11:30 A.M.–2:30 P.M.; dinner, Monday–Thursday, 6 P.M.–10 P.M.; Friday and Saturday, 6 P.M.–11 P.M.

Along with the Mediterranean-influenced food, Eno specializes in wine. Savor a glass of champagne at a sidewalk table, or a bottle of your favorite vintage in the comfortable dining room.

ESPN Zone ★★

3030 Peachtree Road
(404) 682-3776

Daily, 11:30 A.M.–midnight.

With 34,000 square feet, this Buckhead eatery is also an entertainment destination. Salmon and steak are delivered to your table in the Screening room, which features thirty-six-inch video monitors and a sixteen-foot screen. Get comfy in the "Zone Throne"—a high-tech armchair with individual audio controls and a tray for your munchies. You won't miss a minute of the action, even in the bathrooms, built with more than a dozen TVs.

Fado Irish Pub ★

3035 Peachtree Road
(404) 841-0066

Daily, 11 A.M.–11 P.M.

Almost as intriguing as the lineup of potent Irish potables is this pub building itself. The place was shipped over from the old country and reassembled into different rooms designed around a huge bar. Sandwiches and snacks are available, along with hearty entrees of Guinness-battered fish and chips, Irish stew, cottage pie, corned beef and cabbage, salmon, and steak. Weekend brunches are packed with eggs, rashers, tomatoes, beans, and toast.

Flying Biscuit Café ★

1655 McLendon Avenue
(404) 687-8888

Daily, 8:30 A.M.–10 P.M.

Gigantic piping hot biscuits are a meal in themselves, but leave room for the rest of the good things on the menu. Sandwiches, salads, stir-fry, trout, hazelnut chicken, turkey meatloaf, and an assortment of vegetarian specials are added to the breakfast lineup, which is available all day.

Food 101 ★★

4969 Roswell Road
(404) 497-9700

Lunch, Monday–Friday, 11:30 A.M.–2:30 P.M.; dinner, Monday–Thursday

Food that Mom used to make fills the menu and your stomach. Chicken alphabet soup, pork chops, and Yankee pot roast share the table with sea bass, trout, shrimp scampi, and New York strip steak.

The Food Studio ★★★
887 W. Marietta Street
(404) 815-6677

Dinner, daily from 5:30 P.M.

Tucked into the Kind Plow Arts Center, the Food Studio has two seating levels and a lavish bar carved out of a former warehouse space. The food is Southern—lots of pork, rabbit, quail, and sweetbreads—with a continental flair.

Fusebox ★★★
3085 Piedmont Road
(404) 233-3383

Lunch, Monday–Friday, 11:30 A.M.–2:30 P.M.; dinner, Sunday–Saturday, from 5:30 P.M.–11:00 P.M.

CITY FACT

Many of Atlanta's main roads follow old Indian trails through the hills. That's why what often seems like a shortcut is anything but! Keep a good street map handy for finding your way around.

East meets West at this popular fusion restaurant where beef tenderloin comes in a ginger crust and the rack of lamb arrives with Chinese mustard and roasted lotus root.

Greenwoods on Green Street ★
1087 Green Street
Roswell
(770) 992-5383

Dinner, Wednesday–Saturday, 5 P.M.–10 P.M.; Sunday, 11:30 A.M.–2:30 P.M. and 5 P.M.–9 P.M.

Honey-pepper fried chicken, crab cakes, and giant helpings of fresh veggies will fill you up, so take home one of Green's famous apple pies, baked fresh daily. No credit cards, but personal checks are welcome.

Holyfield's New South Grill ★★★

6075 Roswell Road
(404) 531-0300

Lunch, Monday–Friday, 11:30 A.M.–2:30 P.M.; dinner,
Monday–Thursday, 5:30 P.M.–10:30 P.M.; Friday and Saturday,
5:30 P.M.–11:30 P.M.

Owner Evander Holyfield and other sports celebrities make occasional appearances at this Sandy Springs restaurant, where the focus is American food with a Southern accent.

Horseradish Grill ★★

4320 Powers Ferry Road
(404) 255-7277

www.horseradishgrill.com

Lunch daily from 11:30 A.M.; dinner daily from 5:30 P.M.; Sunday brunch from 11 A.M.–2:30 P.M.

Georgia mountain trout, grilled venison chop, and shrimp grits are among the favorites at this comfortable restaurant, where award-winning chefs pick the freshest vegetables from their year-round kitchen garden. A spacious outdoor patio overlooks Chastain Park.

Imperial Fez ★★★★

2285 Peachtree Road
(404) 351-0870

www.mindspring.com/~rafih

Dinner daily, 6 P.M.–11 P.M.

Leave your shoes and shyness at the door before pulling up a cushion on the thick Oriental rug and ordering Moroccan delicacies from the prix fixe six-course menu ($45 per person, without wine). In between courses of couscous, lamb, and soup, veiled belly dancers sashay among the tables.

Indigo Coastal Grill ★★

1397 North Highland Avenue
(404) 876-0676

Monday–Thursday and Sunday, 5:30 P.M.–10 P.M.; Friday and
Saturday, 5:30 P.M.–11 P.M.

Fresh seafood specialties with Caribbean influences will keep you
coming back. Save room after the shrimp, sole, catfish, scallops, or
salmon for Indigo's classic key lime pie.

Killer Creek Chop House ★★★

1700 Mansell Road
Alpharetta
(770) 649-0064

Dinner, Monday–Thursday, 5 P.M.–11 P.M.; Friday, 5 P.M.–midnight;
Saturday, 4 P.M.–midnight; Sunday, 4 P.M.–10 P.M.

Start with the mussels and oysters on the raw bar and work your way
up to a killer steak, from prime rib and London broil to filet mignon
and porterhouse. Smaller appetites can select from the seafood,
chicken, and pasta items.

Kobe Steaks ★★★

5600 Roswell Road
(404) 256-0810

Monday–Thursday, 5 P.M.–10:30 P.M.; Friday and Saturday,
5 P.M.–11:30 P.M.; Sunday, 4:30 P.M.–10 P.M.

The accomplished Japanese chefs show off at your table while whip-
ping up filet mignon, shrimp, crab, salmon, and swordfish.

La Grotta Ristorante ★★★

2637 Peachtree Road
(404) 231-1368

Monday–Saturday, 6 P.M.–10:30 P.M.

A secluded corner of Italy awaits on the lower level of the Buckhead
building that houses La Grotta. Classic Italian veal, chicken, quail,
beef, and lamb dishes lead the menu.

Maggiano's Little Italy ★★

3368 Peachtree Road
(404) 816-9650

Sunday–Thursday, 11:30 A.M.–10 P.M.; Friday and Saturday, 11: 30 A.M.–11 P.M.

Does anyone leave this New York–style Italian restaurant without a doggie bag? The portions of traditional favorites, from fettuccine Alfredo to rigatoni, are so big that even the waiters frequently suggest sharing.

Max Lager's ★★

320 Peachtree Street
(404) 525-4400

Daily, 11 A.M.–midnight.

Beer brewed on-site, wood-fired ovens, and hip industrial decor make this downtown restaurant a hit. Diners on the second-floor deck overlook Peachtree Street and the city skyline while enjoying dinner steaks, seafood, and pastas; a lighter menu of sandwiches, salads, and pizza priced under $10 is served continuously.

Mick's ★

116 E. Ponce de Leon Avenue
Decatur
(404) 373-7797

Service daily, 11 A.M.–10 P.M.; Saturday and Sunday brunch, 11 A.M.–3 P.M.

The big burgers, penne pasta, and fried chicken salad are best-sellers at this casual family-friendly eatery. Look for other Mick's restaurants at Underground Atlanta, Midtown, Lenox Square, and Buckhead.

Mumbo Jumbo ★★★

89 Park Place
(404) 523-0330

Lunch, Monday–Friday, 11:30 A.M.–2:30 P.M.; dinner, Sunday–Saturday, 6 P.M.–11:30 P.M.

This downtown spot is frequented for its enormous and comfortable bar, as well as an eclectic menu of lamb, chicken, rabbit, and seafood. Among the Southern sweets are pecan tart with bourbon ice cream, buttermilk pie, and doughnuts with chocolate sauce.

Nava ★★

3060 Peachtree Road
(404) 240-1984

Lunch, Monday–Friday, 11:30 A.M.–2:30 P.M.; dinner, Monday–Friday, 5:30 P.M.–11 P.M.; Sunday, 5:30 P.M.–10 P.M.

This upscale Southwestern eatery is spread across three tiers and includes one of the prettiest patios on Peachtree. The menu focuses on flavor, with specialties of beef tenderloin in a roasted garlic sauce and corn-crusted snapper.

Nikolai's Roof ★★★★

225 Courtland Street—in the Atlanta Hilton and Towers
(404) 221-6362

Dinner daily, 6 P.M.–9:30 P.M.

The view is almost as delicious as the French and Russian specialties at this fine dining room atop the Atlanta Hilton. The fixed price menu includes six courses for $67.50 or $85 per person, depending on the chef's specials selected.

OK Café ★

1284 West Paces Ferry Road
(404) 233-2888

Service continuously, Sunday–Thursday, 6 A.M.–4 A.M.; Friday and Saturday, twenty-four hours.

A throwback to the roadside cafés of yesteryear, the OK features home-style Southern cooking and rib-sticking breakfasts all day long.

103 West ★★★

103 West Paces Ferry Road
(404) 233-5993

Dinner Monday–Saturday, 6 P.M.–11 P.M.

Continental cuisine with a French flair is the focus of this Mobil Four Star restaurant, noted for its service and elaborate decor.

Palm Restaurant ★★★

3391 Peachtree Road—in the Swissôtel
(404) 814-1955

Service from 11:30 A.M. Monday–Friday, and noon to midnight on Saturday and Sunday.

Possibly the biggest lobsters in town wind up on the tables at the Palm, where six- and seven-pound shellfish are the norm. Beneath the smiling caricatures of regular clients adorning the walls, diners will also delight in prime aged steaks, chops, veal, and pasta.

Pano's and Paul's ★★★

1232 West Paces Ferry Road
(404) 261-3662

Dinner, Monday–Saturday, 5:30 P.M.–10 P.M.

Pano's dispels the myth that good restaurants can't survive in shopping centers. For more than twenty years, this Buckhead eatery has been wowing Atlantans with specialties from the 12-ounce fried lobster tails to roasted pheasant.

Park 75 ★★

75 14th Street—in the Four Seasons Hotel
(404) 253-3840

www.fourseasons.com

Lunch, Monday–Saturday, 11:30 A.M.–2 P.M.; dinner, Monday–Saturday, 5:30 P.M.–10:30 P.M.; Sunday brunch, 11 A.M.–2 P.M.

Bison, free-range chicken, oven-roasted lobster, poached lamb, and an array of exquisite desserts are among the menu offerings served by an attentive staff at this elegant eatery.

Pricci ★★

500 Pharr Road
(404) 237-2941

Lunch, Monday–Friday, 11 A.M.–5 P.M.; dinner, Monday–Thursday, 5 P.M.–11 P.M.; Friday and Saturday, 5 P.M.–midnight; Sunday, 5 P.M.–10 P.M.

Authentic Italian cuisine in a sleek, contemporary setting is Pricci's hallmark. Homemade pasta, pizza, seafood, beef, and chicken dishes precede the luscious desserts.

Public House ★★

805 S. Atlanta Street
Roswell
(770) 992-4646

Lunch, Monday–Friday, 11:30 A.M.–2:30 P.M.; Saturday and Sunday, 11:30 A.M.–3 P.M.; dinner, Monday–Saturday, 5:30 P.M.–11 P.M.; Sunday, 5:30 P.M.–9 P.M.

Anchoring a corner of the historic Roswell square, the Public House is a favorite for lunch and dinner. The menu highlights classic American cooking, with a Southern twist: sautéed chicken arrives with spoonbread; catfish comes with black-eyed peas, corn, and green beans.

The Rose and Crown ★

288 East Paces Ferry Road
(404) 233-8168

Monday–Saturday, 11:30 A.M.–3 A.M.; Sunday, 12:30 P.M.–3 A.M.

British pub favorites fish and chips and shepherd's pie go well with the English ales on tap at this fun spot with a spacious patio and bar.

Ruth's Chris Steakhouse ★★★
267 Marietta Street
(404) 223-6500

950 East Paces Ferry Road
(404) 365-0660

5788 Roswell Road
(404) 255-0035

Lunch, 11:30 A.M.–3 P.M.; dinner, Monday–Saturday, 5 P.M.–11 P.M.; Sunday, 5 P.M.–10 P.M.

Juicy, succulent cuts of beef keep diners coming back to Ruth's, where meat gently sautéed in butter is the main à la carte menu item. The Marietta Street location features an outdoor patio overlooking Centennial Olympic Park.

South City Kitchen ★★
1144 Crescent Avenue
(404) 873-7358

Daily, 11 A.M.–11 P.M.

Regional flavors with Southwestern influences are the mainstay of the South City kitchen. Don't miss the she-crab soup or the crab hash—two poached eggs over jumbo lump crab meat and topped with hollandaise.

Sun Dial ★★★
210 Peachtree Street—in the Westin Peachtree Plaza Hotel
(404) 589-7506

Lunch and dinner daily, 11:30 A.M.–2:30 P.M.; 6 P.M.–11 P.M.

Along with the seafood, steaks, and peach biscuits, the Sun Dial offers one of Atlanta's most spectacular vistas. The entire restaurant rotates ever so slowly to give diners a 360-degree view of the skyline and beyond.

The Tap Room ★★
231 Peachtree Street
(404) 577-7860

Monday–Saturday, 11 A.M.–2 A.M.

Billed as an "urban bar and grill," the Tap Room boasts more than forty beer and twelve martini selections to go with the American cuisine, from barbecued chicken breast sandwiches to country pot pie and a lineup of daily seafood specials.

Thai Chili ★
2169 Briarcliff Road
(404) 315-6750

Lunch, Monday–Friday, 11 A.M.–2:30 P.M.; dinner, Monday–Thursday and Sunday, 5 P.M.–10 P.M.; Friday and Saturday, 5 P.M.–11 P.M.

Chicken, beef, and pork specialties, seafood, and vegetarian entrees get the spicy treatment at this popular spot.

Three Dollar Café ★
3002 Peachtree Road
(404) 266-8667

Open daily, 11 A.M.–midnight.

Though most of the extensive menu is priced above $3, this casual eatery packs people in with big portions and plenty of variety. Entrees run the gamut from chicken teriyaki and shrimp linguine to baby back ribs and baked catfish. Its enormous patio right on Peachtree is one of the city's best people-watching spots.

Van Gogh's ★★★
70 W. Crossville Road
Roswell
(770) 993-1156

Monday–Saturday, 11:30 A.M.–midnight; Sunday, 5 P.M.–10 P.M.

Lamb in dried blueberry, shallot, and beet sauce, salmon in pineapple vinaigrette, and filet mignon with wild rice potato cakes are a few of Van Gogh's inventive entrees. In keeping with its name, the walls (even in the bathrooms) are adorned with colorful artwork.

Villa Christina ★★★
4000 Perimeter Summit Boulevard
Dunwoody
(404) 303-0133

Lunch, Monday–Friday, 11:30 A.M.–3 P.M.; dinner, Monday–Saturday, 6 P.M.–10 P.M.

Tucked into the heart of an office complex, this Italian eatery might be hard to find—but it's worth the hunt. Ask for directions if you're interested in well-done rabbit, lamb, sea bass, veal, and salmon entrees all cooked in classic Italian style.

Vortex Bar & Grill ★
878 Peachtree Street
(404) 875-1667

Open Monday–Friday, 8 A.M.–1:45 A.M.; Saturday and Sunday, 11 A.M.–1:45 A.M.

438 Moreland Avenue
(404) 688-1828

Open daily, 11 A.M.–1:45 A.M.

Juicy burgers, big beefy hot dogs, and a crazy decor of peculiar collectibles will please the kids; Mom and Dad can dig into hot chicken wings and oversized salads.

Zocalo ★★
187 10th Street
(404) 249-7576

Lunch, Monday–Friday, 11:30 A.M.–2:30 P.M.; dinner, 5:30 P.M.–11 P.M.; Sunday, 2:30 P.M.–10 P.M.

One of the best Mexican eateries around, Zocalo has a menu that mixes traditional fajitas and quesadillas with specialties of beef, shrimp, and chicken.

Shopping

Buckhead—the city's premier shopping district—is home to Lenox Square and Phipps Plaza, two of the Southeast's leading malls. But it's also rich with pockets of small retail centers where one-of-a-kind boutiques, antique stores, and specialty shops abound. Along East Andrews Drive, the Cates Center and Andrews Square are two small centers with shops dedicated to consignments, home accents, gardens, clothing, stationery, and jewelry. Miami Circle is the place where the interior designers snag their best finds, but many of the stores are open to the public. Bennett Street, off Peachtree on the south end of Buckhead, is lined with crammed antique stores and the Tula Arts Complex, where artists' studios and galleries are open for browsing.

The community of East Atlanta, south of I-20 around Flat Shoals and Glenwood Avenues, has gained enormous popularity in recent years. The area is home to several restaurants and coffeehouses as well as music stores, antique shops, and specialty stores.

Not far from East Atlanta, on the north side of I-20, the Little Five Points district draws shoppers and tourists from around the city. This funky intersection supports several restaurants, a natural foods store, one of the last remaining places to buy vinyl albums, and several consignment shops, as well as a few places to pick up vintage clothes and unusual jewelry. The district is particularly popular with teens and college-age kids searching for good deals on everything from '70s disco wear to cargo pants.

The intersection of Virginia and Highland Avenues in Midtown sports the same sort of stores as Little Five Points, but draws a more upscale, older crowd. The restaurants are more sophisticated, as are the antique and gift shops.

But even inside the city limits you don't have to pay full price. Outlet shopping abounds along Chattahoochee Industrial Boulevard, where the scenery is largely rows of railroad tracks, but the savings on shoes, clothing, and jewelry can be substantial. The Midtown Outlets off Amsterdam Avenue sell home accents, designer shoes, clothing, furniture, and kitchenware.

SHOPPING AREAS IN THE SUBURBS

Almost every county seat in the Atlanta metro area boasts a court-house square that doubles as the town's leading commercial district. From Canton in Cherokee County to McDonough in Henry County, there are quaint small town centers lined with antique shops, stores, and occasionally a drug store that still boasts a soda fountain. Some squares are thriving: in Cobb, Marietta's square is anchored by several restaurants and a theater. The heart of Decatur in DeKalb County offers several places to eat, to linger over coffee, and to pick up a best-selling book. Fayetteville in Fayette, Lawrenceville in Gwinnett, Jonesboro in Clayton, and Conyers in Rockdale also have busy down-town districts.

In addition to the county seats, many small towns have quaint historic centers, anchored by city halls instead of county buildings. It's easy to spend a leisurely afternoon meandering around Roswell and Alpharetta in north Fulton, Vinings and Kennesaw in Cobb, Norcross and Buford in Gwinnett, Stone Mountain in DeKalb, and Sharpsburg and Senoia in Coweta.

SHOPPING MALLS

Information about Atlanta's leading malls is available on the Internet at *www.realmalls.com.*

Arbor Place

6700 Douglas Boulevard
Douglasville
(770) 947-4244

Monday–Saturday, 10 A.M.–9 P.M.; Sunday, noon–6 P.M.

Opened in 1999, this 1.4-million-square-foot mall has ninety-one stores, including Dillard's, Parisian, and Sears. There's also a 1,000-square-foot soft play area for the kiddies and an environmental wall that teaches them about water conservation and wetlands.

The Avenue East Cobb

4475 Roswell Road, Marietta
(770) 303-2306

Monday–Saturday, 10 A.M.–9 P.M.; Sunday, noon–6 P.M.

Opened in 1999, this 236,000-square-foot mall was among the first to ride the retro wave back to open-air designs. The layout allows shoppers to pull up right in front of their favorite stores, such as Victoria's Secret, Williams-Sonoma, Talbots, and Smith & Hawken.

Cumberland Mall

I-285 and I-75 at Cobb Parkway
(770) 435-2206

Monday–Saturday, 10 A.M.–9 P.M.; Sunday, noon–6 P.M.

Rich's, Macy's, Sears, and J.C. Penney anchor this 1.2-million-square foot mall across from the Galleria. Along with 145 specialty stores, there's a Mick's restaurant and more than a dozen food court outlets.

Galleria Specialty Mall

1 Galleria Parkway
(770) 955-9100

Monday–Saturday, 10 A.M.–9 P.M.; Sunday, noon–6 P.M.

Along with a variety of specialty clothing and furniture stores, the Galleria houses an 108,000-square-foot exhibition hall, an eight-screen theater, and a number of restaurants.

Greenbriar Mall

2841 Greenbriar Parkway
(404) 344-6611

Monday–Saturday, 10 A.M.–9 P.M.; Sunday, noon–6 P.M.

One of the metro area's first malls, this 678,000-square-foot center houses Rich's, Magic Johnson Theatres, and specialty shops that cater to the predominantly African American clientele.

Gwinnett Place

2100 Pleasant Hill Road
Duluth
(770) 476-5160

Monday–Saturday, 10 A.M.–9 P.M.; Sunday, noon–6 P.M.

The county's original mall, Gwinnett Place boasts Macy's, Rich's, Sears, Parisian, and J.C. Penney, as well as a variety of restaurants and specialty stores.

Lenox Square

3393 Peachtree Road
(404) 233-6767

Monday–Saturday, 10 A.M.–9 P.M.; Sunday, noon–6 P.M.

Macy's, Neiman Marcus, and Rich's, along with several fine dining restaurants, a food court, and FAO Schwartz, are located at Lenox, Atlanta's first major "suburban" mall. Today, it's situated in the heart of Buckhead, adjacent to the Lenox MARTA station.

The Mall at Peachtree Center

231 Peachtree Street
(404) 654-1296

Monday–Saturday, 10 A.M.–6 P.M.; restaurants, Monday–Saturday, 7 A.M.–6 P.M.

In the heart of Atlanta's downtown hotel district, Peachtree Center's mall includes more than seventy gift, clothing, and accessory shops as well as hair salons, drug stores, and several restaurants.

Mall of Georgia

3333 Buford Drive
Buford
(678) 482-8788

Monday–Saturday, 10 A.M.–9 P.M.; Sunday, noon–6 P.M.

This sprawling shopping center, one of the metro area's newest, incorporates design elements from various regions of the state into its 1.7 million square feet. Outside the main mall area with Nordstroms, Dilliard's, Rich's, Lord & Taylor, and J.C. Penney, smaller stores, restaurants, movie theaters, and an outdoor performing stage are situated in brick buildings along a Main Street promenade.

Northlake Mall

4800 Briarcliff Road
(770) 938-3564

Monday–Saturday, 10 A.M.–9 P.M.; Sunday, noon–6 P.M.

Among North Lake's 125 shops are Macy's, Sears, J.C. Penney, and Parisian.

Perimeter Mall

4400 Ashford Dunwoody Road
(770) 394-4270

Monday–Saturday, 10 A.M.–9 P.M.; Sunday, noon–6 P.M.

This upscale shopping center boasts the metro area's first Nordstrom's, as well as Rich's, Macy's, and J.C. Penney. The 1.2 million-square-foot space includes several upscale restaurants around the mall.

Phipps Plaza

3500 Peachtree Road
(404) 262-0992

Monday–Saturday 10 A.M.–9 P.M.; Sunday noon–5:30 P.M.

The first two-story mall in the Southeast, Phipps boasts some of the city's poshest boutiques, from Tiffany & Co. to Nike Town. Saks Fifth Avenue and Lord & Taylor are also in the mix, along with several restaurants and a fourteen-screen theater.

Underground Atlanta

50 Upper Alabama Street
Atlanta, GA 30303
(404) 523-2311

www.underatl.com

Monday–Saturday, 10 A.M.–9 P.M.; Sunday, noon–6 P.M.

Yes, it really is underground. This 12-acre, three-level shopping center sits on the site of the city's first buildings in the heart of downtown. An assortment of boutiques and restaurants crowd the cobblestone streets, lined with gas lights and Victorian facades that create an ambience of days gone by.

Nightlife

Night owls, as well those who like to take in a party before hitting the hay, can dance and mingle the night away at Atlanta's various nightspots. Most of these popular hangouts serve limited menus, unless they're part of a larger restaurant complex. Some do charge cover fees if there's a live band, but the prices vary by the time of day, the day of the week, and the musical group performing. Call ahead for specifics on fees.

Beluga

3115 Piedmont Road
(404) 869-1090

Monday–Thursday, 5 P.M.–4 A.M.; Saturday, 7 P.M.–3 A.M.

Whether you're twenty-five or fifty-five, you'll take to the jazz and easy-on-the-ears pop music played at this upscale nightspot.

Blind Willie's

828 N. Highland Avenue
(404) 873-2583

Daily, 8 P.M.–2 A.M.

This small blues bar serves reasonably priced food and drinks to go with the laid-back music performed live every evening.

Champions

Atlanta Marriott Marquis
265 Peachtree Center Avenue
(404) 586-6017

Daily, 11:30 A.M.–2 A.M.

A popular late-night spot with the all-ages intown convention crowd, Champions has twenty-six televisions to capture all the sports action.

The Chili Pepper

208 Pharr Road
(404) 812-9266

Monday–Friday, 9 P.M.–4 A.M.; Saturday, 9 P.M.–3 A.M.

Three levels of bars and dance music are topped by a roof terrace where young revelers can take in the view of Buckhead as well as the party.

Churchill Grounds

660 Peachtree Street
(404) 876-3030

Sunday, noon–6 P.M.; Monday–Thursday, 3 P.M.–2 A.M.; Friday–Saturday, 3 P.M.–3 A.M.

Next door to the Fox Theatre, Churchill's frequently fills up with the decked-out pre- and post-theater crowd as well as casually dressed aging boomers who love the live jazz, gourmet coffee, wine, and cigars.

Cobalt

265 E. Paces Ferry Road
(404) 760-9250

Monday–Friday, 8 P.M.–4 A.M.; Saturday, 8 P.M.–3 A.M.

There's usually a line to get into this high-energy, upscale dance club with VIP rooms as well as five bars that cater to the decked-out crowd of young professionals. DJs spin new wave, alternative, and acid jazz when there isn't a live group.

Dave & Buster's

2215 D&B Drive
Marietta
(770) 951-5554

Monday–Thursday, 11 A.M.–1 A.M.; Friday, 11 A.M.–2 A.M.; Saturday, 11:30 A.M.–2 A.M.; Sunday, 11:30 A.M.–midnight.

This 53,000-square-foot indoor entertainment center appeals to kids who like virtual golf as well as dressed-up adults who enjoy a round of blackjack. (The tykes must be accompanied by an adult, and must leave the premises by 10 P.M.) Billiard tables, shuffleboard courts, and

more than a hundred video and virtual reality games are part of the entertainment. A restaurant serving lunch, dinner, and late-night American fare from $6.50 to $16.95 and a mystery dinner theater ($40 per person for a three-course meal and show) are all under the same roof.

Deux Plex

1789 Cheshire Bridge Road
(404) 733-5900

Tuesday–Friday, 6 P.M.–4 A.M.; Saturday, 6 P.M.–3 A.M.; Sunday, 8 P.M.–2 A.M.

On the main level, Deux Plex is a French bistro serving entrees moderately priced from $8 to $15. Downstairs, the enormous dance floor draws late-night crowds from Gen-Xers pursuing the high-energy party scene to Baby Boomers who just polished off a salmon dinner upstairs.

Frankie's Food, Sports & Spirits

5600 Roswell Road
(404) 843-9444

Daily, 11 A.M.–1 A.M.

Salads, steaks, and sandwiches priced less than $10 are on the menu at this favorite spot for sports enthusiasts of all ages. With 175 televisions and big screens, Frankie's has a sporting event to watch any time of the day or evening.

Jellyroll's
295 E. Paces Ferry Road
(404) 261-6864

Wednesday–Saturday, 7 P.M.–3 A.M.

Dueling pianists face off on gleaming baby grands with rousing performances of favorite rock 'n roll oldies, soft rock, jazz, and blues. The crowd of all ages is encouraged to make requests.

Jocks & Jills Sports Grill
1 CNN Center
(404) 688-4225

Daily, 11 A.M.–11 P.M.

Situated next door to the Georgia Dome and Philips Arena makes Jocks & Jills a favorite for pre- and post-game parties where the onion rings and wings are priced below $10. The fifty satellite televisions show the action outside of town.

Johnny's Hideaway
3771 Roswell Road
(404) 233-8026

Monday–Friday, 11 A.M.–4 P.M.; Saturday, 11 A.M.–3 A.M.

It's smoky and small but Johnny's packs in the older crowd that goes for the free buffets and favorites from the '40s and '50s.

Kaya
1068 Peachtree Street
(404) 874-4460

Wednesday, 7 P.M.–3 A.M.; Thursday, 10 P.M.–4 A.M.; Friday, 9 P.M.–4 A.M.; Saturday, 9 P.M.–3 A.M.; Sunday, 10 P.M.–4 A.M.

This enormous place is part bistro, where tapas and pastas less than $10 are served at an enormous bar, and part dance hall, where those who want to move take to the spacious floor in the back. Different ages come in for different music, from live jazz and poetry readings to reggae, hip-hop, acid jazz, and disco.

Leopard Lounge
84 12th Street
(404) 875-7562

Monday–Thursday, 4:30 P.M.–2 A.M.; Friday, 4 P.M.–4 A.M.; Saturday, 8 P.M.–3 A.M.

Leopard walls, furniture salvaged from the '50s and '60s and a chic two-level lounge give this Midtown spot a retro feel. Swing bands on Friday and Saturday night lure young dancers onto the floor; other nights start off with Rat Pack classics and move into funk and disco.

The Lobby Bar at the Ritz-Carlton Buckhead

3434 Peachtree Road
(404) 237-2700

Monday–Saturday, 6:30 A.M.–10 A.M., 11 A.M.–1 A.M.; Sunday, 6:30 A.M.–noon, 12:30 P.M.–midnight.

This busy bar area is crowded in the early morning when a continental breakfast is served, during high tea in the afternoon, and before and after dinner. A piano player entertains during the day; after dinner, a jazz trio plays a mix of classic and contemporary pieces designed to get the formally attired Boomers and older couples who frequent this chic space out of the overstuffed armchairs and onto the dance floor.

Lulu's Bait Shack

3057 Peachtree Road
(404) 262-5220

Wednesday–Saturday, 7 P.M.–4 A.M.

The view and the live music are two good reasons to party at Lulu's, where the 3,000-square-foot rooftop deck is crowded with casually dressed young people nibbling on the Cajun cuisine and nursing ninety-six-ounce "fish-bowl"-sized drinks.

The Martini Club

1140 Crescent Avenue
(404) 873-0795

Monday–Saturday, 5 P.M.–2 A.M.

A 1930s-style bar and intimate rooms with plenty of plush furniture fill up this former house in Midtown, where the Gen-X crowd dresses up to down some of the most unusual martini mixes around. Live jazz and cigars are on tap, too.

Masquerade

695 North Avenue
(404) 577-8178

Daily, 9 P.M.–4 A.M.

Fans of the gothic, punk, and rock scene flock to this former Midtown factory with a pulsating dance floor as well as a main stage concert hall that books national acts.

Sambuca Jazz Café

3102 Piedmont Road
(404) 237-5299

Monday–Wednesday, 4:30–11 P.M.; Thursday, 4:30 P.M.–midnight; Friday–Saturday, 4:30 P.M.–1 A.M.; Sunday, 4:30–11:30 P.M.

Live jazz groups accompany the Mediterranean menu seven nights a week at this upscale supper club popular with the older set.

Sanctuary
128 E. Andrews Drive
(404) 262-1377

Thursday–Saturday, and each first and third Sunday, 8 P.M.– 3 A.M.

Free salsa lessons early in the evening will get you ready for the hot Latin music that cranks up with live acts and DJs by 9 P.M.

Smith's Olde Bar
1578 Piedmont Avenue
(404) 875-1522

Sunday–Friday, 3 P.M.–4 A.M.; Saturday, 3 P.M.–3 A.M.

Along with the pool tables and food, the casual and laid-back Smith's features local musicians performing rock, blues, and jazz aimed at the thirty-five-and-under set.

Tongue & Groove
3055 Peachtree Road
(404) 261-2325

Tuesday and Thursday, 9:30 P.M.–3 A.M.; Wednesday, Friday, and Saturday, 9 P.M.–3 A.M.

Sophisticated folks of all ages crowd into this Buckhead sushi bar and cocktail lounge where looking good is a must (a dress code is enforced at the door). Wednesday starts off with free salsa lessons.

Professional Sports

AUTO RACING

Atlanta Motor Speedway
Georgia Highway 19 and 41, Hampton
Henry County
(770) 946-4211

Professional auto racing events, including NASCAR competitions in March and November, are staged at this 870-acre complex thirty miles south of the city. Ticket prices range from $6 to more than $100, depending on the event.

BASEBALL

Atlanta Braves

Turner Field
755 Hank Aaron Drive
(404) 577-9100

www.atlantabraves.com

The "Team of the '90s" brought eight straight division titles to Atlanta during the last decade. They've also batted their way into five World Series, including the 1995 championship they won. Tickets $12–$35.

BASKETBALL

Atlanta Hawks

Philips Arena
1 CNN Center
(404) 827-DUNK

www.nba.com/hawks/

Opened in September 1999, this state-of-the-art arena turns into a basketball court for the Hawks, the city's pro team that has enjoyed continued success since 1968. Tickets $10–$400.

FOOTBALL

Atlanta Falcons

Georgia Dome
1 Georgia Dome Drive
(404) 223-9200

www.nfl.com/falcons/

The world's largest cable-supported dome stadium hosted the Super Bowl in 1994 and 2000. When the Atlanta Falcons aren't playing, the field supports a 102,000-square-foot floor where major basketball tournaments and concerts are held. Tickets $25–$41.

ICE HOCKEY

Atlanta Thrashers
Philips Arena
1 CNN Center
(404) 584-PUCK

Though most folks don't think of Atlanta as an ice hockey town, the arrival of this National Hockey League franchise in 1999 has made fans of native Southerners and Northern transplants alike. Tickets $24–$70.

Amateur Sports

CLUBS

Atlanta Club Sport
120 West Wieuca Road
(404) 257-3355

www.usclubsport.com

Co-ed athletic leagues in volleyball, flag football, soccer, ultimate Frisbee, softball, golf, and more, as well as social events, attract active young professionals from around the city. Annual membership $35.

Singles Outdoor Adventures
2055 Mt. Paran Road
(770) 242-2338

Day hikes, canoeing, camping, and backpacking for folks of all skill levels are among the outdoor activities organized by this group, which meets on the third Thursday of every month. Annual membership $25.

BILLIARDS

Buckhead Billiards
200 Pharr Road
(404) 237-3705

Monday, 3 P.M.–2 A.M.; Tuesday and Thursday, 4 P.M.–2 A.M.;
Wednesday, 11 A.M.–2 A.M.; Friday and Saturday, 1 P.M.–3 A.M.;
Sunday, 1 P.M.–1 A.M.

The ten tables in this Buckhead spot are usually crowded with billiard fans and spectators who relax between sets at the full bar. $5.40
per game before 8 P.M.; $7.20 after 8 P.M.; Friday and Saturday, $9.60
after 8 P.M.

BOWLING

Express Bowling Lanes
1936 Piedmont Circle
(404) 874-5703

Open daily, twenty-four hours.

Bowl your heart out day and
night at this Midtown facility,
which includes a snack bar and
lounge. $1.95 per game;
Sunday–Thursday, $2.95 after 6
P.M.; Friday and Saturday, $3.50
after 6 P.M.; shoe rental, $2.50.

GOLF

Alfred Tup Holmes
2300 Wilson Drive
(404) 753-6158

CITY FACT

Atlanta ranked second only to Los Angeles
in population growth from 1990 to 1998.
During those years, Atlanta welcomed
786,559 newcomers; L.A. had more than
1.2 million.

Daily, 7 A.M.–one hour before sunset.

This eighteen-hole course on the city's southside has a clubhouse
and snack bar, and is reputed to be one of the best around. $17–$29
a round.

Bobby Jones

384 Woodward Way
(404) 355-1009

Daily, 7 A.M.–one hour before sunset.

The beautiful greens of this Buckhead course are named for Atlanta's golf legend. Along with the eighteen holes, there's a clubhouse and snack bar. Monday–Friday, $22–$32; Saturday–Sunday, $25–$35.

Candler Park

585 Candler Park Drive
(404) 371-1260

Daily, 8 A.M.–one hour before sunset.

You don't need a tee time to play a round on this nine-hole walking course in the heart of Candler Park. City residents $7; nonresidents $9; resident students $5.50, nonresident students $6.50.

North Fulton Golf Course

216 West Wieuca Road
(404) 255-0723

Daily, 6:30 A.M.–one hour before sunset.

Across the street from Chastain Park in Buckhead, this eighteen-hole course stays busy. Along with the greens, the property includes a clubhouse, pro shop, and snack bar. Monday–Friday, $20–$30, Saturday and Sunday, $25–$35.

RUNNING AND WALKING

Atlanta Track Club

3097 East Shadowlawn Avenue
(404) 231-9065; (404) 262-RACE

More than 11,000 members of this club (which was founded in 1964) participate in monthly races as well as in the city's big events such as the Peachtree Road Race, the Atlanta Marathon, and the Atlanta Half Marathon. Individual annual membership $30.

Walking Club of Georgia

P.O. Box 190011
(770) 593-5817

Race and fitness walkers and hikers at various levels of skill and competitiveness have weekly get-togethers in the Buckhead area to plan hikes and free clinics for beginners. Individual annual memberships $20.

SKIING

Atlanta Ski Club

6255 Barfield Road
(404) 255-4800

The 3,000 members of this long-established club can choose among more than twenty-five trips each year to slopes in the West as well as Europe. In between, they keep busy with about ten social events each month, from symphony concerts and dinners to white-water rafting trips. Individual memberships $65.

MOVING TIP

When selecting a mover, allow plenty of time to check out several before making a decision. Many companies specialize in either local and intra-state moves or long-distance hauls. Check to make sure the company you employ is licensed to do business across state lines—particularly to Georgia!

SWIMMING

Atlanta's Bureau of Recreation maintains fifteen public swimming pools during the summer. Mornings are usually reserved for swimming lessons. Afternoons are free, but after 4:30 P.M. there's a $2 charge per adult; $1 per child ages six through sixteen. For specific information, call the bureau at (404) 817-6778. Here are some of the most popular pools:

John A. White Pool

1101 Cascade Circle
(404) 755-5546

Open June 6–August 13.

Piedmont Pool

400 Park Drive
(404) 892-0119

Open June 6–August 13.

Chastain Pool
235 West Wieuca Road
(404) 255-0863

Open May 26–September 5.

Grant Pool
625 Park Avenue
(404) 622-3041

Open May 26–September 5.

TENNIS

Atlanta Lawn Tennis Association
6849 Peachtree Road
(770) 399-5788

Almost every neighborhood and private club with at least two lighted tennis courts fields an ALTA team. Since its founding in 1971, more than 82,000 Atlantans have joined teams for men, women, juniors, seniors, and wheelchair players that play at public and private facilities around the metro area.

Bitsy Grant Tennis Center
2125 Northside Drive
(404) 609-7193

Daily, 9 A.M.–8 P.M.

$2.25 per hour per person on soft courts; $2 on hard; $2.75 after 6 P.M.

Along with the thirteen clay and ten hard courts under the lights, the Grant center has showers and locker rooms.

Piedmont Park Tennis Center
Piedmont and Park Drive
(404) 853-3461

Monday–Friday, 10 A.M.– 9 P.M.; Saturday and Sunday, 10 A.M.–6 P.M.

$2 per hour per person; $2.50 when lights are on.

This Midtown facility in the heart of the park features twelve outdoor hard courts with lights.

WATER SPORTS

Atlanta Rowing Club

8341 Roswell Road
Roswell
(770) 993-1879

www.atlantarow.org

$235–$370 annual membership; $200-300 initiation fees

From their boathouse across from the Chattahoochee River Park, members of this rowing club train for regattas and races around the area. Novice clinics and events for all skill levels are planned.

Atlanta Whitewater Club

North and North Highland Avenues
(404) 299-3752

The club meets monthly on the first Tuesday at Manuel's Tavern in Virginia-Highland to discuss upcoming white-water paddling trips, races, and social events. Members' skill levels range from beginner to expert. The group also offers clinics and educational programs on river conservation.

Chattahoochee Outdoor Center

1990 Island Ford Parkway
(770) 395-6851

Monday–Friday, 10 A.M.–8 P.M.; Saturday and Sunday, 9 A.M.–8 P.M.

$37.50–$85.

From May until the end of September, "Shooting the Hooch" is a favorite pastime of Atlantans. Grab some friends, some coolers, a four-, six- or eight-person raft or canoe, and go with the flow down the Chattahoochee as it wanders along the Cobb-Fulton border.

Calendar of Events

JANUARY

Cathedral Antiques Show
Cathedral of St. Philip
2744 Peachtree Road
(404) 365-1000

Fabulous finds from around the country are on sale during this three-day event to benefit a local charity. Costs $10.

King Day Celebration
Martin Luther King Jr. National Historic Site
450 Auburn Avenue
(404) 331-6922

A parade, prayers, and remembrances are always part of this national holiday.

FEBRUARY

Black History Month
Various locations around town; prices vary

Lectures, displays, dramatic performances, music, and dance celebrate the African American spirit throughout the entire month. Events are staged across the metro area, from the branches of the Atlanta-Fulton County Public Library to art galleries and colleges.

Official Groundhog Celebration
Yellow River Game Ranch
4525 Highway 78
Lilburn
(770) 972-6643

$6 adults, $5 ages three through eleven

Will General Beauregard Lee see his shadow? Will there be six more weeks of winter? Bundle up the kids and find out firsthand what the South's leading weather forecaster predicts.

Southeastern Flower Show

Atlanta Exposition Center
3650 Jonesboro Road
(404) 366-0833

The city's premier flower and garden event features thousands of budding plants and flowers in professionally landscaped dioramas. Costs $15 per day or $20 for a two-day pass.

MARCH

Atlanta Fair

Turner Field
755 Hank Aaron Drive
(770) 740-1962

This annual fete features music, midway rides, food, prizes, and children's games. Tickets cost $3 for adults and $1 for children.

Atlanta Passion Play

Atlanta Civic Center
395 Piedmont Avenue
(770) 234-8400

An annual production of the First Baptist Church of Atlanta since 1976, the Passion Play is a three-hour depiction of the life and death of Jesus. Costs $8–$16.

Conyers Cherry Blossom Festival

Georgia International Horse Park
1996 Centennial Parkway
Conyers
(770) 918-2169

www.conyerscherryblossom.com

Arts and crafts, international foods, children's events, and sports tournaments mark the budding of the city's beautiful cherry trees. Free with $5 parking fee.

Saint Patrick's Day
Downtown Buckhead

The day usually kicks off with a Mass at the Cathedral of Christ the King in Buckhead, followed by a lively parade through downtown. By late afternoon, the city's pubs are usually crowded with revelers all claiming Irish ancestry.

APRIL

Atlanta Dogwood Festival
Piedmont Park
Piedmont Avenue and 14th Street
(404) 329-0501

www.dogwood.org

Since 1936, this free celebration of Atlanta's favorite tree has hosted thousands of revelers who pack the park for the food, music, hot air balloon floats, art, and magic shows.

Georgia Renaissance Festival
P.O. Box 986
Fairburn
(770) 964-8575

www.garenfest.com

This rollicking outdoor celebration recreates a sixteenth-century English country fair, complete with jousting knights, jugglers, plays, roasted turkey legs, medieval games, and a marketplace. The festival runs weekends April through June. Admission costs $12.95 for adults, $5.75 for children six through twelve, and $11 for seniors.

Inman Park Spring Festival
Inman Park neighborhood
(770) 242-4895

www.inmanpark.org

The enormous block party in this Victorian neighborhood is open to all, with a parade, cloggers, an antiques market, art exhibits, and a home tour. The home tour costs $12–$15; other events are free.

ParkFest

Centennial Olympic Park
International Blvd. and Techwood Drive
(404) 222-7275

Spring is ushered in during this festival of music, food, and crafts at the downtown park. Also beginning in April, the park's free music series kicks off: Music at Noon is held each Tuesday and Thursday at midday; the Wednesday Wind Down features live jazz from 5:30 to 8:30 P.M.

Sheep to Shawl Day

Atlanta History Center
130 West Paces Ferry Road
(404) 814-4000

www.atlhist.org

Shearing, washing, spinning, and weaving—all in one day! Costumed crafters demonstrate the work involved, from start to finish, just to make one article of clothing. Admission costs $10 for adults, $4 for ages six through seventeen, and is free for those five and under.

MAY

Atlanta Celtic Festival

Oglethorpe University
4484 Peachtree Road
(404) 261-1441

For an entire weekend, area folk of Celtic descent party on the Oglethorpe campus with music, a tea room, food, sheep dog exhibitions, and vendors. Tickets cost $5–$10.

Atlanta Jazz Festival

Piedmont Park
Piedmont Avenue and 14th Street
(404) 817-6851

The Memorial Day weekend is packed with free jazz concerts in the park, as well as a handful of other venues around the city.

Music Midtown

Atlanta Civic Center
395 Piedmont Avenue
(404) 233-8889

www.musicmidtown.com

After moving from various city locations, this major music event settled at the Civic Center with multiple stages, kids' activities, an artists' market, and foods from local restaurants. Admission costs $20.

Taste of the South

Stone Mountain Park
Highway 78
Stone Mountain
(770) 498-5702

www.stonemountainpark.org

This four-day event over the Memorial Day weekend features food, crafts, and displays. Admission is free with $6 parking pass.

JUNE

Atlanta Lesbian and Gay Pride Festival

(404) 876-3700

www.Atlantapride.org

The nation's fourth-largest gay and lesbian celebration features a weekend of lectures, readings, and entertainment that wraps up with a Sunday afternoon parade to Piedmont Park.

Georgia Shakespeare Festival

Conant Performing Arts Center
4484 Peachtree Road
(404) 264-0020

www.gashakespeare.org

If you love the Bard, you won't want to miss this covered yet open-air theater where his works—as well as updated versions of those classics—are performed. Tickets cost $20–$26.50.

JULY

Civil War Encampment

Atlanta History Center
130 West Paces Ferry Road
(404) 814-4000

www.atlhist.org

The summer of 1864 is recreated in mid-July with Confederate camps of soldiers, artillery, drills, cavalry, music, and story-telling. Admission costs $10 for adults, $4 for ages six through seventeen, and is free for those five and under.

Fourth of July Fireworks

Lenox Square
3393 Peachtree Road
(404) 233-6767

This free holiday extravaganza with music draws thousands of spectators each year, so plan to be in the parking lot early.

Peachtree Road Race

Peachtree Road from Lenox Square to Piedmont Park

You don't have to be in the horde of runners to enjoy this Fourth of July event. From 8 A.M. until the last runner crosses the finish line, Peachtree is lined with revelers cheering on the participants. The crowd later convenes in the park to find out who won.

AUGUST

Lasershow
Stone Mountain Park
Highway 78
Stone Mountain
(770) 498-5690

www.stonemountainpark.org

An amazing display of lights and music uses the side of the mountain as a backdrop. This specialty continues through the summer. Admission is free with $6 parking pass.

SEPTEMBER

Atlanta Greek Festival
Greek Orthodox Cathedral of the Annunciation
2500 Clairmont Road
(404) 633-5870

Greek heritage is celebrated for three days by thousands of Atlantans who crowd the church grounds for the music, dancing, wine, and food. Tickets cost $3 dollars for adults and $1 for children.

Sweet Auburn Heritage Festival
Auburn Avenue
(404) 525-0205

Crowds take to this historic street in the heart of Downtown to celebrate the culture and contributions of African Americans to the city.

Yellow Daisy Festival
Stone Mountain Park
Highway 78
Stone Mountain
(770) 498-5702

www.stonemountainpark.org

One of the South's biggest craft shows draws more than four hundred artisans and their wares. Free with $6 parking pass.

OCTOBER

Buckhead Art Crawl
Various Buckhead galleries
(404) 467-7607

What started as a small tour of Buckhead galleries has grown to include more than fifty venues. Visitors are shuttled between the galleries of their choice for special exhibits and receptions. Tickets are $15.

Fright Fest
Six Flags Over Georgia
7561 Six Flags Road
Mableton
(770) 948-9290

CITY FACT

The winter of 1999–2000 was one of the city's balmiest yet, with an average temperature of 47 degrees, about four degrees above normal.

Ghosts, goblins, and all the scary rides are part of the Halloween celebration at the area's main amusement park. Tickets cost $37 for adults, half price for children under four feet tall.

Stone Mountain Highland Games
Stone Mountain Park
Highway 78
Stone Mountain
(770) 498-5702

www.stonemountainpark.org

Pipe and drum bands, highland dancing, Scottish food, crafts, and clothes are part of the weekend-long celebration of the clans. Free with $6 parking pass.

NOVEMBER

Lighting of the Great Tree
Lenox Square
3393 Peachtree Road
(404) 233-7575

Free music and dancing accompany the ceremonial lighting of the city's official Christmas tree.

DECEMBER

CITY FACT

Property taxes vary around Atlanta. Some of the lowest are in Clayton and Forsyth counties; the highest can be found in the cities of Atlanta and Decatur.

The Atlanta Ballet's Nutcracker
Fox Theatre
660 Peachtree Street
(404) 873-5811

It wouldn't be Christmas with Clara and the cast of local kids who join the ballet as part of the classic holiday tale. Tickets cost $20–$50.

Candlelight Tours
Atlanta History Center
130 West Paces Ferry Road
(404) 814-4000
www.atlhist.org

Stop to hear carolers on the grounds and sip hot cider while touring the 1928 Swan House, the Tullie Smith Farm, and the grounds of the Atlanta History Center by candlelight. Costs $10 for adults, $4 for ages six through sixteen, and is free for those under five.

Children's Healthcare of Atlanta Christmas Parade

Centennial Olympic Park
International Boulevard and Marietta Street
(404) 325-NOEL

A 1.5-mile parade of bands, clowns, and floats winds its way through downtown to mark the arrival of Santa Claus and the opening of the Festival of Trees.

Festival of Trees

Georgia World Congress Center
285 International Blvd.
(404) 325-NOEL

More than three thousand lavishly decorated trees, wreaths, and holiday scenes bring the season to life. The event also includes children's activities, a kiddy train, and vendors. Proceeds benefit the Children's Healthcare of Atlanta hospitals. Admission costs $8 for adults; $5 for seniors and children ages two through twelve.

Transportation

AIRPORTS

Hartsfield Atlanta International Airport

(404) 530-6830

Atlanta is served by the world's busiest airport, in terms of both passengers and flights. Hartsfield Atlanta International is a 3,750-acre complex that welcomes more than 73 million travelers a year at 170 gates.

Located ten miles south of downtown, Hartsfield is easily reached on I-85 from the north and south, and on I-285 from the east and west.

DeKalb-Peachtree Airport

3915 Clairmont Road
(770) 936-5440

Fulton County Airport
3952 Aviation Circle
(404) 699-4200

McCollum Airport
1723 McCollum Parkway
Marietta
(770) 422-4300

AMTRAK

Brookwood Station
1688 Peachtree Road
Buckhead
(404) 881-3060

Atlanta is served by one Amtrak station in Buckhead's Brookwood neighborhood. Trains heading south to New Orleans and north to New York make one stop each day. Outside the station, there's a cab stand and a bus stop that connects to the MARTA rail line.

BUS STATIONS

Greyhound Bus Lines
232 Forsyth Street
(404) 584-1728; 800-231-2222

Besides the main terminal downtown, Greyhound operates suburban stations in Decatur, Hapeville, Marietta, and Norcross. More than ninety routes arrive in town, with the most frequent runs between Birmingham, Charlotte, Chicago, Detroit, Jacksonville, New York, Orlando, and Washington.

PUBLIC TRANSPORTATION

Metropolitan Atlanta Rapid Transit Authority (MARTA)
2424 Piedmont Road
(404) 848-4711

www.itsmarta.com

MARTA operates buses and trains across Atlanta as well as Fulton County. The north-south trains run from Dunwoody to the airport; east-west lines extend from Decatur to the western city limits. For a complete directory of stations, as well as up-to-date schedules and directions to the city's major attractions, check out the company's Web site.

Generally, buses operate from 5 A.M. to 1 A.M. Monday through Friday, and from 6 A.M. to 12:30 P.M. on weekends and holidays. Trains run weekdays from 5 A.M. to 1 A.M.; 6 A.M. to 12:20 A.M. on weekends and holidays. During the week, trains run very eight minutes; on Saturdays, ten minutes; on Sundays and holidays, fifteen minutes.

Trips on MARTA cost $1.50 each way for adults, $.75 for elderly and disabled. Rolls of twenty tokens sell for $25. Frequent riders will prefer to buy weekly transcards, offering unlimited rides for $12. Monthly passes are an even better deal at $45. Passes and tokens are for sale at MARTA kiosks at the Five Points, Lenox, Airport, and Lindbergh stations.

Cobb Community Transit (CCT)

100 Cherokee Street
Marietta
(770) 427-4444

Since 1989, Cobb County has funded its own buses that crisscross the county, stopping at major retail and business centers, and heading downtown to connect with MARTA rail lines.

Adults pay $1.25 per trip; children less than forty-two inches tall are free. Students under eighteen pay $.80; seniors and disabled passengers pay $.60. CCT operates weekday express buses to downtown Atlanta that cost $3 one way or $4 round trip for adults; $1.60 one way or $2.55 round trip for students. Monthly express passes are also available.

CCT runs express buses to all Falcons home football games at the Georgia Dome for a $5 round-trip fare.

TAXIS

Atlanta Taxicab Bureau

818 Pollard Blvd.
(404) 658-7600

Fares charged by Atlanta's taxicab companies are regulated by the city, which has established a flat rate structure. For example:

- From the airport to downtown, fares are $18 for one passenger, $20 for two, and $8 each for three or more passengers. There's also a 7 percent tax.
- From the airport to Buckhead, fares are $28 for one passenger, $30 for two, and $10 per person for three or more. The fare is not to exceed $30; add $1 to the fare for each additional Buckhead destination.
- Between downtown and Buckhead, the flat rate is $5 for one person; add $1 for each additional person.
- All other destinations are $1.60 for the first seventh of a mile, with $.21 for each additional seventh of a mile and $1 per each extra passenger—all of which include the tax. The per-hour waiting time is $15, and additional space for luggage costs $5.

CAB COMPANIES

Ambassador Taxi
1874 Piedmont Road
(404) 724-0220

American Cab
1075 Brady Avenue
(404) 873-1410

Atlanta Lenox Taxi
2015 Rockledge Road
(404) 872-2600

Atlanta Royal Cabbies
418 Whitehall Street
(404) 584-6655

Atlanta Yellow Cab
55 Milton Street
(404) 521-0200

Buckhead Safety Cab
254 East Paces Ferry Road
(404) 233-1152

Checker Cab
563 Trabert Avenue
(404) 351-1111

Metropolitan Cab Company
755 Virginia Avenue
(404) 525-5466

Southern Taxi & Limo
2791 Clairmont Road
(404) 633-0030

United Taxi Cab Company
298 Grant Street
(404) 658-1638

CHAPTER 7

What's Out of Town

Although there's plenty to do in and around Atlanta, sometimes you just feel the need to get out of town. Beyond the boundaries of the metro area, Georgia offers a wealth of entertainment, whether your interest lies in history, nature, music, or just sightseeing.

Atlanta, though situated in the northern part of the state, is actually centrally located to the rest of Georgia. And with the accessibility to the major interstates that crisscross the city, it's an easy drive to the southern wetlands of the Okefenokee Swamp or the cool waterfalls of the North Georgia mountains. In addition, Birmingham, Alabama, and Chattanooga, Tennessee, are only two hours from town.

But before you venture across the state line, take a look at some of the attractions at home in Georgia.

The Mountains

When the heat of the city gets too oppressive and nothing but a cooling mountain breeze will lower your temperature, head for the hills across the state's northern arc. Beautifully pristine, this southern tip of the Appalachian range offers a welcome respite from Atlanta's sizzling summers. Even when the weather's chilly, the quaint mountain towns offer opportunities for antiquing, dining, and curling up in front of a fire in a log cabin.

NORTHWEST MOUNTAINS

Civil War battlefields blanket much of the state's northwest quadrant, along the routes where Union and Confederate forces fought their way from Chattanooga to Atlanta. Towns such as Ringgold, Resaca, Adairsville, Dalton, Chickamauga, Cartersville, and Rome line the Blue and Gray Trail (770-387-1357). Along the way are town squares, country stores, and military parks—places that were stopovers for the Union Forces during the sweltering summer of 1864.

Vestiges of the Native Americans who first settled the area are found along the Chieftains Trail, a 150-mile loop lined with attractions from the Etowah Indian Mounds in Cartersville to the Chieftains Museum in Rome (800-733-2280).

The mountains also offer a variety of camping, canoeing, fishing, swimming, horseback riding, and hiking opportunities. For details, contact one of the following welcome centers:

Blue Ridge
(800) 899-6867

Calhoun-Gordon County
(800) 625-5062
www.info@gordonchamber.org

Cartersville
(800) 733-2280
www.notatlanta.org

Chatsworth
(706) 695-6060

Ellijay
(706) 635-7400

Rome
(800) 444-1834
www.romegeorgia.com

Take I-75 north out of Atlanta toward Chattanooga and you'll discover the following spots in less than two hours:

Apple Orchard Tour
Ellijay
(706) 635-7400

Known as the "Apple Capitol of Georgia," Ellijay prides itself on its bountiful apple orchards. From roadside stands to tractor-drawn carts that deliver you right to the tree to pick your own, there are plenty of places to find an apple assortment. Call the chamber of commerce for a map with driving routes to eighteen orchards. Ellijay also features a quaint square with antique shops and several restaurants. The Cartecay River is a popular spot for canoeists and white-water rafters.

Cave Spring

3 Georgia Avenue
Cave Spring
(706) 777-3382

The limestone cave that gave the town its name is a natural spring where visitors can fill up their own containers with the clear water that flows at a constant fifty-six degrees. The adjacent Rolater Park boasts the second-largest swimming pool in the state that filled with chlorinated spring water from the cave. The cave is open on weekends during the winter and daily during the summer from 10 A.M.–5 P.M. Admission is $1 per person.

The pool opens on weekends from Memorial Day until the first of June, when it's open daily except Monday from 10 A.M.–6 P.M. Admission is $3 for adults; $1.50 for children.

Chickamauga-Chattanooga National Military Park

3370 LaFayette Road
Fort Oglethorpe
(706) 866-9241

The country's first and largest national military park offers battlefield tours and monuments. A visitor's center, book store, and museum are open 8 A.M.–4:45 P.M.; park hours are dawn to dusk. $3 adults; $1.50 children.

MOVING TIP

You can save money on a move by packing your own items. But be forewarned: Many professional moving companies won't insure your items unless they're packed by the company's professional crew.

Chief Vann House

82 Georgia Highway 225 N
Chatsworth
(706) 695-2598

Built in 1804, the Federal-style mansion was built by Chief James Vann, and has been dubbed the "showplace of the Cherokee nation." Take a tour Tuesday through Saturday, 9 A.M.–5 P.M.; Sunday, 2 P.M.–5:30 P.M. Admission is $2.50 for adults; $1.50 for children; age five and under, free.

Chieftains Museum

501 Riverside Parkway
Rome
(706) 291-9494

A national historic landmark, this 1794 log cabin belonged to Major Ridge, a prominent Cherokee leader whose signature on the New Echota Treaty led to the "Trail of Tears," the march that drove the Cherokee tribe across the country. Hours are Tuesday through Saturday, 10 A.M.–4 P.M. Admission is $3.

Cloudland Canyon State Park

122 Cloudland Canyon Park Road
Rising Fawn
(800) 864-7275

Perched on the edge of Lookout Mountain, this state park includes sweeping views across a deep gorge. It's a favorite spot for hang gliders—and the spectators who watch them sail out over the valley. Hiking trails, tennis courts, a pool, picnic areas, and waterfalls are also on the grounds. The park is open daily, 7 A.M.–10 P.M..

Etowah Indian Mounds State Historic Site

813 Indian Mounds Road
Cartersville
(770) 387-3747

This Mississippian Indian site with ceremonial mounds was used from 1000 to 1500 A.D. Some of the mounds have been fitted with stairs for visitors to climb; the tallest is sixty-three feet. A museum houses artifacts unearthed in the area. Hours are Tuesday through Saturday, 9 A.M.–5 P.M.; Sunday, 2 P.M.–5:30 P.M. Admission is $3 adults; $2 ages six through eighteen; under six, free.

New Echota State Historic Site

1211 Chatsworth Highway
Calhoun
(706) 624-1321

New Echota was the Cherokee nation's capital until the tribe's forced relocation in 1838 (also known as the "Trail of Tears"). Original and reproduction buildings give a glimpse of life in the early 1800s. The site is open Tuesday through Saturday, 9 A.M.–5 P.M.; Sunday, 2 P.M.–5:30 P.M. Admission is $3 adults; $2 students; age five and under free.

Oak Hill

2277 Martha Berry Highway
Mount Berry
(800) 220-5504
www.berry.edu/oakhill

The 1847 mansion of Martha Berry, a nationally recognized educator and founder of Berry College, is surrounded by lavish gardens, nature trails, and a museum of memorabilia from the educator's life. Oak Hill is open Monday through Saturday, 10 A.M.–5 P.M.; Sunday, 1 P.M.– 5 P.M. Admission is $5 adults; $3 children.

Red Top Mountain State Park
781 Red Top Mountain Road
Cartersville
(800) 864-7275

Open daily, 7 A.M. –10 P.M., this 1,950-acre park offers swimming, fishing, and hiking. A thirty-three-room lodge and restaurant includes cottages and a marina.

Rock City Gardens
1400 Patten Road
Lookout Mountain
(800) 854-0675

www.seerockcity.com

Those "See Rock City" bird feeders all over Atlanta came from this fourteen-acre attraction of natural rock formations. Suck your tummy in while passing through the "fat man's squeeze," then see how many states you can spot from the overhang atop Lookout Mountain. The gardens are open daily, 8:30 A.M.–6 P.M. Admission ranges from $4.95 to $8.95.

Weinman Mineral Museum
51 Mineral Museum Drive
Cartersville
(770) 386-0576

See gems, minerals, and rocks from Georgia and around the world here. The museum also holds exhibits about mining in the area and the state. Open Tuesday through Saturday, 10 A.M.–4:30 P.M.; Sunday, 1 P.M.–4:30 P.M. Admission is $3.50 adults; $2.50 children.

City Fact

New home sales have been brisk in the Midtown area of the city, where more than 300 properties sold for an average of $210,326 in 1998.

NORTHEAST MOUNTAINS

The northeast mountains are an outdoor lover's dream. Packed with places to play, hike, boat, swim, and fish, they make it easy to see why the traffic backs up along I-85 on every warm weekend. But the interstate accesses only a small portion of this area, where the predominant roads are two-lane mountain trails past waterfalls and breathtaking views. Most of these destinations are less than a two-hour drive from Atlanta, but be prepared to go slowly along the steep and winding roads.

For detailed information about Georgia's northeastern regions, contact one of the following:

Alpine Helen-White County
(800) 858-8027

www.helenga.org

Banks County
(800) 638-5004

bccvb@aol.com

Dahlonega-Lumpkin County
(800) 231-5543

www.dahlonega.org

Gainesville-Hall County
(770) 536-5209

www.ghcc.com

Rabun County
(706) 782-4812

www.gamountain.com/rabun

Taccoa-Stephens County
(706) 886-2132

tocoaga@alltel.net

Towns County
(706) 896-4966

Amicalola Falls State Park
418 Amicalola Falls Lodge Road
Dawsonville
(706) 265-8888

The crown jewel of this park is the 729-foot waterfall. Hiking, trout fishing, and camping are also available. The park is open daily, 7 A.M.–10 P.M.

Anna Ruby Falls
Georgia Highway 356
Helen
(706) 878-3574

A half-mile trail through the Chattahoochee National Forest leads to these twin waterfalls. Make the trek any day, 9 A.M.– 8 P.M.

Babyland General Hospital

73 West Underwood Street
Cleveland
(706) 865-2171

Kids still go crazy for Cabbage Patch dolls, and at this special turn-of-the-century "hospital" you can watch the newest ones come into the world. The hospital also keeps the dolls' "adoption" records. There's no charge for tours, offered Monday through Saturday, 9 A.M.–5 P.M.; Sunday, 10 A.M.–5 P.M.

Brasstown Bald

Georgia Highway 180
Blairsville
(706) 745-6928

This is Georgia's highest mountain, 4,784 feet tall. The observation deck, picnic area, and hiking trails are open Memorial Day through October, 10 A.M.–6 P.M. Admission is free, but there's a $2 parking fee.

Chateau Elan Winery and Resort

100 Rue Charlemagne
Braselton
(800) 233-9463

Wine tastings, vineyard tours, fine dining, an authentic Irish pub, a health spa, tennis, golf, and horseback riding are part of the fun at this elegant chateau.

You don't have to be a guest at the resort to take a free tour or sample the latest wines.

Consolidated Gold Mines

185 Consolidated Road
Dahlonega
(706) 864-8473

Tour a real gold mine on a forty-minute underground excursion. Then try your luck at planning for gold and gemstones. The mines are open daily, 10 A.M.–4 P.M. Admission is $10 adults; $5 children.

MOVING TIP

Label moving boxes with contents and the room where they belong. This small step saves time, and, if you're paying movers who charge by the hour, money.

Crawford W. Long Museum

28 College Street
Jefferson
(706) 367-5307

This museum, named for the doctor who developed anesthesia, sits on the site of the first painless operation. Exhibits include an 1840s doctor's office, a general store, and the offices of the Jackson County Historical Society. Hours are Tuesday through Saturday, 10 A.M.–4 P.M. Admission is $2 for adults; $1 for children.

Dahlonega Gold Museum

Public Square
Dahlonega
(706) 864-6962

In 1828, this north Georgia town was the site of the country's first gold rush. The restored county courthouse in the middle of the town retells the history of mining in Georgia. Open Monday through Saturday, 9 A.M.–5 P.M.; Sunday, 10 A.M.–5 P.M. Admission is $2.50 for adults; $1.50 for ages six to eighteen; five and under, free.

Georgia Mountain Museum

311 Green Street
Gainesville
(770) 536-0889

More than twenty-five exhibits tell the story of local and regional history in northeast Georgia. Hours are Tuesday

through Saturday, 10 A.M.–5 P.M. Admission ranges from $1 to $2.

Gold 'n Gem Grubbin' Mine

75 Gold Nugget Lane
Cleveland
(800) 942-4436

www.goldngem@ngweb.net

You can pan for gold year-round, 9 A.M. to 6 P.M., at this one hundred-acre park where miniature golf, fishing, and camping are also available. Admission ranges from $3.50 to $5.

Lake Lanier Islands

6950 Holiday Road
Gainesville
(800) 840-LAKE

This family facility around Lake Lanier includes the Lake Lanier Islands Hilton and the Renaissance Pine Isle Resort, two premier places to stay that also offer golfing, boating, tennis, and swimming.

The Lake Lanier Islands Water Park sits at the water's edge. You'll find paddle boats and canoes on the beach, and water slides, a wave pool, and other wet rides around the grounds. The park opens on weekends in the spring and fall, then daily 10 A.M.–6 P.M. during the summer.

Admission is $21.99 for adults; $13.99 for children.

Museum of the Hills
8590 Main Street
Helen
(706) 878-3140

This charming museum tells the story of Helen, an Alpine town tucked into Georgia's mountains. It also includes the Fantasy Kingdom of Fairytales, an exhibit of the fables' favorite characters. Drop by between 10 A.M. and 9 P.M. Admission is $5 adults; $3.50 children.

Nantahala Outdoor Center
851-A Chattooga Ridge Road
Clayton
(800) 232-7238

Whether you're an experienced rafter or a novice, the center offers a range of rides along the white-water rapids of the Chattooga River. Open daily from mid-March to mid-November; rates range from $42 to $90.

Road Atlanta
5300 Winder Highway
Braselton
(800) 849-RACE

www.roadatlanta.com

Atlanta's premier motor sports center has a 2.54-mile, twelve-turn track that hosts events from motorcycles and vintage cars to sports cars. Admission and hours vary by event.

Sautee Nacoochee Indian Mound
Georgia Highway 75 and Georgia Highway 17
Helen
(706) 878-2181

Experts estimate that this mound dates to 10,000 B.C. Now close to the highway, it's easily viewed for no charge.

Sky Valley Resort
1 Sky Valley
Sky Valley
(800) 437-2416

If you want to ski and can't go far from home, Sky Valley is the only place you'll find in Georgia to do it. The 2,300-acre resort also features plenty of warm-weather activities, from golfing and swimming to tennis and hiking. Elevations range from 3,000 to 4,000 feet. Rates at the resort run from $100 to $250 per person.

Tallulah Gorge State Park
U.S. Highway 441
Tallulah Falls
(706) 754-7979

One of the most breathtaking gorges in the southeast, Tallulah runs two miles at a depth of almost 1,000 feet. Camping, swimming, and hiking trails are available daily from 8 A.M. until dark.

Toccoa Falls
Georgia Highway 17
Toccoa Falls
(706) 886-6831

Check out the 186-foot waterfalls from 9 A.M. to sundown daily.

Unicoi State Park
Georgia Highway 356
Helen
(706) 878-2201

www.gastateparks.org

Just two miles outside of Helen lies this mountain area, which includes trails, camping, tennis, and a lodge. Hours are 7 A.M.–10 P.M. daily.

Georgia Central

Georgia's heartland includes the former capital in Milledgeville, as well as the state's second-largest city, Macon. Much of the area is rural, but rich in history. Macon is easily reached in about two hours by driving south along I-75. But if you're not in a hurry, follow the Antebellum Trail from Athens, home of the University of Georgia, to Macon along less-traveled back roads. This route winds its way through several small towns that were thriving long before the Civil War. Many boast restored town squares and renovated historic homes. Among the highlights are Madison, Eatonton, and Watkinsville. Other charming small cities in the vicinity (also accessible by I-20 east) include two with Hollywood connections: for years, Covington was the set of the television series *In the Heat of the*

CITY FACT

Stop and smell the roses at the Atlanta Botanical Garden, where admission is free every Thursday after 3 P.M.

Night, while Juliette provided the backdrop for the movie *Fried Green Tomatoes.* Oxford, across I-20 from Covington, is home to Oxford College, the original site of Emory University.

All of these destinations are less than a two-hour drive from Atlanta. These local visitor's centers can provide extensive information:

Athens-Clarke County
(800) 653-0603

www.visitathensga.com

Covington-Newton County
(800) 616-8626

www.citybreeze.com

Eatonton-Putnam County
(706) 485-7701

www.oconee.com

Macon-Bibb County
(800) 768-3401

www.maconga.org

Madison-Morgan County
(800) 709-7406

www.citybreeze.com

Milledgeville-Baldwin County
(800) 653-1804

www.milledgevillecvb.com

Watkinsville
(706) 769-5197

www.oconeecountry.com

Alice Walker Driving Tour
Eatonton
(706) 485-7701

Drop by the chamber of commerce for a map that leads around the hometown of writer Alice Walker.

Flannery O'Connor Room
N. Clark Street and W. Montgomery Street Milledgeville
(912) 445-4047

Manuscripts and memorabilia from the Georgia writer's life are housed in the Ina D. Russell Library on the campus of Georgia College. There's no charge to stop by Monday through Friday, 9 A.M.–noon and 1 P.M.–4 P.M.

Geri Wayne Emu & Petting Ranch
12818 Alcovy Road Covington
(770) 786-0755

Tours and hayrides around this ranch show off the six-foot emus, pot-bellied pigs, and other creatures. Admission is $5 by appointment.

Georgia Music Hall of Fame
200 Martin Luther King Jr.
Boulevard
Macon
(912) 750-8555

From Little Richard to Otis Redding, the Hall of Fame includes the state's great artists of rock, R&B, jazz, gospel, country, and blues with more than eighty hours of music and videos. Open Monday through Saturday, 9 A.M.–4:30 P.M.; Sunday, 1 P.M.–4:30 P.M. Admission is $8 for adults; $3.50 for children ages four through sixteen.

Georgia Sports Hall of Fame
301 Cherry Street
Macon
(912) 752-1585

www.gshf.org

Drive a NASCAR simulator, kick field goals, and shoot hoops at this museum, which honors Georgia's sports legends, both professional and amateur. Hours are Monday through Saturday, 9 A.M.–5 P.M.; Sunday, 1 P.M.–5 P.M. Admission is $6 for adults; $3.50 children ages six to sixteen.

Georgia Museum of Art
90 Carlton Street
Athens
(706) 542-4662

The state's collection includes more than twenty exhibitions annually, as well as a permanent display of seven thousand items. Drop by Tuesday through Saturday, 10 A.M.–5 P.M.; Friday, 10 A.M.–9 P.M.; Sunday, 1 P.M.– 5 P.M. There is no admission fee.

Hay House
934 Georgia Avenue
Macon
(912) 742-8155

Built between 1855 and 1859, this antebellum mansion is home to the Georgia Trust for Historic Preservation. Tours are $6 for adults and $1 for children, and are offered every thirty minutes between 10 A.M. and 4:30 P.M. daily.

Jarrell Plantation
Jarrell Plantation Road
Juliette
(912) 986-5172

More than twenty buildings dot this restored plantation, which dates to 1847 and houses an extensive collection of farm tools, machinery, and family artifacts. Hours are Tuesday through Saturday, 9 A.M.–5 P.M.; Sunday, 2 P.M.–5:30 P.M. Admission is $3.50 for adults and $2 for children ages six through eighteen.

Lake Tobesofkee

6600 Moseley-Dixon Road
Macon
(912) 474-8770

This 1,750-acre lake is surrounded by campgrounds and
parks with playgrounds, picnic
pavilions, and fishing spots. A
protected beach is perfect for
swimming. The lake area is open
daily, 6 A.M.–9:30 P.M.
Admission is $3, with children
under six free.

Madison-Morgan Cultural Center

434 South Main Street
Madison
(706) 342-4743

Housed in a former grade school
built in 1895, the cultural center
is this Victorian town's heart. It
includes a theater, history
museum, art galleries, and a
turn-of-the-century classroom.
Hours are Tuesday through
Saturday, 10 A.M.–4:30 P.M.;
Sunday, 2 P.M.–5 P.M. Admission
is $3 for adults and $1 for children.

Museum of Arts and Sciences

4182 Forsyth Road
Macon
(912) 477-3232

You'll find a planetarium, science
exhibits, hiking trails, interactive

displays, and a two-story banyan
tree on the grounds of the
museum, which is open Monday
through Thursday and Saturday,
9 A.M.–5 P.M.; Friday, 9 A.M.–9
P.M.; Sunday, 1 P.M.–5 P.M. Tickets
are $2 to $5.

Old Governor's Mansion

120 South Clark Street
Milledgeville
(912) 445-4545

A National Historic Landmark,
this building—which was the
home of nine Georgia gover-
nors—dates to 1839. Tours are
given at the top of each hour,
Tuesday through Saturday from
10 A.M.–4 P.M.; Sunday, 2 P.M.–4
P.M. Admission is $5 adults; $2
children.

Old State Capitol Building

201 East Greene Street
Milledgeville
(800) 653-1804

Milledgeville was the state capitol from 1803 to 1868, and its
Gothic-style statehouse now
houses the Georgia Military
College. Visitors may tour the
grounds daily at no charge.

Rock Eagle Effigy

Highway 41 N
Eatonton
(706) 484-2831

For more than five thousand years, this rock outcropping—which resembles a bird with outspread wings—has fascinated visitors. Drive by during daylight hours for the best view.

CITY FACT

It will soon be easier than ever to walk to the train. Plans are underway to include more residential housing in the mix of projects going up around the Lenox, Brookhaven, Lindbergh, Sandy Springs, and Ashby stations.

State Botanical Gardens of Georgia
2450 South Milledge Avenue
Athens
(706) 542-1244

The grounds of this beautiful garden spot include eleven plant collections and a conservatory. Take in the sights daily, 8 A.M.–8 P.M., or wander through the visitors' center Monday through Saturday, 9 A.M.–4:30 P.M.; Sunday, 11:30 A.M.–4:30 P.M. Admission is free.

Tubman African American Museum
340 Walnut Street
Macon
(912) 743-8544

This is the state's largest museum dedicated to the history and culture of African Americans. Open Monday through Friday, 9 A.M.–5 P.M.; Saturday, 10 A.M.–5 P.M.; Sunday, 2 P.M.–5 P.M. A $3 donation is requested.

Uncle Remus Museum
U.S. Highway 441 S
Eatonton
(706) 485-6856

Built from two log cabins, the museum houses memorabilia belonging to author Joel Chandler Harris and his Uncle Remus stories. Hours are Monday through Saturday, 10 A.M.–5 P.M.; Sunday, 2 P.M.–5 P.M.; closed Tuesdays, September through May. Visitors are invited to make a donation.

Warner Robins Air Force Base and the Museum of Aviation

Highway 247 and Russell Parkway
Warner Robins
(912) 926-6870

The SR-71 Blackbird, the fastest plane on earth, resides here, along with ninety other historic aircraft and missiles. Exhibits retell aviation contributions to World War II, Korea, Desert Storm, and more. The Georgia Aviation Hall of Fame is also located there. The free museum is open daily, 9 A.M.–5 P.M.

South and West

It's about a three-hour drive due south to Thomasville or southwest to Columbus, two towns where history and beauty abound. Columbus sits at the end of I-185, a spur of I-85 that streaks past Pine Mountain and the lavish Callaway Gardens attraction and Warm Springs, the home of Franklin Delano Roosevelt's "Little White House." Both attractions are well worth the detour.

En route to Thomasville along I-75, you'll come across several areas that offer a glimpse into the life of a small Southern town. The quaint squares and shops of Albany, Vienna, Cordele, or Moultrie, or the race track at Hawkinsville, make great side trips. In Thomasville, Georgia's "City of Roses," amble through the public rose gardens and a restored Victorian downtown district. Andersonville, the Civil War camp where thousands of Union soldiers perished, is a moving monument to the horrors of war. Nearby is Plains, the boyhood home of President Jimmy Carter.

For more details, contact the following welcome centers:

Albany
(912) 434-8700

Americus-Sumter County
(912) 924-2646

www.americustourism.com

Bainbridge
(912) 246-4774

www.bainbridgega.com

Columbus
(800) 999-1613

www.columbusga.com

MOVING TIP

Be prepared to pay extras for moving large or unusual items, such as pianos, waterbeds and antiques.

Pine Mountain
(800) 441-3502

Plains
(912) 824-7477

Thomasville
(912) 227-7099

www.thomasvillega.com.

Warm Springs
(800) 337-1927

Andersonville National Historic Site
Highway 49
Andersonville
(912) 924-0343

The 475-acre site includes two museums and driving routes through one of the Civil War's largest prisoner of war camps.

A national POW museum and cemetery is on the grounds. Open daily, 8 A.M.–5 P.M. Admission is free.

Callaway Gardens
Highway 27
Pine Mountain
(800) CALLAWAY

A 14,000-acre nature-lover's paradise! There's almost too much to see and do in one day. Highlights include the butterfly greenhouse, canoeing, hiking, paddle boats, swimming, tennis, waterskiing. The property includes a lodge and rental cabins, sixty-three holes of golf, and special events each month. Hours are 9 A.M.–6 P.M. daily. An all-inclusive admission is $10 for adults, thirteen and older; $5 for children ages six to twelve.

Coca-Cola Space Science Center
701 Front Avenue
Columbus
(706) 649-1470

An observatory, theater, and various hands-on activities are part of this free center, open Tuesday through Friday, 10 A.M.–4 P.M.; Saturday, 1:30 P.M.–9 P.M.; Sunday, 1:30 P.M.–4 P.M.

Habitat for Humanity— International Headquarters

419 Church Street
Americus
(800) 422-4828

The world headquarters for the affordable housing organization includes a free museum that's open Monday through Friday, 8 A.M.–4 P.M.

Hollywood Connection

1683 Whittlesey Road
Columbus
(706) 571-3456

This family entertainment center boasts ten theaters with stadium seating, a skating rink, rides, laser tag, miniature golf, and an arcade. Sunday through Thursday, 11:30 A.M.–9 P.M.; Friday and Saturday, 11:30 A.M.–midnight. Tickets vary by activity; it's $5 to skate and $7 to see a movie; individual amusement rides run from $1.50 to $5.

Jimmy Carter National Historic Site

300 North Bond Street
Plains
(912) 824-4104

The restored Plains High School is now a free museum that tells the story of the thirty-ninth president, Jimmy Carter. Daily, 9 A.M.–5 P.M.

Little White House

401 Little White House Road
Warm Springs
(706) 655-5870

Built in 1932 for President Franklin D. Roosevelt, this modest white home was close to the therapeutic springs where he was treated for polio. The rooms are maintained as they were on the day Roosevelt died there. A museum on the grounds includes rare footage of the handicapped president and his hand-controlled automobiles and wheelchairs. Hours are 9 A.M. –5 P.M. daily. Admission is $5 adults; $2 for children aged six to eighteen.

Pebble Hill Plantation

Highway 319 S
Thomasville
(912) 226-2344

Built as a shooting lodge for wealthy owners, this house museum has collections of art, antiques, vintage cars, and carriages. Open Tuesday through Saturday, 10 A.M.–5 P.M.; Sunday, 1 P.M.–5 P.M. Admission to the grounds is $3, and visitors are invited to wander at their leisure. House tours are $7 for those thirteen and older; $5 for children.

Woodruff Museum of Civil War Naval History

U.S. 280 and Veterans Parkway
Columbus
(706) 327-9798

Relics and artifacts from the Confederate Navy are on display, along with hulls of the ironclad *Jackson* and gunboat *Chattahoochee*. It's free Tuesday through Friday, 10 A.M.–5 P.M.; 1 P.M.–5 P.M. Saturday and Sunday.

The Coast

You've got about a five-hour drive before you can hit the white sand of Georgia's beaches. But the history, fun, and beauty of the coast makes it worth the ride. Golf courses also abound, along with a wealth of restaurants, cushy resorts, campgrounds, and quaint bed-and-breakfast inns. And of course, there's Savannah, the town made famous for its "Garden of Good and Evil," where shady squares are lined with mansions. For information about places to stay and see, call the following:

Augusta
(706) 724-4067
www.augustaga.org

Brunswick Golden Isles
(912) 265-0629
www.bgivb.com

St. Simons Island
(912) 638-9014

Savannah
(912) 944-0460
www.savcvb.com

CITY FACT

Coldwell Banker/Buckhead Brokers offers a home price comparison guide that looks at real estate prices in Atlanta and the U.S. It also gives you an idea of how much home you can buy in Atlanta, depending on the area of the country you're moving from. For a copy, call (888) 574-SOLD.

Waycross

(912) 283-3742

www.gacoast.com

Bonaventure Cemetery

330 Bonaventure Road
Savannah
(912) 233-4709

The riverfront burial place of statesmen and soldiers was immortalized in the book *Midnight in the Garden of Good and Evil.* Visitors may wander the grounds from dawn to dusk.

Fort Frederica

Frederica Road
St. Simons Island
(912) 638-3639

The British built this fort in 1736 to keep out Spanish invaders. Tour on foot or by car every day, 9 A.M.–5 P.M. Admission is $4 per carload.

Jekyll Island

Jekyll Island Causeway
(912) 635-2626

www.jekyllisland.com

From 1886 to 1942, Jekyll was the winter home of America's wealthiest families. The Rockefellers, Goodyears, Morgans, and others built mansions that today are part of the island's historic district. You'll also find public beaches, hotels, a water park, golf courses, tennis courts, and a shopping area on the island.

Okefenokee National Wildlife Refuge

Route 2
Folkston
(912) 496-7836

Walk or boat around this wildlife preserve, which includes a restored homestead, animal displays, picnic facilities, an observation tower, and a 4,000-foot boardwalk. Open daily, 7 A.M.–7:30 P.M. Admission is $5 per carload.

River Street Riverboat

9 E. River Street
Savannah
(912) 232-6404

The *Savannah River Queen*, a 325-passenger boat, cruises the river with dinner, entertainment, and Sunday brunch. Prices vary by activity and day.

Beyond Georgia

BIRMINGHAM

A two-hour drive along I-20 west takes visitors to Birmingham, Alabama. The state capital hosts year-round events that attract crowds. It's an entertaining place for a relaxing weekend getaway. And it's in the Central Time Zone, so you'll be an hour ahead of the crowd back home. For more information, contact the Birmingham Convention and Visitors Bureau, (800) 458-8085.

Alabama Jazz Hall of Fame

1140 5th Avenue
Birmingham
(205) 254-2731

Local jazz artists, including Birmingham's own Erskine Hawkins, are honored in this hall. Open Tuesday through Saturday, 10 A.M.–5 P.M.; Sunday, 1 P.M.–5 P.M. There's no admission fee.

Birmingham Botanical Gardens

2612 Lane Park Road
Birmingham
(205) 414-3900

Take a stroll through gardens bursting with blooms of native plants. Open every day, dawn to dusk, and it's free.

Birmingham Civil Rights Institute

520 16th Street
Birmingham
(205) 328-9696

Learn about the struggles and events that brought Martin Luther King Jr. to town to help the cause of Alabamians fighting for civil rights. Hours are Tuesday through Saturday, 10 A.M.–5 P.M.; Sunday, 1 P.M.–5 P.M. Admission is free.

Birmingham Museum of Art

2000 8th Avenue
Birmingham
(205) 254-2565

A sculpture garden and collections of American, Oriental, and African art are free to the public, Tuesday–Saturday, 10 A.M.–5 P.M.; Sunday, noon–5 P.M.

Birmingham Race Course

1000 John Rogers Drive
Birmingham
(205) 838-7500

You can place your bets on grey-hound races and simulcasts of horse racing events from around the country at this course on the eastern edge of town.

Sloss Furnaces

20 32nd Street
Birmingham
(205) 324-1911

An industrial museum dedicated to the city's iron and steel roots, the Furnaces now serves as a venue for music events. Take a free tour Tuesday through Saturday, 10 A.M.–4 P.M.; Sunday, from noon to 4 P.M.

CHATTANOOGA

The city immortalized in the big-band song lies two hours north of metro Atlanta on I-75. Another great weekend getaway, Chattanooga offers shopping, dining, sightseeing, and outdoor activities for all ages. Detailed information is available from the visitors' center, (800) 322-3344, or *www.chattanoogafun.com.*

Chattanooga Choo-Choo

1400 Market Street
Chattanooga
(800) TRACK 29

www.choochoo.com

The old train station is now a mall surrounded by gardens, antique rail cars, shops, and restaurants. Make reservations ahead to stay or dine in a restored train car at the Chattanooga Holiday Inn. Open-air trolley travel around the complex for a nominal charge.

MOVING TIP

The state of Georgia regulates what moving companies may charge within the state. Those prices must be itemized in the moving agreement.

Creative Discovery Museum
4th and Chestnut Streets
Chattanooga
(423) 756-2738

The kids will stay busy on a dinosaur dig, puttering in the inventor's workshop, drawing in the artist's studio, and making music in a recording studio. Open daily, 10 A.M.–6 P.M. in the summer, with scaled-back hours in the fall and winter. Prices are $7.95 for adults; $4.95 for children ages two to twelve.

Ruby Falls
1720 South Scenic Highway
Chattanooga
(423) 821-2544

A tour guide leads the way 1,100 feet into the heart of Lookout Mountain, along a trail crowded with rock formations. The trek ends in the cavern where the 145-foot Ruby Falls cascade. The cave is open 8 A.M.–9 P.M. in the summer; 8 A.M.–6 P.M. in the winter. Tickets are $9.50 for adults; $4.50 for children ages three to twelve.

Tennessee Aquarium
1 Broad Street
Chattanooga
(800) 262-0695

This is one of the largest aquariums in the world, boasting six thousand species of water animals in their natural habitats. Hours are daily from 9 A.M.–6 P.M. Admission is $11.95 for adults; $6.50 for children ages three to twelve.

CHAPTER 8

Volunteer and Community Involvement

Settling into a new job, hunting for a place to live, and finding your way around a strange town can fill most of the hours in a day. But there's good news: The transition period eventually ends, and you may find yourself looking for ways to get involved and make new friends. One of the best ways to do that is to volunteer.

Atlanta is a very giving town. Through the strong community of churches, social service organizations, and philanthropic agencies, opportunities abound to share your energy, insight, and talent. The city features an array of groups that support various causes and concerns, from serving lunch to elderly shut-ins and people with AIDS to helping troubled teens with homework. The vast majority of these organizations are constantly in need of helping hands. You can volunteer by contacting the agency directly or through the United Way of Metro Atlanta, which sponsors a 211 hotline to hook up volunteers with nonprofit groups looking for supporters. (You can also reach the United Way's main office at 100 Edgewood Avenue at 404-614-1000.)

Most of Atlanta's large churches sponsor hundreds of community outreach programs. Through the church of your choice, you can get involved in philanthropic programs with folks of similar ages and backgrounds.

MOVING TIP

Don't leave packing to the last minute! The moving experts suggest tackling at least one box a day beginning a month prior to the big day.

Atlanta also abounds with cultural organizations that thrive through volunteer-supported activities. Whether it's conducting a tour of the Fox Theatre for the Atlanta Preservation Center or organizing the annual outdoor gala at Zoo Atlanta, there's plenty of work to do!

And if you don't have the time to roll up your sleeves for hands-on volunteering, there's usually some event going on each week that combines partying with a purpose. Wine-tasting parties, dinners, socials, fun runs, tours, and auctions that raise funds for a variety of worthy causes abound around town.

Here's some information on various nonprofit groups that welcome volunteers.

AID Atlanta
1438 West Peachtree Street
(404) 872-0600

www.aidatlanta.org

The city's leading AIDS support group raises funds and awareness through a variety of volunteer projects.

The Alliance Theatre
1280 Peachtree Street
(404) 733-4650

www.alliancetheatre.org

The auxiliaries supporting the Alliance plan fundraisers from auctions to galas.

American Red Cross
1925 Monroe Drive
(404) 881-9800

www.redcross.org

From blood drives to emergency response services, the American Red Cross always needs volunteers to help in a variety of functions.

Atlanta Botanical Garden

1345 Piedmont Avenue
(404) 876-5859

www.atlantabotanicalgarden.org

Children's programs, tours, the gift shop, and a variety of fundraising events run with the help of garden-loving volunteers.

Atlanta Community Food Bank

970 Jefferson Street
(404) 892-9822

Food from area stores and restaurants is donated to the Food Bank, which redistributes it to people living in poverty. Volunteers sort and pack food boxes.

Atlanta Day Shelter for Women and Children

1039 Marietta Street
(404) 876-2894

This shelter provides basic necessities for women and their children and helps them on the path to a productive life. Volunteers help in the office, sorting clothes, running children's programs, and offering job counseling.

Atlanta History Center

130 West Paces Ferry Road
(404) 814-4000

www.atlhist.org

There's a year-round calendar of events at the History Center that keeps volunteers busy, from working in the gift shop to assisting with tours. The Center is also home to the Swan Coach House gift shop and art gallery, staffed by volunteers who are members of the Forward Arts Foundation.

Atlanta Humane Society

981 Howell Mill Road
(404) 875-5331

www.hsma-atl.org

Volunteers pitch in at the Society's animal shelter, organize fundraising events, and sponsor animal adoption clinics.

Atlanta Interfaith AIDS Network

1053 Juniper Street
(404) 874-8686

www.whosoever.org

Several faith communities have formed this coalition to serve people with HIV/AIDS. Volunteers assist in a variety of social and support services, from an annual fundraising gala to lunch at a day center for HIV victims.

The Atlanta Junior Chamber of Commerce

1401 Peachtree Street
(404) 881-1676

Young professionals from twenty-one to forty years of age are invited to join this community-service organization, which sponsors the annual Empty Stocking Fund for needy children.

The Atlanta Opera

728 W. Peachtree Street
(404) 881-8801

www.atlantaopera.org

Opera supporters work behind the scenes to raise funds and awareness about this cultural art form.

The Atlanta Preservation Center

537 Peachtree Street
(404) 876-2040

www.preserveatlanta.com

Learn about Atlanta's past as a tour guide for the APC, which offers walking tours of the city's historic neighborhoods and buildings.

The Atlanta Symphony Orchestra

1293 Peachtree Street
(404) 733-4900

www.atlantasymphony.org

Among various events organized by volunteers is the ASO's annual home tour.

Atlanta Union Mission

165 Alexander Street
(404) 588-4000

www.aum-atl.org

Hot meals, night shelters, and an array of rehabilitative programs are offered by the Mission, located in the heart of downtown.

Big Brothers/Big Sisters of America

1410 Loch Lomond Trail
(404) 629-2000

www.bbbsa.org

Volunteer youth mentors are paired with boys and girls across the city.

Boys and Girls Clubs of Metro Atlanta

100 Edgewood Avenue
(404) 527-7100

www.bgca.org

Educational and motivational programs for kids of all ages are supported by volunteers. Clubs are located in several metro counties as well as in Atlanta.

The Bridge Family Center

1559 Johnson Road
(404) 792-0070

Homeless and runaway teens find residential treatment at the Bridge, where volunteers run school and mentoring classes.

Buckhead Christian Ministry

2461 Peachtree Road
(404) 239-0058

BCM provides emergency financial assistance to homeless and working poor. Volunteers stock the BCM food pantry and thrift store and counsel clients.

Capitol Area Mosaic

341 Kelly Street
(404) 524-1751

Aimed at residents in the Capitol Homes area in southwest Atlanta, the Mosaic provides education, economic, social, and spiritual enrichment opportunities.

Carpenter's House

2355 Bolton Road
(404) 350-9691

Volunteers participate in therapeutic art and poetry groups at Carpenter's House, where men recovering from drug and alcohol addiction make the transition to a productive lifestyle.

Central Night Shelter

201 Washington Street
(404) 659-0274

Central Presbyterian Church downtown operates a volunteer-supported night shelter and dinner program for homeless men.

CITY FACT

The Atlanta metro area has three area codes: 770, 404, and 678. Every local call—even if it's to the neighbor down the block—must include the three-digit code.

Childkind

828 West Peachtree Street
(404) 892-8313

www.childkind.org

Childkind provides daycare, education, and support programs for medically fragile children, many with HIV/AIDS.

Children's Healthcare of Atlanta

1405 Clifton Road
(404) 325-6000

www.choa.org

This group of children's hospital volunteers sponsors fundraising events throughout the year, including the Festival of Trees and the annual Christmas Parade.

CITY FACT

You can be part of the CNN action as an audience member in the station's Talk Back Live program. To reserve free tickets, call (800) 410-4CNN.

CHRIS Home

1447 Peachtree Street
(404) 876-2768

This group home provides support for children from six to seventeen years old. Adults are needed for mentoring programs.

Christmas in April Atlanta

70 Courtland Street
(404) 577-2350

www.christmasinapril.org

This program engages the energies of volunteers to rehabilitate housing of the elderly and disabled. The projects usually extend over the last two weekends of April.

Clifton Night Hospitality

369 Connecticut Avenue
(404) 373-3253

This facility provides shelter and hospitality for thirty homeless men every day. The shelter also supports Joe's Place, a transitional housing program that uses volunteers in life-skill classes, counseling, and mentoring.

Couples' Shelter at the Temple

1589 Peachtree Street
(404) 873-1731

The Jewish Temple in Midtown supports a shelter and dinner program for couples.

Fairhaven Inn

(770) 457-4673

Fairhaven provides confidential crisis intervention and housing for battered women and their children.

Families First

1105 West Peachtree Street
(404) 853-2800

www.familiesfirst.org

This child service and family counseling center helps strengthen families. Volunteers are particularly needed in the pregnancy prevention campaign.

FCS Community Economic Development

750 Glenwood Avenue
(404) 627-4304

FCS maintains two resale stores, Home Resources & Furniture Center and the Family Store. These two outlets provide employment training and low-cost goods and services to the community.

Habitat for Humanity Atlanta

419 Memorial Drive
(404) 223-5180

www.habitat.org

One of the metro area's largest volunteer organizations, Habitat builds affordable housing for low-income families. Trained builders teach volunteers everything they need to know about putting a house together from the ground up. In addition to Atlanta proper, Habitat groups are active in most of the metro area counties.

Hands On Atlanta

931 Monroe Drive
(404) 872-2252

Volunteers fan out across the city to work on cleanup and improvement projects in parks and neighborhoods.

High Museum of Art

1280 Peachtree Street
(404) 733-4400

www.high.org

Volunteers work throughout the museum and support a number of fundraising projects. The Young Careers organization involves young professionals in social and cultural events.

The Junior League of Atlanta

3154 Northside Parkway
(404) 261-7799

The League sponsors a variety of educational, civic, and cultural programs across the city.

Kiwanis Club of Atlanta

2211 Atlanta Gas Light Tower
(404) 521-1443

www.commandcorp.com

This social and civic group supports several citywide programs.

Life Span

3003 Howell Mill Road
(404) 237-7307

Life Span provides services to adults age fifty-five and older, and seeks volunteers to assist with transportation, minor home repairs, and home visits.

MOVING TIP

Never place flammable and perishable items in storage!

Literacy Volunteers of America

1776 Peachtree Street
(404) 239-9104

www.literacyvolunteers.org

Pitch in to help adults learn to read. Volunteers also conduct classes in English as a second language.

Metro Atlanta Chamber of Commerce

235 International Boulevard
(404) 880-9000

www.metroatlantachamber.com

One of the city's leading business networks, the Chamber of Commerce supports a variety of causes. One of the most successful is the Partners in Education program, which pairs companies with public schools and encourages employees to volunteer in the classrooms.

Metro Atlanta Furniture Bank

538 Permalume Place
(404) 355-8530

The Furniture Bank redistributes new and used furniture and household items to formerly homeless families moving out of shelters and into permanent housing.

Nicholas House

1790 Lavista Road
(404) 633-8386

This transitional housing facility provides evening meals and a place to stay, as well as tutoring, to homeless families.

Partnership Against Domestic Violence

1475 Peachtree Street
(404) 870-9600

Volunteers man crisis hotlines for victims of domestic violence.

Pets Are Loving Support

1438 West Peachtree Street
(404) 876-7257

www.palsatlanta.org

Volunteers care for the pets of people with HIV/AIDS.

Prison Ministries With Women

465 Boulevard
(404) 622-4314

Volunteers participate in programs to support women in prison and their families.

Project Open Hand Atlanta

176 Ottley Drive
(404) 872-6947

www.projectopenhand.org

Volunteers package and deliver meals to people with HIV disabilities throughout the metro area.

Rotary Club of Buckhead

235 Peachtree Street
(404) 522-2767

This civic organization supports a variety of philanthropic and educational causes.

The Salvation Army

740 Marietta Street
(404) 522-9783

www.redshield.org

The Salvation Army operates several thrift stores, community centers, and emergency services programs around the metro area.

Shepherd Center

2020 Peachtree Road
(404) 352-2020

www.shepherd.org

This hospital, specializing in the treatment of spinal injuries, recruits volunteers to help with patient programs as well as fundraising events.

Support to Employment Project

236 Forsyth Street
(404) 577-7312

S.T.E.P. provides assistance and training to those seeking serious employment. Volunteers help with career mentoring and office management.

Zoo Atlanta

800 Cherokee Street
(404) 624-5600

www.zooatlanta.org

Help out with children's activities, fundraisers, and tours at one of the Southeast's leading zoos.

Finding the Essentials

CHAPTER 9

Important Places to Know

Getting settled in your new town requires more than finding a place to live. You don't want to give up Friday night videos and doing the laundry! Here's a handy list of key locations where you'll find what you need to get life back to normal.

Appliance Stores

Appliance Showcase
2235 Cheshire Bridge Road
(404) 728-0036

Best Buy
1201 Hammond Drive
(770) 392-0454

Bob Carroll Appliance Co.
2122 N. Decatur Road
Decatur
(404) 624-2411

Roberds Inc.
2755 Piedmont Road
(404) 467-9363

Sewell Appliance Sales
6125 Roswell Road
(404) 255-0640

Banks

CITY **FACT**

Atlanta is home to one of the country's leading jazz stations. WCLK, 91.9 FM, is a public radio affiliate based at Clark-Atlanta University.

Buckhead Bank
3520 Piedmont Road
(404) 261-0700

Capitol City Bank & Trust
2358 Cascade Road
(404) 755-4254

562 Lee Street
(404) 756-0477

Citizens Trust Bank
2840 East Point Street
(404) 768-0920

Bank of America
411 Flat Shoals Avenue
(404) 330-0750

www.bankofamerica.com

1700 Monroe Drive
(404) 881-3574

600 Peachtree Street
(404) 607-4850

3116 Peachtree Road
(404) 262-6340

133 Peachtree Street
(404) 330-0755

712 W. Peachtree Street
(404) 881-6879

75 Piedmont Avenue
(404) 659-5959

Colonial Bank
3379 Peachtree Road
(404) 261-2612

Fidelity National Bank
235 Peachtree Street
(404) 524-1171

3490 Piedmont Road
(404) 814-8114

First Union Bank
921 Abernathy Boulevard
(404) 865-2140

www.firstunion.com

55 Park Place
(404) 865-3410

241 Peachtree Street
(404) 865-5480

999 Peachtree Street
(404) 865-3010

Regions Bank
6637 Roswell Road
(404) 255-8550

3655 Roswell Road
(404) 233-1199

SouthTrust Bank
874 Abernathy Boulevard
(404) 752-8400

www.southtrust.com

2318 Cascade Road
(404) 752-8410

2349 Cheshire Bridge Road
(404) 321-3008

79 West Paces Ferry Road
(404) 841-2720

Wachovia
1878 Piedmont Road
(404) 841-7816

4454 Roswell Road
(404) 851-2960

1330 Spring Street
(404) 853-1975

Cable TV Services

BellSouth Entertainment
660 Hembree Parkway
Roswell
(770) 360-4640

CableVision
3075 Breckinridge Boulevard
Duluth
(770) 806-7070

Comcast Communications
3425 Malone Drive
Chamblee
(770) 451-4785

www.connectedtoyou.com

MediaOne
2841 Greenbriar Parkway
(404) 349-2657

Time Warner Cable
923 Elnora Drive
Marietta
(770) 926-0334
www.twonline.com

Car Rentals

Accent Rent-a-Car
4208 Peachtree Road
(404) 264-1773

Alamo Rent-a-Car
188 Piedmont Road
(404) 768-4161
www.alamo.com

Atlanta Rent-a-Car
2800 Campbellton Road
(404) 344-1060

Avis
143 Courtland Street
(404) 659-4814
www.avis.com

Budget Rent-a-Car
140 Courtland Street
(404) 530-3000
www.budget.com

Car Temps
2980 Piedmont Road
(404) 816-6770

Enterprise
3088 Piedmont Road
(404) 261-7337
www.enterprise.com

Hertz
3300 Lenox Road
(404) 237-2660
www.hertz.com

Southern
1120 Abernathy Boulevard
(404) 753-6100

Thrifty
100 Courtland Street
(404) 524-2843

Car Repair

Bavarian Imports
1505 Howell Mill Road
(404) 351-2002

Beaudry Ford
141 Piedmont Avenue
(404) 659-3673

Brookwood Auto Service
1776 Peachtree Street
(404) 876-7766

Decatur Automotive Center
2928 East Ponce de Leon Avenue
Decatur
(404) 373-3897

Firestone Car Service
3369 Lenox Road
(404) 261-8561

2460 North Druid Hills Road
(404) 325-8802

NAPA AutoCare Centers
2810 Clairmont Road
(404) 636-0333

Penske Auto Center
2581 Piedmont Road
(404) 261-5390

Pep Boys Automotive Centers
2399 Piedmont Road
(404) 231-0032

Precision Tune Auto Care
1689 Howell Mill Road
(404) 351-7611

Road Britannia Foreign Car Service
3190 Roswell Road
(404) 266-1699

Tune-Up Clinic
2778 Clairmont Road
(404) 325-3440

230 Moreland Avenue
(404) 659-6225

Churches

AFRICAN METHODIST EPISCOPAL

Big Bethel AME
220 Auburn Avenue
(404) 659-0248

St. Philip AME
240 Candler Road
(404) 371-0749

St. Mark AME
3605 Campbellton Road
(404) 349-6800

BAPTIST

Druid Hills Baptist
1085 Ponce de Leon Avenue
(404) 874-5721

Northside Drive Baptist
3100 Northside Drive
(404) 237-8621

Ebenezer Baptist
407 Auburn Avenue
(404) 688-7263

Second Ponce de Leon Baptist
2715 Peachtree Road
(404) 266-8111

First Baptist Church of Atlanta
4400 North Peachtree Road
(770) 234-8300

Wieuca Road Baptist
3626 Peachtree Road
(404) 814-4460

First Baptist Church of Decatur
308 Clairemont Avenue
Decatur
(404) 373-1653

www.mindspring.com/
~fbcdecatur

Zion Hill Baptist
815 Lynhurst Drive
(404) 691-8025

CATHOLIC

Cathedral of Christ the King
2699 Peachtree Rod
(404) 233-2145

Holy Spirit
4465 Northside Drive
(404) 252-4513

Our Lady of Lourdes
25 Boulevard
(404) 522-6776

Sacred Heart
353 Peachtree Street
(404) 522-6800

Shrine of the Immaculate Conception
48 Martin Luther King Jr. Drive
(404) 521-1866

MOVING TIP

Instead of moving it, donate it! Unwanted items taken to local charities or groups such as the Salvation Army may even qualify for a tax deduction.

CHRISTIAN—DISCIPLES OF CHRIST

Brookhaven Christian
4500 Peachtree Road
(404) 237-3030

First Christian Church of Decatur
601 West Ponce de Leon Avenue
Decatur
(404) 378-3621

Peachtree Christian Church
1580 Peachtree Street
(404) 876-5535

CHRISTIAN SCIENCE

Fifth Church of Christ Scientist
1685 Martin Luther King Jr.
Drive
(404) 755-5141

First Church of Christ Scientist
1235 Peachtree Street
(404) 892-7838

CHURCH OF GOD

Mount Paran
2055 Mt. Paran Road
(404) 261-0720

Perimeter North
3878 Chamblee Dunwoody Road
(770) 457-9094

EPISCOPAL

All Saints
634 West Peachtree Street
(404) 881-0835

Church of Our Savior
1068 North Highland Avenue
(404) 872-4169

Cathedral of St. Philip
2744 Peachtree Road
(404) 365-1000

Saint Anne's
3098 Northside Parkway
(404) 237-5589

JEHOVAH'S WITNESSES

Ben Hill
1891 Fairburn Road
(404) 344-3654

Buckhead
258 West Wieuca Road
(404) 255-0030

LATTER DAY SAINTS

Atlanta
1450 Ponce de Leon Avenue
(404) 378-0488

LUTHERAN

Grace Lutheran
1155 North Highland Avenue
(404) 875-5411

Lutheran Church of the Redeemer
731 Peachtree Street
(404) 874-8664

www.redeemer.org

Peachtree Road Lutheran
3686 Peachtree Road
(404) 233-7031

St. Luke Lutheran
3264 Northside Parkway
(404) 237-4413

METHODIST

Ben Hill United Methodist
2099 Fairburn Road
(404) 344-0618

Druid Hills United Methodist
1200 Ponce de Leon Avenue
(404) 377-6481

First United Methodist
360 Peachtree Street
(404) 525-2385

Glenn Memorial United Methodist
1660 North Decatur Road
(404) 634-3936

Northside United Methodist
2799 Northside Drive
(404) 355-6475

www.nsideumc-atl.org

Peachtree Road United Methodist
3180 Peachtree Road
(404) 266-2373

NON-DENOMINATIONAL

Buckhead Community Church
700 Galleria Parkway
(770) 952-8834

PRESBYTERIAN

Central Presbyterian
201 Washington Street
(404) 659-0274

Clifton Presbyterian
369 Connecticut Avenue
(404) 373-3253

Columbia Presbyterian
711 South Columbia Drive
Decatur
(404) 284-2441

Druid Hills Presbyterian
1026 Ponce de Leon Avenue
(404) 875-7591

First Presbyterian of Atlanta
1328 Peachtree Street
(404) 892-8461

Morningside Presbyterian
1411 North Morningside Drive
(404) 876-7396

North Avenue Presbyterian
607 Peachtree Street
(404) 875-0431

Peachtree Presbyterian
3434 Roswell Road
(404) 842-5800

Trinity Presbyterian
3003 Howell Mill Road
(404) 237-6491

QUAKER

Religious Society of Friends
701 West Howard Avenue
Decatur
(404) 377-2474

SEVENTH-DAY ADVENTIST

Berean Seventh-Day
312 Hightower Road
(404) 799-7288

West End Seventh-Day
845 Lawton Street
(404) 755-5927

UNITARIAN

First Existentialist
470 Candler Park Drive
(404) 378-5570

Unitarian Universalist Congregation of Atlanta
1911 Cliff Valley Way
(404) 634-5134

CITY FACT

Pine Log Mountain in Cherokee County is the area's tallest, at 2,320 feet. Other area high spots include Sawnee Mountain in Forsyth, 1,902 feet; Kennesaw Mountain in Cobb, 1,808 feet; and Stone Mountain in DeKalb County, 1,683 feet.

Government Offices

CITY

Atlanta City Hall
55 Trinity Avenue
(404) 330-6000

COUNTY

Clayton County
112 Smith Street
Jonesboro
(770) 473-3900

Cobb County
100 Cherokee Street
Marietta
(770) 528-1000

DeKalb County
1300 Commerce Drive
Decatur
(404) 371-2000

Douglas County
8700 Hospital Drive
Douglasville
(770) 920-7286

MOVING TIP

Take family heirlooms, fragile items, and sensitive electronic devices in a car, not the truck.

Fayette County
140 West Stonewall Avenue
Fayetteville
(770) 460-5730

Fulton County
141 Pryor Street
Atlanta
(404) 730-4000

Gwinnett County
75 Langley Drive
Lawrenceville
(770) 822-8000

Henry County
345 Phillips Drive
McDonough
(770) 954-2400

STATE

Georgia State Office
106 Washington Street
(404) 656-2000

Furniture Rental

Aaron Rents Furniture
2173 Piedmont Road
(404) 873-1455

Cort Furniture Rental
2970 Peachtree Road
(404) 467-1110

Easy Rental
568 Lee Street
(404) 758-9446

3563 Martin Luther King Jr.
Drive
(404) 691-7000

First American Rental
*3050 Martin Luther King Jr.
Drive*
(404) 691-1779

1599 Memorial Drive
(404) 377-5666

General Furniture Leasing
*4209 Northeast Expressway
Doraville*
(770) 939-8461

Rent-A-Center
530 Ashby Street
(404) 752-5119

Renter's Choice
3369 Buford Highway
(404) 982-1070

2924 Campbellton Road
(404) 758-2555

*2636 Martin Luther King Jr.
Drive*
(404) 699-1373

Grocery Stores

Cub Foods
2841 Greenbriar Parkway
(404) 346-4750

2625 Piedmont Road
(404) 842-3800

DeKalb Farmers Market
3000 East Ponce de Leon Avenue
(404) 377-6400

Harris Teeter
1799 Briarcliff Road
(404) 607-1189
www.harristeeter.com

3954 Peachtree Road
(404) 814-5990

Kroger
590 Cascade Road
(404) 756-1140

3425 Cascade Road
(404) 505-8855

235 Central Avenue
(404) 586-7390

1715 Howell Mill Road
(404) 355-7886

1700 Monroe Drive
(404) 872-0782

3330 Piedmont Road
(404) 237-8022

725 Ponce de Leon Avenue
(404) 875-2701

MOVING TIP

Don't forget to make proper arrangements for the transfer of your medical records. Your physician, dentist, optometrist, and veterinarian will have files containing prescriptions, dental x-rays, and immunization history. Contact the American Medical Records Association to determine your state's procedure.

Piggly Wiggly
2112 Candler Road
Decatur
(404) 288-4528

230 Cleveland Avenue
(404) 559-9586

Publix
3655 Cascade Road
(404) 505-2870

2868 Peachtree Road
(404) 848-0330

1544 Piedmont Avenue
(404) 898-1850

Sevananda Natural Foods
457 Moreland Avenue
(404) 681-2831

Sweet Auburn Curb Market
209 Edgewood Avenue
(404) 659-1665

Hardware and Home Improvement

Ace

2301 Cheshire Bridge Road
(404) 636-1401

1709 Howell Mill Road
(404) 351-4240

2365 Peachtree Road
(404) 841-9525

1544 Piedmont Avenue
(404) 872-1000

4405 Roswell Road
(404) 255-2411

626 Glen Iris Drive
(404) 872-6651

1231 Glenwood Avenue
(404) 627-5757

3910 Campbellton Road
(404) 346-1552

1248 West Paces Ferry Road
(404) 266-8944

Cofer Brothers

2300 Main Street
Tucker
(770) 938-3200

General Hardware

4218 Peachtree Road
(404) 237-5209

Highland Hardware

1045 North Highland Avenue
(404) 872-4466

Home Depot

3885 Jonesboro Road
(404) 361-5634

www.homedepot.com

815 Sidney Marcus Blvd.
(404) 231-1411

1032 Research Center Atlanta
Drive
(404) 691-2077

2295 Lawrenceville Highway
Decatur
(404) 315-0015

Intown Hardware

854 North Highland Avenue
(404) 874-5619

True Value

2891 Church Street
East Point
(404) 761-2640

Hospitals and Emergency Rooms

Children's Healthcare of Atlanta
1405 Clifton Road
(404) 325-6411

Crawford Long
550 Peachtree Street
(404) 686-4411

Decatur Hospital
450 North Candler Street
Decatur
(404) 501-6700

DeKalb Medical Center
2701 North Decatur Road
(404) 501-5200

Emory University
1364 Clifton Road
(404) 712-3411

Georgia Baptist
303 Parkway Drive
(404) 265-4000

www.gbhcs.org

Grady Memorial
80 Butler Street
(404) 616-4307

www.gradyhealthsystem.org

Hughes Spalding Children's Hospital
35 Butler Street
(404) 616-6600

Northside
1000 Johnson Ferry Road
(404) 851-8000

Piedmont Hospital
1968 Peachtree Road
(404) 605-5000

St. Joseph's
5665 Peachtree Dunwoody Road
(404) 851-7500

South Fulton Medical Center
1170 Cleveland Avenue
(404) 305-3500

Southwest Hospital
501 Fairburn Road
(404) 699-1111

Laundries and Dry Cleaners

Family Clothes Care Center
857 Collier Road
(404) 351-3024

Grant Park Coin Laundry
1328 Boulevard
(404) 624-1466

Laundry Lounge
1544 Piedmont Avenue
(404) 876-3517

Midtown Laundry Center
670 Myrtle Street
(404) 875-5872

Peachtree Hills Coin Laundry & Cleaning
174 Peachtree Hills Avenue
(404) 237-3634

Piedmont Laundry & Cleaners
1000 Piedmont Avenue
(404) 875-0999

Star Laundry
551 10th Street
(404) 897-3899

Pharmacies

APP Pharmacy
710 Peachtree Street
(404) 881-0838

Bolton Professional Pharmacy
2608 Bolton Road
(404) 351-3811

CVS
2076 Campbellton Road
(404) 758-4526

www.cvs.com

2738 North Decatur Road
(404) 377-8122

3788 Roswell Road
(404) 233-6730

Drug Emporium
2953 Druid Hills Road
(404) 636-6108

www.drugemporium.com

2625 Piedmont Road
(404) 233-1201

Eckerd Drugs
1410 Moreland Avenue
(404) 622-5348

www.eckerd.com

1512 Piedmont Avenue
(404) 876-2263

4540 Roswell Road
(404) 257-1873

King's Drugs
2345 Peachtree Road
(404) 233-2101

MOVING TIP

Liquor store boxes, designed to carry heavy yet breakable items, making great moving cartons. The sturdier boxes from grocery stores are also good choices.

Kroger
235 Central Avenue
(404) 586-7399
www.eckerd.com

1715 Howell Mill Road
(404) 355-7889

2205 LaVista Road
(404) 633-4201

1700 Monroe Drive
(404) 872-0785

Little Five Points Pharmacy
484 Moreland Avenue
(404) 524-4466

Mid-Towne Medicine
699-B Piedmont Avenue
(404) 888-9834

North Avenue Pharmacy
150 North Avenue
(404) 659-4300

Patient's Pharmacy
1874 Piedmont Avenue
(404) 870-9999

699 Piedmont Avenue
(404) 873-1337

Tuxedo Pharmacy
4411 Roswell Road
(404) 255-3022

Wender and Roberts Drugs
1262 West Paces Ferry Road
(404) 237-7551

Post Offices

For general information, including zip codes for all areas, call (800) 275-8777.

Atlanta

Ben Hill
2260 Fairburn Road

Briarcliff
3104 Briarcliff Road

Brookhaven
3851 Peachtree Road

Buckhead
1 Buckhead Loop Road

Cascade
2414 Herring Road

Central City
183 Forsyth Street

Civic Center
570 Piedmont Avenue

Druid Hills
1799 Briarcliff Road

East Atlanta
1273 Metropolitan Avenue

Greenbriar
2841 Greenbriar Parkway

Hartsfield Airport
In the Atrium

Howell Mill
1984 Howell Mill Road

Little Five Points
455 Moreland Avenue

Midtown
1072 W. Peachtree Street

Morris Brown
50 Sunset Avenue

North Highland
1190 North Highland Avenue

Northlake
2312 Northlake Parkway

Peachtree Center
240 Peachtree Street

Pharr Road
575 Pharr Road

Ralph McGill
822 Ralph McGill Blvd.

West End
848 Oglethorpe Avenue

Decatur
DeKalb County
5200 West Ponce de Leon Avenue

Douglasville
Douglas County
6000 Stewart Parkway

Fayetteville
Fayette County
250 Georgia Avenue E.

Jonesboro
Clayton County
255 North Main Street

Lawrenceville
Gwinnett County
121 East Crogan Street

Marietta
Cobb County
257 Lawrence Street

McDonough
Henry County
100 Postmaster Drive

Roswell
Northern Fulton County
8920 Eves Road

Union City
Southern Fulton County
5050 Union Street

Real Estate Brokers

W.T. Adams & Co.
458 Cherokee Avenue
(404) 688-1222

Barbara Alexander Realty Co.
2125 Headland Drive
East Point
(404) 761-1222

Buy Owner
6309 Roswell Road
(404) 252-7653

www.by-owner-ol.com

Century 21 Gold Medal Realty
2857 Henderson Mill Road
Chamblee
(770) 621-9009

www.c21gm.com

Coldwell Banker—Buckhead Brokers
5395 Roswell Road
(404) 252-7030

www.bhbrokers.com

Coldwell Banker—Bullard Realty Co.
238 Stockbridge Road
Jonesboro
(770) 477-6400

Coldwell Banker—The Condo Store
900 Peachtree Street
(404) 292-6636

www.condostore.com

ERA MBA Properties
2100 Roswell Road
Marietta
(770) 973-6000

Fourteen West Realtors
1311 North Highland Avenue
(404) 874-6357

Harry Norman
77 West Paces Ferry Road
(404) 233-4142

Jenny Pruitt & Associates
3405 Piedmont Road
(404) 814-9000

Metro Brokers/Better Homes and Gardens
415 East Paces Ferry Road
(404) 843-2500

www.metrobrokers.com

Northside Realty
6065 Roswell Road
(404) 252-3393

MOVING TIP

Most storage facilities base their costs on size. Don't pay to stash items you don't really need or want.

Prudential Atlanta Realty
863 Holcomb Bridge Road
Roswell
(770) 992-4100

RE/MAX of Georgia
1100 Abernathy Road
(770) 393-1137

Spas

Cortex Midtown Spa
1121 Peachtree Walk
(404) 607-0700

Don & Sylvia Shaw Day Spa
4505 Ashford Dunwoody Road
(770) 394-4603

Jolie The Day Spa
3619 Piedmont Road
(404) 266-0060

Key Lime Pie Salon
806 North Highland Avenue
(404) 873-6512

Mila European Spa
3167 Peachtree Road
(404) 233-2588

Perfect Touch
2531 Briarcliff Road
(404) 636-8875

Philip John Salon
3209 Paces Ferry Place
(404) 231-3477

Quintessence
3220 Peachtree Road
(404) 364-0474

Spa Sydell
3060 Peachtree Road
(404) 237-2505

Toosies Beyond Beauty
2291 Cascade Road
(404) 755-5656

Storage Centers

A Action Storage & U-Haul
1170 Howell Mill Road
(404) 881-0100

www.selfstorage.net/aaction

211 Moreland Avenue
(404) 222-9000

Dobbins Mini-Warehouses
1108 Chattahoochee Avenue
(404) 352-2638

www.thedobbinsco.com

Public Storage
1067 Memorial Drive
(404) 525-8711

134 John Wesley Dobbs Avenue
(404) 588-9430

2519 Chantilly Drive
(404) 321-2733

1387 Northside Drive
(404) 351-8415

Veterinary Hospitals

Ambery Animal Hospital
1400 Howell Mill Road
(404) 351-5960

Animal Doctors
468 Boulevard SE
(404) 627-7879

736 Ponce de Leon Avenue
(404) 584-8387

Animal Emergency Clinic
288 Sandy Springs Place
(404) 252-7881

Aynsley Animal Clinic
593 Dutch Valley Road
(404) 873-1786

Belle Isle Animal Clinic
216 East Belle Isle Road
(404) 252-3587

Briarcliff Animal Clinic
1850 Johnson Road
(404) 874-6393

Buckhead Animal Clinic
1911 Piedmont Circle
(404) 873-3771

Cheshire Animal Clinic
2206 Cheshire Bridge Road
(404) 320-6555

Emory Animal Hospital
1226 Clairmont Road
(404) 633-6163

LaVista Animal Hospital
2804 LaVista Road
Decatur
(404) 325-9924

Northside Drive Pet Hospital
1634 Northside Drive
(404) 350-9827

Pets Are People Too
1510 Piedmont Road
(404) 875-7387

Petsmart Veterinary Services
3221 Peachtree Road
(404) 237-7455

Pharr Road Animal Hospital
553 Pharr Road
(404) 237-4601

West End Animal Hospital
801 Lee Street
(404) 753-1114

Wieuca Animal Clinic
4589 Roswell Road
(404) 252-8676

Video Stores

Blast Off Video
1133 Euclid Avenue
(404) 681-0650

Blockbuster Video
1145 Abernathy Blvd.
(404) 753-9975

3425 Cascade Road
(404) 699-6046

3934 North Druid Hills Road
(404) 636-0064

2002 Howell Mill Road
(404) 609-9565

2161 LaVista Road
(404) 634-8850

985 Monroe Drive
(404) 876-0433

3515 Northside Parkway
(404) 261-7177

3944 Peachtree Road
(404) 233-1189

2099 Peachtree Street
(404) 352-4252

1544 Piedmont Avenue
(404) 872-6339

882 Ponce de Leon Avenue
(404) 872-8898

6660 Roswell Road
(404) 705-9269

Hollywood Video
1944 Candler Road
(404) 288-3173

590 Cascade Road
(404) 753-4230

Movie Gallery
1715 Howell Mill Road
(404) 350-9347

The Movie Store
595 Piedmont Avenue
(404) 815-9616

4920 Roswell Road
(404) 847-0554

Movies Worth Seeing
1409 North Highland Avenue
(404) 892-1802

Video Hits
2072 DeFoors Ferry Road
(404) 355-6073

Video Update
299 Moreland Avenue
(404) 658-1772

CHAPTER 10

Local Schools and Colleges

From kindergarten to college, Atlanta abounds with educational opportunities. Each metro county has a school system from kindergarten through high school, as well as a variety of independent and religious schools. Along with the county schools, the cities of Marietta in Cobb, Decatur in DeKalb, and Buford in Gwinnett have separate systems.

Two of the country's top colleges—Emory University and Georgia Institute of Technology—are located here. In addition, there's a well-established system of state colleges and universities that offer all levels of higher learning.

Students in both pre-kindergarten and college benefit from the Georgia lottery. Proceeds of the game are channeled into pre-K programs for three- and four-year-olds and HOPE (Helping Outstanding Students Educationally) scholarships that pay tuition at state universities for students who maintain a B average in high school.

Child Care and Preschool

Childcare and preschool programs abound around the metro area. Many are offered through community churches; others are run by professional childcare companies. The cost to enroll your child varies by location and the type of program you're joining (after-school care versus full day care). Some companies offer discounts to families with more than one child enrolled. For specific details, be sure to contact the individual center.

Bright Horizons Family Solutions

644 West Peachtree Street
Atlanta
(404) 881-3790

www.brighthorizons.com

Family events, after-school activities, and summer camp are a few of the programs at the seven area locations. About 900 children aged from six weeks to twelve years attend one or more of the programs.

Childcare Network, Inc.

3025 University Avenue
Columbus
(706) 562-8600

www.childcarenetwork.net

This Columbus-based company has eleven Atlanta locations with more than 1,100 students. Ages range from six weeks to twelve years. Summer camps are offered.

Children's World Learning Centers

1835 Savoy Drive
Atlanta
(770) 458-4646

www.childrensworld.com

Dance, karate, computers, gymnastics, and music are among the special programs offered at the twenty-one centers around town. About 1,200 students aged from six weeks to twelve years attend one or more of the programs.

MOVING TIP

Keep a phone book from the city you left. No matter how well you planned your relocation, there will be loose ends to tie up.

Creme de la Creme

4669 Roswell Road
Atlanta
(404) 256-4488

www.cremechildcare.com

Five metro locations offer French, computers, music, art, ballet, sports, and summer camps to more than 1,000 children, aged six weeks to nine years.

Discovery Point

1140 Old Peachtree Road
Duluth
(770) 622-2112

www.discoverypoint.com

The sixteen Discovery Point centers enroll 2,500 children, from six weeks to twelve years old. Summer camps are offered, along with usual preschool programs.

Kids "R" Kids Quality Learning Centers

1625 Executive Drive South
Duluth
(770) 279-7777

www.kidsrkids.com

With forty-four locations around town, this child center program is one of the area's largest, enrolling about 8,000 children aged six weeks to twelve years. It offers programs in language arts, science, math, and reading, as well as field trips and after-school care.

KinderCare Learning Centers

850 LeCroy Drive
Marietta
(770) 578-3005

www.kindercare.com

Special programs in phonics and writing are part of the curriculum at the thirty-nine KinderCare Centers. More than 3,900 children aged six weeks to twelve years attend.

La Petite Academy

1100 Mount Bethel Drive
Marietta
(770) 977-8892

www.lapetite.com

About 4,000 kids from six weeks to twelve years old are enrolled in the academy's forty metro-area locations. Along with preschool programs, the academy offers a summer camp.

Primrose Schools

199 South Erwin Street
Cartersville
(770) 606-9600

www.primroseschools.com

Along with infant and toddler care, Primrose offers four- and five-year-old kindergarten programs and after-school care.

With twenty-nine metro are locations, Primrose enrolls 4,350 students.

YMCA of Metro Atlanta
100 Edgewood Avenue
Atlanta
(404) 588-9622

www.ymcaatl.org

Seven YMCAs across the city draw more than 1,400 kids. Each center tailors its programs to suit the needs of the surrounding community. Many offer before- and after-school care, summer camps, and preschool programs.

Public Elementary, Middle, and High Schools

In the metropolitan Atlanta area, school districts are drawn by county. In addition, the cities of Atlanta, Buford, Decatur, and Marietta have their own systems, separate from their home counties. Statistical information, such as test scores and enrollment numbers for all the schools in the state, is available through the Georgia Department of Education, (404) 656-2800. Many of the counties also have free new-comer packets that include the same information.

To help you narrow the school search, the transportation department of each county's school district will provide specific information about which elementary, middle, and high schools are located in the neighborhoods where you're house or apartment shopping.

All of Georgia's public schools follow these criteria for enrollment:

- Students must be five years old before September 1 to enter kindergarten, and six years old before September 1 to enter first grade. Kindergartners who are younger but have attended an accredited school in another state must be five before December 31; first-graders in the same situation must be six before December 31.

- Students arriving from out of state should contact the school board in the district they'll be attending to make sure their past education credits will be accepted. A transcript or record of the student's history is usually required.

- Students entering public school must have an immunization certificate for the following: measles, rubella, tetanus, diphtheria, polio, mumps, and whooping cough. Sixth-graders must have at least one additional measles, mumps, and rubella booster. In addition, students must provide documentation of eye, ear, and dental exams.

- Students must have a Social Security number.

Atlanta City Schools

210 Pryor Street
(404) 827-8000

www.atlanta.k12.ga.us

More than 58,000 students are part of the Atlanta school system, which includes sixty-nine elementary, seventeen middle, and eleven high schools. The overall student-teacher ratio is 16 to 1.

The system includes pre-kindergarten programs and three adult education centers. In addition the Magnet School Program has sixteen areas of study where students can obtain extensive education in subjects such as performing arts, math, international studies, communications, hospitality, retailing, and health care.

About 70 percent of Atlanta school graduates receive college prep diplomas. The annual dropout rate is about 4 percent.

Clayton County

120 Smith Street
Jonesboro
(770) 473-2700

www.ccps.ga.net

About 45,000 students attend forty-eight schools in this southside county. The student-teacher ratio is approximately 17 to 1. Seventy percent of Clayton's seniors receive college prep diplomas. The dropout rate is about 3.5 percent. The system also supports alternative and evening schools.

MOVING TIP

Don't forget to return the videos and pick up the dry cleaning. Having to take care of this by mail is a hassle.

Cobb County

14 Glover Street
Marietta
(770) 426-3300

www.cobb.k12.ga.us

One of the largest school systems in the state, Cobb enrolls more than 94,000 students in sixty-one elementary schools, nineteen middle schools, and thirteen high schools. The student-teacher ratio is about 20 to 1.

Along with the traditional schools, Cobb supports an adult education center, an open-campus high school, and four magnet programs in performing arts, math, science and technology, and the International Baccalaureate. About 78 percent of Cobb students receive college prep degrees. The dropout rate is around 1 percent.

DeKalb County

3770 North Decatur Road
Decatur
(404) 297-1200

www.dcss.dekalb.k12.ga.us

DeKalb enrolls about 93,000 students in eighty-two elementary schools, twelve middle schools, and eighteen high schools. The student-teacher ratio is approximately 26 to 1.

DeKalb offers magnet programs in math, science, computers, performing arts, writing, and foreign languages. Special education classes and an international center are also available. About 82 percent of students receive college prep diplomas. The dropout rate is about 2.5 percent.

CITY FACT

Forsyth County northeast of Atlanta leads the metro area in growth, increasing its population to 86,130, a 92 percent increase from 1990 to 1998. It was followed closely by Henry County on the southside, where 104,667 residents marked an increase of 75 percent during the same period. The slowest-growing area was DeKalb County, where the 593,850 headcount represents an increase of 8 percent.

Douglas County

9030 Georgia Highway 5
Douglasville
(770) 920-4000

www.myschoolonline.com

With about 17,000 students attending sixteen elementary, six middle and four high schools, Douglas is one of the area's smaller school systems. The student-teacher ratio averages 20 to 1. Approximately 64 percent of seniors receive college prep diplomas. The dropout rate is 3 percent.

Fayette County

210 Stonewall Avenue
Fayetteville
(770) 460-3535

www.fcboe.org

Fayette schools have an enrollment of about 19,300 students attending twenty-five schools. The system also offers alternative and evening programs. The student-teacher ratio is approximately 22 to 1. Almost 76 percent have college prep degrees; the dropout rate is less than 1 percent.

Fulton County

786 Cleveland Avenue
Atlanta
(404) 763-6820

www.fulton.k12.ga.us

Approximately 67,000 students are enrolled in Fulton County's forty-five elementary, thirteen middle, and twelve high schools, which serve all of the county except the city of Atlanta. Magnet programs are offered in math, science, international studies, and visual and performing arts. The system also boasts the first elementary school in Georgia to hold classes year-round.

About 86 percent of Fulton students receive college prep diplomas. The dropout rate is about 2.2 percent.

Gwinnett County

52 Gwinnett Drive
Lawrenceville
(770) 963-8651

www.gwinnett.k12.ga.us

There are eighty-six schools in the Gwinnett system, with a student population of about 105,500—one of the biggest in the state. The district includes vocational and special education centers. The student-teacher ratio is about 25 to 1. More than 84 percent of seniors receive college prep degrees. The dropout rate is less than 2 percent.

Henry County
396 Tomlinson Street
McDonough
(770) 957-6601

www.henry.k12.ga.us

About 22,000 students attend school in Henry County, in seventeen elementary schools, six middle schools, and five high schools. The district also supports an alternative high school and an evening school. The teacher-student ratio is about 21 to 1. Fifty-seven percent of students receive college prep diplomas. The dropout rate is 5.5 percent.

Independent Elementary, Middle, and High Schools

Atlanta International School
2890 North Fulton Drive
Atlanta
(404) 841-3840

www.aischool.org

This Buckhead school, with 800 students from fifty-seven countries, was established in 1984 by members of the city's international community. Classes enroll students from kindergarten through twelfth grade, with courses in French, German, and Spanish offered at each level. AIS also offers an International Baccalaureate. Tuition ranges from $9,600 to $11,200.

The Lovett School
4075 Paces Ferry Road
Atlanta
(404) 262-3032

www.lovett.org

Almost 1,500 children, in pre-kindergarten to twelfth grade classes, attend this school on the edge of the Chattahoochee River, which provides a natural outdoor classroom. Tuition goes from $6,200 to $11,645.

The Galloway School
215 West Wieuca Road
Atlanta
(404) 252-8389

www.gallowayschool.org

Almost 800 students are enrolled in pre-kindergarten to twelfth grade. The curriculum combines academics and physical fitness with problem-solving, teamwork, and reasoning.

Tuition ranges from $2,350 to $10,400 annually.

Greater Atlanta Christian School

1575 Indian Trail Road
Norcross
(770) 243-2000

www.gacs.pvt.k12.ga.us

More than 1,400 students, some as young as three years old, attend this suburban Christian school on a seventy-four-acre campus. Classes are offered through grade 12. Tuition is $7,643.

Greenfield Hebrew Academy of Atlanta

5200 Northland Drive
Atlanta
(404) 843-9900

www.ghacademy.org

Almost 600 students, from pre-kindergarten to eighth grade, study at this school, which emphasizes the Hebrew language and Judaic studies. Tuition is $7,975 per year.

Holy Innocents' Episcopal School

805 Mount Vernon Highway
Atlanta
(404) 255-4026

www.hies.org

About 1,300 students, from three-year-olds to twelfth-graders, attend this northside school, which stresses learning in a Judeo-Christian environment. The thirty-three-acre campus includes athletic fields, a fine arts building, and a chapel. Tuition costs $5,500 to $10,400.

Marist School

3790 Ashford-Dunwoody Road
Atlanta
(770) 457-7201

www.marist.com

Students in grades 7 through 12 attend this Catholic school, which has an enrollment of 1,025. Tuition is $8,800 annually.

MOVING TIP

If you are intending to transfer to another college, university, or graduate school, you must send your old school written permission to release your sealed transcript to the new registrar.

Mount Zion Christian Academy
7102 Mount Zion Boulevard
Jonesboro
(770) 478-9842

Almost 1,000 children attend classes from three-year-old kindergarten to twelfth grade. Tuition ranges from $2,400 to $3,900.

Pace Academy
966 West Paces Ferry Road
Atlanta
(404) 262-1345

www.paceacademy.org

Housed on the grounds of a former Buckhead estate, this school property has playing fields and a state-of-the-art performance hall. More than 800 students attend classes from kindergarten through twelfth grade. The curriculum includes advanced classes geared toward a college prep diploma. Tuition runs from $7,600 to $12,300 per year.

The Paideia School
1509 Ponce de Leon Avenue
Atlanta
(404) 377-3491

www.paideiaschool.org

Paideia ("community of learning") teaches about 800 children from three to eighteen years of age. Art, music, and physical education are emphasized. Tuition varies from $9,100 to $10,300.

St. Pius X Catholic High School
2674 Johnson Road
Atlanta
(404) 636-3023

www.spx.org

Grades 9 through 12 enroll 1,065 students at this Catholic school, one of the largest in the metro area. The curriculum is designed with three levels of college prep classes. Tuition is $6,400 per year.

The Walker School
700 Cobb Parkway
Marietta
(770) 427-2689

Almost 900 students, in kindergarten through twelfth grade, are enrolled in this Marietta campus, which boasts computer and science labs, two gyms, and three libraries. Tuition ranges from $5,570 to $9,400 per year.

The Westminster Schools
1424 West Paces Ferry Road
Atlanta
(404) 355-8673

www.westminster.net

Kindergarten through twelfth-grade programs are offered to 1,700 students on Westminster's 171-acre Buckhead campus. The site includes tennis courts, indoor and outdoor pools, gyms, and playing fields. Tuition varies from $7,700 to $12,000 per year.

Founded in 1900 as a military academy, this traditional school now enrolls more than 2,800 students from pre-kindergarten to twelfth grade. The students are divided among three campuses, in College Park, Riverdale, and Duluth. Tuition is $9,200 per year.

Woodward Academy
1662 Rugby Avenue
College Park
(404) 765-8262

www.woodward.edu

Junior Colleges

Atlanta Technical Institute
1560 Metropolitan Parkway
Atlanta
(404) 756-3700

www.atlanta.tec.ga.us

Tuition is $318 per quarter at this public technical school, which offers associate degrees. More than 2,600 students attend.

Chattahoochee Technical Institute
980 South Cobb Drive
Marietta
(770) 528-4500

www.chat-tec.com

More than 2,800 students are enrolled in this two-year public technical institute. Tuition is $326 per quarter.

DeKalb Technical Institute
495 North Indian Creek Drive
Clarkston
(404) 297-9522

www.dekalb.tec.ga.us

Technical associate degrees are offered at this two-year commuter school. Tuition is $999 per year. More than 3,000 students attend.

Georgia Perimeter College

3251 Panthersville Road
Decatur
(404) 299-4000

www.gpc.peachnet.edu

This two-year college enrolls 14,000 students in associate degree programs in arts and sciences. Tuition is $1,440 per year.

Gwinnett Technical Institute

5150 Sugarloaf Parkway
Lawrenceville
(770) 962-7580

www.gwinnett-tech.org

Gwinnett Tech extends associate degrees in a range of occupational programs. There are 3,400 students, paying $1,356 per year.

Colleges and Universities

American InterContinental University

3330 Peachtree Road
Atlanta
(404) 231-9000

www.aiuniv.edu

Tuition is $26,700 at this private university, where 1,975 students specialize in interior design and fine arts.

Art Institute of Atlanta

6600 Peachtree-Dunwoody Road
Atlanta
(800) 275-4242

www.aia.artinstitutes.edu

This private college, with 1,900 students, stresses creative and professional services, from the culinary arts to interior and graphic design. Tuition is $18,100 per year.

 CITY FACT

Metro Atlanta has sixty-three hospitals, eighty-five nursing homes, and more than 4,100 doctors to keep you healthy.

Brenau University
6745 Peachtree Industrial Boulevard
Atlanta
(770) 446-2900

www.brenau.edu

Almost 2,000 students attend the Atlanta campus of this private four-year college, based in Gainesville. The school confers bachelor's and master's degrees in arts, sciences, and education. Tuition is $395 per semester hour.

Clark Atlanta University
223 James P. Brawley Drive
Atlanta
(404) 880-8000

www.cau.edu

This private university is one of the leading institutions of black education. Degrees are offered in arts, sciences, education, social work, and business. Tuition is $16,424 per year.

Clayton College and State University
5900 North Lee Street
Morrow
(770) 961-3400

www.clayton.edu

Home of the acoustically ideal Spivey Hall performance center, Clayton has 4,500 students

majoring in arts, sciences, and music programs. Tuition is $1,808 per year. The college has no residence halls.

DeVry Institute of Technology
250 North Arcadia Avenue
Decatur
(404) 292-7900

www.atl.devry.edu

A private commuter college, DeVry specializes in the sciences. More than 4,000 students attend, at a cost of $3,875 per semester.

Emory University
1380 Oxford Road
Atlanta
(404) 727-6123

www.emory.edu

Founded in 1836, the "Harvard of the South" has almost 12,000 students. Tuition is $31,480 per year. Degree programs are offered at all levels in arts and sciences.

Georgia Institute of Technology
225 North Avenue
Atlanta
(404) 894-2000

www.gatech.edu

Rated one of the country's top science schools, Tech enrolls

14,000 students studying for bachelor's, master's, and doctoral degrees. Tuition is $10,844 per year. The campus, just off the Downtown Connector, includes the Robert Ferst performing arts center.

Georgia State University
1 University Plaza
Atlanta
(404) 651-2000

www.gsu.edu

Almost 24,000 students attend the urban campus of GSU, situated in the heart of the downtown district. Tuition is $9,268 per year. Degree programs include bachelor's, master's, and doctoral programs in business, arts, and sciences. The Rialto Center of the Performing Arts is part of the campus.

Kennesaw State University
1000 Chastain Road
Kennesaw
(770) 423-6300

www.kennesaw.edu

. This public commuter university has more than 13,000 students pursuing bachelor's and master's degrees in the arts, business, education, science, and professional writing. Tuition is $2,928 per year.

Life University
1269 Barclay Circle
Marietta
(770) 424-0554

www.life.edu

This four-year private college specializes in chiropractic education. Cost is $9,282 per year. More than 4,000 students attend.

Mercer University
3001 Mercer University Drive
Atlanta
(770) 986-3300

www.mercer.edu

This private Baptist university enrolls 1,800 students who study for arts, sciences, education, and pharmacology degrees. Tuition is $23,535 per year.

Morehouse College
830 Westview Drive
Atlanta
(404) 681-2800

www.morehouse.edu

Founded in 1879, this historically black men's college has 3,000 students. It offers bachelor's degrees in arts and sciences. Tuition is $14,660 per year.

Morris Brown College

643 Martin Luther King Jr. Drive
Atlanta
(404) 220-0270

Founded in 1881, Morris Brown has long been associated with the African Methodist Episcopal church. More than 2,300 students are working toward bachelor's of arts and science degrees. Tuition is $13,168 per year.

Southern Polytechnic State University

1100 South Marietta Parkway
Marietta
(770) 528-7200

www.spsu.edu

More than 3,600 students attend this Cobb County public university, where the emphasis is on science and math. Tuition is $9,296 per year.

Spelman College

350 Spelman Lane
Atlanta
(404) 681-3643

www.spelman.edu

Since 1881, Spelman has specialized in educating black women. It offers four-year degrees in arts and sciences. Tuition is $17,715 per year.

Finding a Job

CHAPTER 11

Working in the City

It's been a very good few years in Georgia. For a while now, the state's unemployment rate has hovered around 3 percent, lower than the national average (which hit a thirty-year low of 4 percent as of January 2000). In February 2000, Atlanta's unemployment rate was 2.8 percent, one of the lowest in the state. In 1999, 106,300 new jobs were created in the metro area.

Based on statistics compiled by the U.S. Census Bureau, the median household income in the Atlanta area is about $48,000. The cost of living here is slightly higher than the national average (with 100 considered average, Atlanta rates a 103.3; by comparison, New York earned a 232.1, San Diego a 125.6).

A 1999 survey of the Atlanta metro labor market by the Bureau of Labor Statistics revealed the following:

- White-collar workers average $16.67 per hour. The highest paid in this group were electrical engineers, pulling down $32.48 per hour. White-collar employees made up 54 percent of those surveyed.

- Blue-collar workers average $13.09 per hour. They represented 29 percent of those surveyed. Industrial truck operators reported $11.96 per hour; printing press operators, $16.45 per hour.

- The remaining respondents were service workers, who averaged $9.63 per hour.

Several job markets have been particularly strong in the state, and are predicted to continue growing through the middle of the decade. The demand for business and management services, healthcare and child-care workers, educators, engineers, and hospitality employees will grow. In addition, the state's labor department predicts that there will be a particular need for high-tech specialists: technical writers, computer programmers, database administrators, and a range of tech support personnel. Conversely, the demand for workers in manufacturing, farming, and metal industries is expected to decrease.

Service industries play a major role in Atlanta's economy. From restaurants and hotels to fast-food chains and retail stores, those ubiquitous "Now Hiring" signs are in plain view. The metro area's abundance of hospitals and health-related businesses provides another boon to the job market. Real estate, both commercial and residential, is another booming field fueled by a strong economy. Government jobs at the federal, state, and local levels keep almost 600,000 working. Several companies work closely with government projects, including Boeing and Lockheed Martin Aeronautical Systems.

MOVING TIP

Until you've memorized them, keep your new home or P.O. box address and telephone number in your wallet or purse.

For years, Atlanta's downtown district was largely occupied by banking concerns. Today, First Union, Bank of America, Wachovia, and SunTrust are among the area's largest employers. In the past several years, Atlanta has added additional software and telecommunications firms such as GTE and MCI WorldCom to an already lengthy list that includes Compaq Corporation, Mindspring, and Equifax. The Ford Motor Company has an assembly plant near the airport that turns out

Taurus and Mercury Sable models; in Doraville, General Motors maintains a manufacturing facility.

Atlanta is the corporate home of many companies, among them Coca-Cola, Delta Airlines, Home Depot, Georgia-Pacific Corporation, Rollins, Cohn & Wolfe public relations, Mindspring Enterprises, Maxell Corporation, Scientific Atlanta, Kimberly-Clark Corporation, Southern Company, Southwire, and United Parcel Service, as well as the federal Centers for Disease Control and the nonprofit American Cancer Society. Cox Enterprises, which includes the *Atlanta Journal-Constitution* and some television and radio stations and cable services, along with Turner Broadcasting and CNN, offer a wealth of top-notch media positions. Some of the other leading employers are AT&T, AETNA U.S. Healthcare, IBM, Kaiser Permanente, and Georgia Power Company.

One of the most efficient ways of connecting with Atlanta's employers is through direct contact. Most personnel departments of the large corporations accept résumés with query letters through postal and e-mail. Those looking for assistance in their job search will find a plethora of Atlanta companies that specialize in matching employers with employees.

In addition, never underestimate the value of networking. The city's numerous professional organizations and networking groups can open doors to your Atlanta dream job.

Internet Resources

America's Job Bank

www.ajb.dni.us

A joint service of the U.S. Department of Labor and state employment services, this site lists more than 1 million jobs across the country.

Career Path

www.careerpath.com

Job listings from the nation's leading papers give you access to a variety of positions across the country. Search by geographic location, skills, trends, or salary.

Georgia Careers

www.georgiajobs.net

Read features on local companies and find out who's hiring here—this site includes resources, local links, and job-skills matching.

Georgia Department of Labor

www.dol.state.ga.us./lmi

Check this state site for details and statistics about the state's workforce, job training, economic outlooks, and more.

Headhunter.net

www.headhunter.net

You'll find more than 300,000 jobs in sales, marketing, engineering, customer service, and other fields posted on this site, along with tips on job-hunting.

Hot Jobs

www.hotjobs.com

Search for your next job by location or career field. There's also a section where you can post your résumé.

Monster.com

www.monster.com

Send out your résumé and check listings and employer profiles on this super site, which lists more than 385,000 openings.

U.S. Government

www.usajobs.opm.gov

Check out job openings with the federal government and learn about the process required to apply.

Work Atlanta Online

www.ajobs.com

Check out local professional organizations, personnel agencies, government jobs, and networking groups for the Atlanta area.

Networking Groups

Career Transition Ministry

St. Anne's Episcopal Church
3098 Northside Parkway
(404) 684-2858

Every Thursday evening this Buckhead church offers free counseling, résumé review, and networking, as well as seminars on job searches, interviewing skills, and using the Internet.

Crossroads Services

Mount Vernon Baptist Church
850 Mount Vernon Highway
Dunwoody
(404) 255-3133

This group meets on the first Thursday of each month. There's no charge to hear the guest speaker and network with other job-seekers.

CITY FACT

Not that it makes rush hour any easier, but Fulton County does boast the highest number of interstate miles—74.72—of any metro county.

Christ the King Lutheran Church
5918 Spalding Drive
Norcross
(770) 449-1211

Every Tuesday evening the church hosts seminars on job-hunting and networking.

Employment Transition Ministry
2744 Peachtree Road
(404) 240-4764

A ministry of the Episcopal Cathedral of St. Philip, this group meets once a week to work on job leads and resources.

Jewish Family and Career Services
4549 Chamblee Dunwoody Road
(770) 677-9300

www.jfcs-atlanta.org

This organization maintains a job bank of metro-area opportunities, and offers career counseling, résumé assistance, and individual career and educational testing.

Job Network
Peachtree Presbyterian Church
3434 Roswell Road
(404) 842-5800

This Buckhead church hosts Thursday evening sessions on strategies for job-seekers. The bulletin board of openings and jobs wanted is updated regularly.

Job Search Training
All Saints Catholic Church
2443 Mount Vernon Road
Dunwoody
(770) 671-1176

All Saints offers free tips on résumé writing, interviewing, and presentation every Saturday morning. One-on-one counseling is also available.

Jobseekers, USA
Mick's Restaurant
3525 Mall Boulevard
Duluth
(770) 813-5770

This men's employment network welcomes unemployed professionals and executives every Tuesday morning for a light breakfast. Guest speakers, study groups, job leads, and emotional support are among the project's offerings.

Network for Employment Transition
Good Shepherd Presbyterian Church

1400 Killian Hill Road
Lilburn
(770) 921-7434

These Tuesday night sessions, geared toward those making job and career changes, offer tips on networking, interviewing skills, and résumé polishing.

Roswell United Methodist Church

814 Mimosa Boulevard
Roswell
(770) 640-2260

Roswell invites job-seekers to attend Monday evening sessions for networking. A job board posts current positions available.

St. Ann Catholic Church

4905 Roswell Road
Marietta
(770) 998-1373

The church's employment network meets every Tuesday evening.

St. Jude Catholic Church

7171 Glenridge Drive
(770) 394-3896

One of the metro area's oldest and biggest employment groups

meets regularly at St. Jude. It's not unusual to have as many as a hundred people attend the sessions on job-finding strategies.

Sales and Marketing Seekers

814 Mimosa Boulevard
Roswell
(770) 640-2260

Professional salespeople seeking employment meet Monday mornings at Roswell United Methodist Church.

Women's League

1705 Commerce Drive
(404) 351-5939

This nonprofit group offers a free employment guide for midlife and older women that includes a variety of local resources for jobs.

Work Connections

2201 Glenwood Avenue
(404) 373-0456

Goodwill Industries supports this resource center, which provides free job leads.

Newspapers and Publications

Atlanta Business Chronicle
1801 Peachtree Street
(404) 249-1000

www.amcity.com
www.hireatlanta.com

This weekly business journal features business-oriented positions from around the metro area in its pages and on its Internet sites.

MOVING TIP

Employment agencies may charge fees for finding you a job, but some charge the company.

Atlanta Journal-Constitution
72 Marietta Street
(404) 526-5151

www.ajc.com

The Southeast's biggest Sunday paper is packed with classifieds in the Job section. A calendar lists information on networking groups and seminars.

Creative Loafing
750 Willoughby Way
(404) 688-5623

www.cln.com

Each week, this thick free paper, with suburban editions in Gwinnett, North Fulton, and Cobb, is jammed with classifieds from around the city. The employment ads appear on the paper's Internet site every Monday at 5 P.M.

Gwinnett Daily Post
166 Buford Drive
Lawrenceville
(770) 963-9205

www.gwinnettdailypost.com

Check out the paper's classified section for jobs from around Gwinnett and nearby counties.

Marietta Daily Journal
580 Fairground Street
Marietta
(770) 428-9411

This Cobb County daily paper posts employment ads from around the northwest area.

Personnel Agencies

AAA Employment

2814 Spring Road
(770) 434-9232

AAA specializes in finding management, sales, marketing, finance, and technology positions.

Accountancy by Accounts on Call

3355 Lenox Road
(404) 261-4800

www.aocnet.com

Accounting and financial staff, including data entry clerks, bookkeepers, accountants, bankers, and financial managers, are this company's specialty.

Accountants & CPAs

1835 Savoy Drive
(770) 220-2469

This company matches employers with available controllers, accounting managers, CPAs, and financial analysts.

Accountants Inc.

Six Concourse Parkway
(770) 393-2228

Specializing in accounting and finance positions, this company maintains a twenty-four-hour info line. Call (404) 237-8199 for the latest job postings.

MOVING TIP

Network, network, network! Let people know you're looking for employment.

Accountants One

1870 Independence Square
Dunwoody
(770) 395-6969

Accountants One specializes in employment opportunities in accounting, bookkeeping, and finance.

All Medical Personnel

1961 North Druid Hills Road
(404) 320-9125

This Atlanta company works exclusively with the healthcare industry, matching clinical, clerical, and technical employees with full- and part-time jobs.

America Employment, Inc.
3390 Peachtree Road
(404) 239-5777

Sales, management, secretarial, and technical support positions are the mainstay of this Buckhead company.

AppleOne Employment Services
3330 Piedmont Road
(404) 240-2880

AppleOne offers assistance with résumés, skills analysis, and computer training as well as job referrals.

MOVING TIP

Most agencies do not prepare résumés, though they do make suggestions. A good résumé should be tailored to the job you're seeking and include a chronological list of work history, complete with dates.

Boreham International
275 Carpenter Drive
(404) 252-2199

Boreham recruits employees for international trade, accounting, sales, marketing, and office support positions.

Cambridge Placements Inc.
1 Piedmont Center
(404) 842-2800

Employers pay this agency's fees for finding legal secretaries, paralegals, receptionists, secretaries, and word processors.

Careers@Work
1615 Peachtree Street
(404) 873-1345

www.careersatwork.org

For more than twenty-five years, these job-referral experts have conducted workshops on résumé development and offered career counseling and testing for Atlanta-area job-seekers.

Catalina Resources
4470 Chamblee Dunwoody Road
(770) 220-0770

www.catalinaresources.com

Catalina specializes in finding employees in business and technical services, accounting, finance, office support, medical, sales, and marketing.

ComputerXperts

1360 Peachtree Street
(404) 888-0800

www.vanstar.com

This job source for the computer industry maintains a twenty-four-hour hotline of available positions; call (404) 237-8152 for an update.

Corporate Search Consultants Inc.

47 Perimeter Center East
(770) 399-6205

www.rothberg.com

Corporate Search matches job-seekers with engineering, manufacturing, data processing, sales, secretarial, accounting, insurance, and medical backgrounds with positions at local companies.

DDS Staffing

9755 Dogwood Road
Roswell
(770) 998-7779

This Roswell company works exclusively with those seeking positions in the dental and medical fields.

Dunhill Professional Search

3340 Peachtree Road
(404) 261-3751

For more than thirty-five years, this Buckhead company has matched job-seekers with positions in accounting, sales, and finance.

Executive Placement Services

5901 Peachtree Dunwoody Road
(770) 396-9114

www.execplacement.com

This company brokers a variety of opportunities in the hospitality and retailing fields.

The Hart Group

3200 Professional Parkway
(770) 541-7823

www.thehartgroup.com

Hart offers referrals for job-seekers with healthcare, management, office support, data entry, and customer service backgrounds.

Initial Staffing Services

1355 Peachtree Street
(404) 607-7776

Office support positions, including word processors, receptionists, secretaries, and data entry clerks, are featured, along with some light industrial and technical support jobs.

International Insurance Personnel Inc.

300 West Wieuca Road
(404) 255-9710; (800) 235-9710

Since 1982, this Buckhead group has focused on finding positions for underwriters, customer service personnel, claims adjusters, examiners, and insurance agents.

King Personnel Consultants

3390 Peachtree Road
(404) 266-1800; (800) 466-1804

For more than forty years, King has worked with people seeking jobs in fast food management, telecommunication sales, underwriting, and more.

Legal Professional Staffing

Two Ravinia Drive
(770) 392-7181

Legal positions in law firms as well as corporate law departments have been the focus of this company since 1987.

Management Professional Group

778 Rays Road
Stone Mountain
(404) 298-9121

Full-time restaurant administration—from assistant managers and supervisors to general managers—is this firm's exclusive focus.

MarketPro

2211 New Market Parkway
Marietta
(770) 951-9181

This Cobb County company specializes in recruiting and placing marketing professionals.

Med Pro Personnel, Inc.

1955 Cliff Valley Way
Suite 116
(404) 633-8280

The employers pay the fees for finding employees in medical support positions, as well as nurses, physician's assistants, nurse practitioners, and X-ray technicians.

Meridian Healthcare Staffing

24 Perimeter Center East
(770) 351-0500; (800) 540-9666

Meridian recruits for support staff in a range of healthcare positions, from administration to billing and marketing.

Millennium Staffing

3355 Lenox Road
(404) 264-0001

This Buckhead group recruits executive assistants, desktop publishers, word processors, and graphic designers.

More Personnel Services Inc.

4501 Circle 75 Parkway
(770) 955-0885

www.job-morepersonnel.com

With more than twenty-five years experience, this firm has placed workers in sales, marketing, finance, insurance, and business jobs around the Atlanta area.

The Morgan Group

100 Galleria Parkway
(770) 956-4050

Since 1982, this group has recruited employees for high-tech, financial, legal, sales, management, and restaurant jobs.

New Boston Select Staffing

3391 Peachtree Road
(404) 266-1969

New Boston recruits administrative assistants, banking and customer service specialists, and data entry clerks, as well as packers and shippers, machine operators, telemarketers, and word processors.

NPS of Atlanta

900 Circle 75 Parkway
(770) 984-6778

Since 1976, this firm has placed employees in the fields of finance, accounting, information

technology, office support, and customer service.

Paces Personnel

235 Peachtree Street
(404) 688-5307

All fees paid are paid for employees placed in the legal, medical, and secretarial fields. Office management, receptionist, accounting, and marketing and sales positions are also featured.

MOVING TIP

Know the company you're interviewing with—bone up in advance.

Perimeter Placement Inc.

24 Perimeter Center East
(770) 393-0000

Office staff specialties have been the focus of this company since 1970. Accountants, administrative assistants, executive secretaries, office managers, receptionists, and people looking for jobs in sales and marketing will find useful postings.

Personalized Management Associates Inc.
1950 Spectrum Circle
Marietta
(770) 916-1668

www.pmasearch.com

With more than forty years' experience, this firm has focused on management recruiting for the restaurant, retail, and service industries.

Personnel Opportunities, Inc.
5064 Roswell Road
(404) 252-9484

This agency recruits for jobs in accounting, administration, data processing, engineering, sales, manufacturing, and medical support.

Phoenix Technical Solutions
1447 Peachtree Suite
(404) 888-9938

www.technical-solutions.com

This company works extensively with programmers, analysts, Web-based designers, database administrators, and technical support workers, and also maintains a healthcare division.

P. J. Reda & Associates
1955 Cliff Valley Way
Suite 117
(404) 325-8812

For more than twenty years, this company has specialized in restaurant and hotel work, placing employees in a variety of positions from entry level to executive management.

CITY FACT

One of the area's lowest unemployment rates is in Forsyth County, where only 2.1 percent of the population is out of work. The highest number of unemployed are in DeKalb County, which has a 4.1 percent unemployment rate.

Portfolio
1330 West Peachtree Street
(404) 817-7000

www.portfolio.com

Creative types looking for jobs as graphic designers, art directors, illustrators, copywriters, and photographers will find assistance and advice here.

Progressive Personnel Services Inc.
1349 West Peachtree Street
(404) 870-8240

Legal staffing experts since 1985, Progressive Personnel reps have recruited secretaries, paralegals, receptionists, and word processors for a variety of area firms.

ProLink Staffing
1827 Powers Ferry Road
(770) 226-0909

ProLink works extensively with support and clerical positions for sales, accounting, and technical firms.

Remedy Intelligent Services
990 Hammond Drive
(770) 804-8036

Remedy locates staff for customer services, word processing, clerical, manufacturing, and packing and distribution positions.

Restaurant & Hospitality Recruiters of America, Inc.
2479 Peachtree Road
(404) 233-3530

For more than twenty-five years, this firm has recruited employees for positions in the restaurant and hospitality industry.

Resources in Food Inc.
1627 Peachtree Street
(404) 897-5535

This agency recruits for positions in restaurant management and hospitality.

Don Richard Associates of Georgia
3475 Lenox Road
(404) 231-3688

Accountants, bookkeepers, controllers, and CFOs are recruited by this CPA-owned firm. Call the twenty-four-hour info line, (404) 237-8139.

Romac International
3 Ravinia Drive
(770) 604-3880

www.romacintl.com

Romac recruits controllers and accounting managers as well as systems designers and programmers.

City Fact

The annual average pay of Georgia workers in 1998 was $30,873.

Shepard refers job-seekers with backgrounds in manufacturing, engineering, and health care.

Software Search

2163 Northlake Parkway
Tucker
(770) 934-5138

www.softwearsearch.com

Since 1965, this Tucker firm has recruited computer programmers, systems analysts, administrators, and salespeople.

Rowland & Associates, Inc.

4 Executive Park
(404) 325-2189

www.rmasales.com

Rowland recruits employees in sales, management, information technology, telecommunications, manufacturing, and medical fields.

The Shepard Group Inc.

999 Whitlock Avenue
Marietta
(770) 794-1117

Sterling Legal Search, Inc.

5180 Roswell Rod
(404) 250-9766

Full-time legal staffing is Sterling's specialty.

Tanner Personnel Service

3312 Piedmont Road
(404) 231-9303

This service focuses on medical personnel, from nurses to X-ray technicians, as well as support workers.

Professional Organizations

No matter what your chosen field, you're likely to find a professional organization of your peers that meets in and around Atlanta. Most of these groups list only phone numbers; their meeting times and places are subject to change. Call in advance for additional information on the following groups.

American Association of Occupational Nurses
(404) 262-1162

American Association of Records Managers and Administrators
(404) 881-7000

American Institute of CPAs
(404) 231-8676

American Institute of Graphic Artists
(770) 479-8280

American Marketing Association
(404) 222-2779

American Society for Public Administrators
(404) 331-2475

American Society for Training and Development
(404) 845-0522

American Society of Mechanical Engineers
(770) 512-6397

American Society of Women Accountants
(404) 874-7244

Association for Systems Management
(770) 677-9097

MOVING TIP

Agencies not only set up interviews, many help you practice your interviewing skills—goals, interests, job history.

Atlanta Ad Club
(770) 642-6687

Atlanta Human Resources Planning Group
(770) 840-8696

Atlanta Press Club
(404) 892-2582

Business Marketing Association
(770) 931-9677

Commercial Real Estate Women
(404) 874-0908

Creative Club of Atlanta
(404) 874-0908

Financial Women International
(770) 479-2111

Georgia Society of Association Executives
(770) 986-0700

Georgia Society of Professional Engineers
(404) 355-0177

Greater Atlanta Home Builders
(770) 938-9900

Institute of Internal Auditors
(404) 215-5000

International Association of Business Communicators
(770) 642-6687

International Customer Service Association
(404) 612-2586

International Society of Certified Employee Benefits Specialists
(404) 365-1976

Meeting Professionals International
(770) 489-9622

National Association of Business Economists
(404) 888-8049

National Association of Fundraising Executives
(404) 350-7310

National Association of Legal Secretaries
(404) 817-8511

National Association of Purchasing Management
(404) 753-9712

National Association of Women in Construction
(770) 277-2997

National Black MBA Association
(404) 572-8001

National Contract Management Association
(404) 679-4055

Professional Secretaries International
(770) 428-9439

Public Relations Society of America
(404) 612-7463

Society for Human Resources Management
(770) 886-1800

Society of Logistics Engineers
(770) 793-0507

MOVING TIP

Call the Georgia Association of Personnel Services at (770) 952-3178 to obtain a detailed list of member employment firms and their areas of job expertise.

Society of Marketing Professional Services
(770) 988-3210

Women in Communications
(404) 325-7031

State Employment Offices

All offices are open 9 P.M. to 4:30 P.M., Monday through Friday.

Clayton County
1193 Forest Parkway
Lake City
(404) 363-7643

DeKalb County
3879 Covington Highway
Decatur
(404) 298-3970

Cobb County
465 Big Shanty Road
Marietta
(770) 528-6100

Gwinnett County
1535 Atkinson Road
Lawrenceville
(770) 995-6913

North Metro
2943 North Druid Hills Road
(404) 679-5200

South Metro
2636 Martin Luther King Jr.
Drive
(404) 656-6000

Temporary Agencies

Accountants on Call
3355 Lenox Road
(404) 261-4800

www.aocnet.com

This agency features temporary jobs for data entry, bookkeepers, accountants, and other aspects of the banking and finance world.

Accountant-Source Temps
4170 Ashford Dunwoody Road
(404) 250-4444

Clerks, bookkeepers, accountants, controllers, and financial analysts can find temporary positions here.

Accountemps
3424 Peachtree Road
(404) 846-9010

www.accountemps.com

This Buckhead firm specializes in accounting, bookkeeping, data entry, credit, and collections jobs.

Adecco Employment Services
1201 Peachtree Street
(404) 249-7770

www.adecco.com

There's no fee charged to applicants seeking temporary secretarial, clerical, data input, and accounting positions.

CITY FACT

Some of Atlanta's top employers include Delta Airlines (more than 27,550 employees); BellSouth (more than 19,500 employees), and Emory University (14,000 employees).

Atlanta Technical Support
9000 Central Parkway
(770) 390-9888

www.atsjobs.com

This agency recruits for technical specialties in more than a hundred industries, and offers vacation and holiday pay, insurance, pension, and employer-paid fees.

ATS Staffing
8343 Roswell Road
Dunwoody
(770) 649-1011

ATS fills temporary openings in accounting, assembly, clerical, computer, and light industrial fields.

Butler International
4960 Peachtree Industrial Boulevard
Norcross
(770) 448-9220

Since 1974, this firm has placed trained professionals in aerospace, energy, computer information, pharmaceutical, and telecommunications companies.

ComputerXperts
1360 Peachtree Suite
(404) 888-0800

www.vanstar.com

Graphic artists, technical writers, and desktop publishers, as well as database experts, secretaries, and programmers are recruited—with vacations, holiday pay, and benefits.

e-staff
3210 Peachtree Road
(404) 846-9979

Check out e-staff listings for temporary positions for graphic designers, Web page designers, and desktop publishers.

Excel Temporary Services
2900 Peachtree Road
(404) 266-8484

Excel specializes in filling administrative, clerical, production and distribution, and technical short-term jobs.

FirstPRO
3859 Peachtree Road
(404) 365-8367

FirstPRO needs temporary employees for accounting, secretarial, word processing, data entry, and customer service positions. It also recruits skilled electricians and construction workers.

CITY FACT

Just in 1999, 106,300 new jobs were created in Atlanta.

Food Team Inc.
1627 Peachtree Street
(404) 897-5535

The Team recruits banquet servers, cooks, bartenders, chefs, and housekeepers for the hospitality industry as well as private functions.

Hire Intellect Inc.
2401 Lake Park Drive
Smyrna
(770) 435-2111

This Cobb County firm recruits marketing contractors in public relations, multimedia, internal communications, and marketing research.

Kelly Services
2000 Powers Ferry Road
Marietta
(770) 952-2551

Kelly fills a variety of temporary jobs in technical, scientific, and support service industries.

Labor Ready
485 N. Central Avenue
Hapeville
(404) 559-8300

www.laborready.com

From offices around the metro area, Labor Ready supplies workers for construction, manufacturing, and light industrial firms.

Norred Personnel Services, Inc.
3420 Norman Berry Drive
(404) 761-5058

Norred conducts extensive background checks on the skilled laborers it recruits for positions in warehousing, shipping, freight handling, forklift operating, data entry, and janitorial services.

Norrell Staffing Services
303 Peachtree Street
(404) 577-6679

www.norrell.com

Norrell supplies temporary workers in a variety of clerical, receptionist, data entry, industrial warehouse, manufacturing and accounting jobs. Vacation, holiday pay, and pension plans are featured.

Randstad

43 West Paces Ferry Road
(404) 264-9600

www.randstadstaffing.com

Short- and long-term positions are available in administrative, technical, clerical, legal, medical, and hospitality fields—with benefits.

TempWorld

2140 Peachtree Road
(404) 351-2077

TempWorld fills short-term clerical, secretarial, and light industrial positions, and provides vacation and holiday pay for its workers.

Western Staff Services

2200 Century Parkway
(404) 633-2722

Since 1948, this firm has recruited temporary workers for office, clerical, light industrial, accounting, programming, and engineering positions.

WPPS

1175 Peachtree Street
(404) 815-0440

www.wpps.com

This company specializes in placing skilled software workers in temporary office positions.

INDEX

About

Because moving affects almost *every aspect* of a person's life, Monstermoving.com is committed to improving the way people move. Focusing on an individual's needs, timing, and dreams, the site provides everything for the entire lifestyle transition and every stage of the move. Free service provider content, interactive products, and resources give consumers more control, saving them time and money, and reducing stress. Site features include cost-of-living comparisons, home and apartment searches, mortgage calculators and services, an interactive move-planning application, an address change service, relocation tax advice, and virtual city tours. Monstermoving.com is committed to remaining the most effective, comprehensive, and lifestyle-centric point of service for everyone involved in moving.

Monstermoving.com is part of the Interactive Division of TMP Worldwide (NASDAQ: "TMPW;" ASX: "TMP"). For information, visit *www.monstermoving.com* or call (800) 567-7952.

Bekins is pleased to offer you the following extra value services and cost savings on your next out of state move.

You will receive:

- A minimum discount of 52% off a move between 5,000–7,999 lbs., or a minimum discount of 55% off a move 8,000 lbs. and over.
- Free First Day Service – Bekins will unpack up to 5 cartons of essential items that you will need upon arriving at your new home.
- The FAS-Hotline – Instant access to a powerful collection of relocation assistance services such as a preferred mortgage program, cost of living reports and much more.
- Firm Pick-Up and Delivery Dates on shipments greater than 5,000 lbs.

To find the participating agent nearest you, please use our agent locator at www.bekinsagent.com, or look in the yellow pages under the "movers" heading.

Terms & Conditions

You must have a minimum weight of 5,000 lbs. within the continental U.S. to qualify for the discounts. The rules and restrictions of all programs are described in and governed by HGB 400-M tariff and section 13 of the HGB 104-F tariff, or as amended or reissued.

Coupon must be presented at the time of the estimate, must accompany your moving documents, has no cash value, is void where prohibited, may not be combined with any other discount and is subject to service availability. Coupon sets forth minimum discount level; final discount offer may be affected by prevailing market conditions. Offer is valid at participating Bekins agents only and cannot be used if estimate has already been performed. Offer is not valid for local or intrastate moves. DOT52793. Shipment must be registered using corporate code number 31402.

$10 Off an Avis Weekend Rental

Rent an Avis car for a minimum of two consecutive weekend days and you can save $10 off your rental.
For reservations and information, call your travel consultant or Avis toll free at: 1-800-831-8000.

- Rental must begin by December 31, 2001.
- Valid on an Intermediate through Full Size four-door car.
  - Valid at participating locations in the contiguous U.S.
  - Subject to complete Terms and Conditions on reverse side.
  - An advance reservation is required
  - Visit Avis Online at www.avis.com

Coupon # **MUWA014**

Bekins is pleased to offer you the following extra value services and cost savings on your next out of state move.

You will receive:

- A minimum discount of 52% off a move between 5,000–7,999 lbs., or a minimum discount of 55% off a move 8,000 lbs. and over.
- Free First Day Service – Bekins will unpack up to 5 cartons of essential items that you will need upon arriving at your new home.
- The FAS-Hotline – Instant access to a powerful collection of relocation assistance services such as a preferred mortgage program, cost of living reports and much more.
- Firm Pick-Up and Delivery Dates on shipments greater than 5,000 lbs.

To find the participating agent nearest you, please use our agent locator at www.bekinsagent.com, or look in the yellow pages under the "movers" heading.

Terms & Conditions

You must have a minimum weight of 5,000 lbs. within the continental U.S. to qualify for the discounts. The rules and restrictions of all programs are described in and governed by HGB 400-M tariff and section 13 of the HGB 104-F tariff, or as amended or reissued.

Coupon must be presented at the time of the estimate, must accompany your moving documents, has no cash value, is void where prohibited, may not be combined with any other discount and is subject to service availability. Coupon sets forth minimum discount level; final discount offer may be affected by prevailing market conditions. Offer is valid at participating Bekins agents only and cannot be used if estimate has already been performed. Offer is not valid for local or intrastate moves. DOT52793. Shipment must be registered using corporate code number 31402.

Coupon valid on an Intermediate (Group C) through a Full Size four-door (Group E) car. Minimum two day weekend rental required. Coupon must be surrendered at time of rental; one per rental. May not be used in conjunction with any other coupon, promotion or offer. Coupon valid at participating Avis locations in the contiguous United States. Weekend rental period begins Thursday noon and car must be returned by Monday 11:59 p.m. or a higher rate may apply. Offer may not be available during holiday and other blackout periods. Offer may not be available on all rates at all times. **An advance reservation is required.** Cars subject to availability. Taxes, local government surcharges vehicle licensing fee no higher than $1.93/day in CA, $.35/day in FL, $.55/day in UT, $1.42/day in Montana, and $1.65/day in Texas, airport recoupment fee up to 15% and optional items, such as LDW ($19.99/day or less), additional driver fee and fuel service, are extra. Renter must meet Avis age, driver and credit requirements. Minimum age is 25, but may vary by location. Rental must begin by 12/31/01.

Rental Sales Agent Instructions

At checkout:
- In CPN, enter **MUWA014**
- Complete this information:

RA # _____

Rental location_____

* Attach to coupon tape.